The Future of Pentecostalism
in the United States

The Future of Pentecostalism in the United States

EDITED BY ERIC PATTERSON
AND EDMUND RYBARCZYK

LEXINGTON BOOKS

A division of
ROWMAN & LITTLEFIELD PUBLISHERS, INC.
Lanham • Boulder • New York • Toronto • Plymouth, UK

LEXINGTON BOOKS

A division of Rowman & Littlefield Publishers, Inc.
A wholly owned subsidiary of The Rowman & Littlefield Publishing Group, Inc.
4501 Forbes Boulevard, Suite 200
Lanham, MD 20706

Estover Road
Plymouth PL6 7PY
United Kingdom

British Library Cataloguing in Publication Information Available

Library of Congress Cataloging-in-Publication Data

The future of Pentecostalism in the United States / edited by Eric Patterson and Edmund
Rybarczyk.
    p. cm.
  Includes bibliographical references and index.
  ISBN-13: 978-0-7391-2102-3 (cloth : alk. paper)
  ISBN-10: 0-7391-2102-2 (cloth : alk. paper)
  ISBN-13: 978-0-7391-2103-0 (pbk. : alk. paper)
  ISBN-10: 0-7391-2103-0 (pbk. : alk. paper)
 1. Pentecostalism—United States. 2. Pentecostal churches—United States. I.
Patterson, Eric, 1971– II. Rybarczyk, Edmund J. (Edmund John), 1961–
  BR1644.5.U6F88 2007
  277.3'083—dc22

                                                            2007031766

Printed in the United States of America

⊖™ The paper used in this publication meets the minimum requirements of American
National Standard for Information Sciences—Permanence of Paper for Printed Library
Materials, ANSI/NISO Z39.48–1992.

For my mother and teacher, Dwayla Patterson
E.P.

*For Cecil M. Robeck, Jr., who taught me to love the
beauty of my own Pentecostal tradition*
E.R.

Contents

Foreword

Harvey Cox

Outside observers and scholars who try to understand Pentecostalism often throw up their hands in despair. The movement is baffling and perplexing. It continues to expand at a rapid pace and is growing everywhere on the globe. Theories of why it has spread so quickly come and go, but none seems satisfactory. Never exclusively a faith of the urban poor, or of rural uneducated (as some writers once contended), one can find Pentecostal churches in hamlets, villages, small cities, and in different sections of the sprawling urban complexes of every continent. Further, Pentecostalism also seems to be mutating into a variety of shades and colorations. Some now speak of "neo-Pentecostalism," and even of "post-Pentecostalism" to refer to congregations and denominations that exhibit some of the characteristics of "classical Pentecostalism," but deviate in ways that appear highly suspect to those who adhere to previous "Pentecostal" configurations. This term ("post-Pentecostal") for example, is now often applied to the Universal Church of the Kingdom of God, founded less than thirty years ago in Brazil, but now with congregations in over seventy countries. In addition, one of the fastest growth areas for Pentecostalism is *within* other denominations, such as the emergence of the "charismatic movement" in the 1980s in which those who testified to being baptized in the Spirit and the gift of tongues and healing still chose to remain within the Catholic, Lutheran, or Methodist churches. But even before that, in the 1940s, such figures as T.L. Osborne and Oral Roberts led movements in which healing and prophecy and tongues were in evidence, but did not join Pentecostal denominations.

No wonder observers of what some have called a "new reformation" (the Pentecostal "movement" or "movements?") are confused. The object of their investigation is just too elusive, even mercurial. What, exactly, counts or does not count as "Pentecostal?" Nowadays whole congregations sometimes adopt a Pentecostal style of worship wholesale but do not change the sign on the door that says "Baptist" or "Roman Catholic." Sometimes the "full Gospel" congregations within a denomination band together, as has happened among Black Baptists, but sometimes they do not. To make things more complicated many so-called "mega-churches" adopt some, but only some, Pentecostal forms of praise but often preach a self-help message that is worlds removed from the core doctrines of classical Pentecostals. Meanwhile, in the "mainline" churches healing

services, praying with arms stretched toward heaven and even bodily movements in the aisles are no longer uncommon. Recently an Episcopalian reporter
for *The Christian Century*, the flagship journal of the mainline churches, visited
the annual assembly of the United Church of Christ in Massachusetts, widely
thought to be a "liberal" denomination. She was astonished at the swaying, aisle
dancing and emotional testimonies she witnessed. When I was in Salvador (Ba-
hia) Brazil in July 2005 someone pointed out the huge, impressive building of
the "First Baptist Church" of that city, and told me it was now—and had been
for a few years—a Pentecostal congregation, but stayed within the Brazilian
Baptist organization and retained the large "Baptist" sign on the front. What is
going on? It is enough to make any researcher run to look for other things to
study.

Amidst this confusion and puzzlement, the present volume is a welcome one.
Moving away from too much theorizing, the writers focus on the specifics. They
enable us to feel our way into the heartbeat, the actual life, of a variety of Pentecostal movements. This is a valuable corrective to the over-theorizing that has
sometimes plagued this field of study. But these writers are also not overly cautious. They are willing to hazard informed guesses about what we might expect
next from this fascinating spiritual revolution. Taken together, these well-
researched and engagingly written essays contribute an indispensable basis for
further study, observation, participation and—eventually—theorizing.

I invite the reader to view this volume not as an answer book, but as an invitation to father thought and reflection. Having myself observed the Pentecostal
movement, as a sympathetic outsider, for over fifty years now, I find that my
own questions about it change as time goes by. What gives it its continuing zest
and its astonishing appeal? Surely the power of the Spirit is within it. But just
how does the Spirit work? What about eschatology? If the Lord has not yet appeared in glory, though the early founders expected he would—momentarily—
are Pentecostals prepared for a much longer haul? What might happen
next? Will the constant divisions within the movement ultimately weaken it, or
will they make it more attractive to more and different kinds of people? Will the
alleged "middle-class-ification" of the movement cause it to forget the special
mission its early leaders once felt for the socially marginalized? How will the
ethnic subdivisions that characterize Pentecostalism (Black, Latino, Asian, Anglo, etc.) shape its future?

There are other questions. Will Pentecostals succumb to the new wave of
pyrotechnic apocalypticism dramatized by the "Left Behind" series of novels,
with an eschatology derived from fundamentalist dispensationalism, historically
at variance with Pentecostal beliefs? Or will Pentecostalism become so "respectable" it will lose its cutting edge? Will the Pentecostals' earnest search for a
viable social theology continue and deepen, or will the Pentecostal movement
turn in on itself with the smugness and complacency that often mars the more
"established" churches? What will happen along the already blurred boundary
between Pentecostals and other bodies of Christians, with Catholics, Orthodox,
Evangelicals, and "Mainline" churches? There also questions that are now al-

lowed and even welcomed among Pentecostals that until very recently would simply not have been entertained at all. One such query is how will Pentecostals pursue the pressing question of how the Christian faith, and especially the tradition they represent, relate to other religious and spiritual traditions? Another is, will the Pentecostal search for a viable social theology succeed? Might there one day even be a Pentecostal Social Gospel?

The reader should be forewarned that this volume will not answer all these questions. But, as I read them I did find valuable hints and provocative suggestions. Still these essays also demonstrate that the movement is just too lively to analyze with any finality. And this as it should be.

Standing on the threshold of a new century, threatened by new plagues, nuclear weapons and deep divisions between haves and have-nots, the whole world desperately needs a basic spiritual renewal. I say "the world," not just the church. It was to the world that God sent his Son, and it was on "all flesh" that He poured out the Holy Spirit. Therefore I suppose my largest question about the Pentecostal movement would have to be expressed in the form of a prayer. It would be one of the oldest prayers Christians have ever uttered: "Come Holy Spirit, Bless Thy whole creation." Will it happen? I hope so.

Preface

2006 marked the centenary of the Azusa Street revival, the cradle of twentieth century Pentecostalism and related charismatic Christian movements. In the 100 years since a one-eyed black minister led a heterogeneous, working class congregation in a Los Angeles industrial neighborhood, the movement has become the fastest growing religion in the world and claims more than 500 million adherents worldwide—over one fourth of all Christians.

In 2004 I assumed that someone was writing "the book" on the present and future of Pentecostalism in the US, timed for publication with the Azusa Street anniversary. I queried members of my university's religion department, my limited network of contacts on the issue, and members of the Society for Pentecostal Studies—the main academic forum for such work. To my utter astonishment the consistent reply was, "No one is writing *that* book."

My colleague Ed Rybarczyk quickly came on board as an equal partner in this endeavor. We decided on a two-pronged approach: an edited volume and a survey. For the former we approached the best scholars on Pentecostalism to contribute to an interdisciplinary volume that looked beyond theology and history to the present and future of the Pentecostal movement itself. Although not everyone we contacted chose to participate, we nonetheless were able to organize a superior company of scholars to engage the issues.

We asked them to begin by answering two simple questions: is there a future for Pentecostalism in the US? If so, what will it look like in fifty years? Furthermore, we asked them to relate their unique expertise and life experiences to the issue. The book in your hands is the fruit of their reflections.

The second track of our project was to survey Pentecostal thinkers on these same questions. We developed an electronic mail questionnaire that simply asked the same two questions and allowed for any additional voluntary responses. The questionnaire was distributed to a database we developed of over 500 Pentecostal thinkers, most of them educators or administrators at Bible schools, institutes, colleges, and universities. A small minority of those contacted were senior Pentecostal denominational officials for whom we were able to track down email addresses.

The response was silence. Deafening silence. We sent the questionnaire to the entire list twice, but in the end received less than a dozen responses. We were stunned, in part because our personal and scholarly credentials demonstrate long term engagement with the movement and its challenges.

This silence parallels a strange void in the literature regarding the future of Pentecostalism in its birthplace. Volumes of history, by friends and foes, were churned out in the decade preceding the Azusa Street centenary, but no prognostications on its future. A massive literature, from *Newsweek* and *The Economist* to the most exclusive scholarly presses, has reported on Pentecostalism in the developing world, but remained mostly mute on the United States. Furthermore, theologians debate American Pentecostalism as text, subtext, and even heresy but largely fail to forecast how this fluid yet unique set of doctrinal positions may evolve in the United States of the twenty-first century.

Consequently, the focus of this book is those two questions: will there be Pentecostalism(s) in the United States in 2050, and what will it/they look like? These questions hide a third: what is the state of the movement and its auxiliaries today? These questions are important because during the twentieth century the United States was the epicenter of global Pentecostalism. However, a century after Azusa Street, the United States is losing its leadership role. Is this a natural development, the loss of "the fire," an abdication of responsibility, or something else?

Hence, this work. The book before you focuses on the vitality and trajectory of American Pentecostalism from a variety of perspectives (e.g. sociology, theology, education) and on numerous issues (e.g. music, church practices, race, denominational dynamics). In other words, the volume is purposefully interdisciplinary and directed not only to academics, but to the wider universe of all interested in the present and future of Pentecostalism in the United States.

This collection began and ended as a labor of love. I am grateful to my friend and co-editor Edmund Rybarczyk for his wisdom and diligent work on this project. We deeply appreciate our friends and especially our families for supporting these efforts, and we thank Lexington Books for publishing this book.

Eric Patterson

Chapter 1

Introduction: American Pentecostalism: Challenges and Temptations

Edmund J. Rybarczyk

Among Pentecostals the name "Azusa Street" carries almost mythic proportions. The reasons for this status are understandable and varied. Visitors to Los Angeles's 40-by-60 foot Azusa Street mission described a "heavenly atmosphere" that could be felt blocks away.[1] Pentecostals consistently purport that the Holy Spirit can be "felt," and so the visage of an atmosphere that extended for blocks seizes the Pentecostal imagination. For his part, Frank Bartleman, an itinerating minister and some-time pastor, added to Azusa Street's legendary character when he described the racial mixing that occurred in the wooden livery turned Christian revival center by uttering a phrase that itself has become famous, "the color line has been washed away in the blood."[2] Pentecostals believe that the post-resurrection day of Pentecost of Acts 2 foreshadowed the eschatological renewal of God's creation; Pentecost was a day when diverse people became united, when the curse of sin's alienation was overturned by the unity of the Spirit. If racial lines were being ameliorated at Azusa Street's worship gatherings in the era of the Jim Crow laws, it was (and is) rightly asked, who but God's Spirit could be at work?

At a simple historical level much of what would later characterize the global Pentecostal movement took place first at the Azusa Street mission: miraculous healings through the laying on of hands, speaking and singing in tongues, the sharing of testimonies, waiting upon the Lord in corporate silence, prophecies, a vibrant and kinetic worship style,[3] spiritual trances, altar calls (for salvation, sanctification, or Spirit-baptism), renewed love for other Christians and a renewed burden for the lost, a heightened eschatological awareness (both in terms of Christ's return and the realization that "today is the day of salvation" for the non-believer), baptism in the Holy Spirit,[4] and an emphasis upon spreading the Gospel. Led by its blind-in-one-eye African American pastor, William Seymour (1870–1922), the Azusa Street mission became the *de facto* "mother church" for Pentecostalism as curious ministers and evangelists from all over the United

States heard or read about the revival that was occurring in Los Angeles and in turn boarded ships and trains to experience the phenomenon first hand. After spending between a few days and several weeks these Christian leaders would re-board the ships and trains and often take the new way of being Christian back to their homelands.

Although the mission was demolished in 1931, today almost all Pentecostals trace their historical roots back to or through the Azusa Street Mission.[5] Zealous, invigorated, and Spirit-empowered folks left Los Angeles and within years of the mission's revivalist zenith (1906–1908) they could be found scattered not only across the United States and Canada, but also in Mexico, South Africa, the Congo, Liberia, India, England, Germany, France, Norway, Sweden, the Netherlands, Russia, Estonia,[6] Egypt, Chile, Argentina, and Brazil.[7] From the few hundred congregants under Seymour's leadership the Pentecostal movement has grown to number some 523 million. This means that of the roughly 2 billion people who are identified as Christian, more than one-fourth of them belong to a movement that has only been extant for a century. Only the Roman Catholics, with approximately 1 billion, comprise a larger group. To help put it into perspective, Pentecostals outnumber all the other Protestants in the world combined.[8]

These numbers are impressive, especially for the value system of our market-driven society, but the qualitative impacts of the movement are just as important and so deserve mention. First, due at least initially to the presence of the Pentecostal movement Western Christendom has witnessed the rise, spread, and acceptance of a broadly charismatic ethos: a general openness to such things as the dynamic activity of the Holy Spirit,[9] the recognition that God's Spirit speaks personally and contemporaneously through the Scriptures,[10] the reality and influence of the supernatural, the conviction that prevailing, or intercessory, prayer avails with God, and a fresh re-appreciation of the a-rational.[11] Just one way to note how this charismatic ethos has made its mark is that roughly one-tenth of all Roman Catholics now identify themselves as charismatics—those who accept and practice the Holy Spirit-impelled gifts referenced and affirmed in Paul the apostle's letters: prophecies, healings, miracles, words of wisdom, and speaking in tongues.

A second qualitative impact stems from Pentecostalism's populist character, that dynamic by which the sixteenth century Reformation's anthem of "the priesthood of all believers" is not only intellectually affirmed, but intentionally and practically implemented. Especially formative within this populist ecclesial character (often categorized together with "low-church" or "free-church" groups) is the conviction that all believers are given spiritual gifts—*charismata*—for both the edification of the church and cooperation with the Spirit of God in establishing the Kingdom of God. This perspective, then, is not merely a democratic affirmation of the rites or equality of all (as though this populist orientation were only an ideological vehicle), but a biblically and theologically based impetus that seeks to involve each believer in the life and work of the church. Further on this point, Pentecostalism's populist character works together with the aforementioned charismatic emphasis so that the church is turned away from the hierarchy (or institution) and toward, by, and from the people.[12] The ecclesial ramifications at this level are both enormous and profound but cannot herein be developed.

Third, a qualitative impact can be seen within both the twenty-first century academy and the larger sweeps of Christendom where there is a fresh re-appreciation for the role of the experiential, spiritual, existential, and even mystical dimensions of what it means to be human. This broad move toward the subjective may have more to do with the emergence of postmodern ways of framing exploratory questions and thinking about existence than with the influence of Pentecostalism, but we recall that the latter predated the former by several decades. Pentecostals were acting in what might be described as postmodern ways before the term was used.[13] Indeed, it is true that first-generation Pentecostals were characterized by an anti-intellectual streak, so that one might suppose they simply turned to a-rational means of knowing as a means of sociological separation, so as to establish their unique identity. But the truth is that they positively and purposefully affirmed a-rational means of knowing and interpreting life specifically because they believed those were inherent in a biblical world-view. And again, the historic churches are embracing this a-rational type of knowing today.

Those qualitative elements are briefly noted precisely to make the point that Christendom has been, as the Pentecostal biblical scholar Russell Spittler said, "Pentecostalized" both in the United States and around the globe. The Christian churches are not what they were one hundred years ago, and to an important extent this is due to the rise and influence of the Pentecostals.

A Typology of Pentecostalism

The focus of this book is the future of Classical Pentecostalism in the United States. The reason for this specific aim is simple: because the Classical Pentecostals are the oldest members of the Pentecostal family tree, both informed exploration and heuristic supposition, especially as those concern the land of their origins, are warranted. The reason for our focus so stated, it seems prudent to make at least some introductory typological clarifications between Classical Pentecostals, Charismatics, and neo-Charismatics.

Classical Pentecostals are comprised of those who, when the movement began in the early decades of the twentieth century, deemed it necessary to break way from the historic denominations and form their own denominations. Especially in the movement's first forty-to-fifty years this saw Classical Pentecostals as being provincial, arrogant, and sectarian; frankly, the movement in the United States continues to so suffer.[14] Classical Pentecostals consist of three primary trajectories: Wesleyan-Holiness denominations, the Reformed-Higher Life denominations, and the Oneness denominations. Theologically, all Classical Pentecostals traditionally aver that the evidence of one's having been baptized in the Holy Spirit is speaking in tongues (*glossolalia*). Together, these three trajectories of Classical Pentecostalism have over 20 million adherents in the United States.[15]

The Wesleyan-Holiness trajectory includes the Church of God (Anderson, Indiana), the Church of God (Cleveland, Tennessee), the Church of God in Christ, the Free Methodists, the International Pentecostal Holiness Church, and the Wesleyan Church. The *Wesleyan* emphasis in this trajectory holds that sanctification is an experience, sometimes referred to as a crisis event, that follows salvation but which precedes baptism in the Holy Spirit. John Wesley himself variously called this experience the "second definite word of grace," "entire sanctification," "Christian perfection," or "perfect love." This experience is understood to cleanse the believer in profound ways, so that God's Spirit, at baptism in the Holy Spirit, is allowed to enter a cleansed vessel. Many Wesleyan Pentecostals believe sanctification roots out the sinful, fallen, Adamic nature. The *Holiness* emphasis in this trajectory not only refers to the experience of sanctification as one enabling and deepening a life of personal holiness, but also denotes the historic emphasis on moral purity and cleanliness that can be traced back into nineteenth-century Methodism.

The Reformed-Higher Life groups are sometimes categorized as Keswick Higher Life Pentecostals, stemming from the early twentieth-century evangelistic movement in Great Britain which emphasized baptism in the Holy Spirit as a means of empowerment for Christian ministry and service, and sometimes described as the Baptistic Pentecostals, as a more narrow construct of the Reformed Protestant tradition. The Reformed-Higher Life Pentecostal branch consists of the Assemblies of God, the International Church of the Foursquare Gospel, and the Open Bible Churches. Heavily influenced during the first generation by both pastors who emigrated from and teachers within the Reformed tradition, these denominations do not believe that sanctification is an experience but a process.

In 1916 the Assemblies of God, a Reformed-Higher Life denomination, endured a rending theological debate. The "New Issue," as it was then called, had to do variously with an understanding of Christ's nature, biblical hermeneutics, Christian initiation rites, and the role and authority (or not) of church tradition. The result was that approximately one-fourth of Assemblies of God ministers left the new denomination to form Oneness denominations: those who deny the doctrine of the Trinity as an unnecessary historical accretion taken from Greek philosophy. Oneness Pentecostals believe the fullest revelation of God is the name "Jesus." This distinctive resulted in Oneness Pentecostals sometimes identifying themselves, or being labeled by outsiders, as "Jesus Name" or "Jesus Only" adherents. Today these include the United Pentecostal Church International and the Pentecostal Assemblies of the World.

Charismatics are distinguished from Classical Pentecostals along the lines of polity, theology and lifestyle. Concerning polity, Charismatics are those members of the vast array of historic Christian traditions and denominations who did not leave their own group when they were filled with the Holy Spirit. Instead, these kinds of Christians remain in their flocks with the hope of being used by God's Spirit to renew the larger church and/or denomination. Concerning theology, Charismatics generally do not believe speaking in tongues is the only sign of baptism in the Spirit, and they are more likely to describe the post-conversion experience of the God's Spirit as being filled with, or renewed by, the Holy Spirit, rather than as baptism in or with the Holy Spirit. For the Charismatics, other signs of this experience include a filling of love, receiving other spiritual gifts, and a sense of cleansing. Finally, concerning lifestyle, Charismatics have not preserved the historic Classical Pentecostal "sin lists": drinking alcohol, smoking or chewing tobacco, social dancing, and the like. All three of these differentiations—affiliation, theology, and lifestyle—have caused staunchly committed Classical Pentecostals to view Charismatics with suspicion.

The third trajectory of Pentecostalism is variously described as the Third Wave (following Classical Pentecostals and Charismatics), the Neo-Pentecostals, or the Neo-Charismatics, the preference herein.[16] Each of these phrases are catch-all phrases to include many independent churches, many "Word of Faith" churches, many Latino Pentecostal churches, and numerous individual healing evangelists, none of whom are affiliated with either of the older Classical Pentecostal or Charismatic trajectories. The single denomination to emerge within this trajectory in the United States is the Vineyard Christian Fellowship. Because they do not stem so immediately from historic Christian traditions, these kinds of Christians are more likely to affirm the indigenous culture. In foreign lands the predilection of Neo-Charismatics to affirm the local culture, as against the older Classical Pentecostal yen to critique culture, sometimes causes other Christians to accuse them of syncretism, the most outstanding forms of which are ancestor worship which gets re-processed in Christian terms in light of the heavenly community or the doctrine of the saints, and witchcraft which gets re-processed in terms of the charisms of spiritual/apostolic power and/or authority. In the United States this culture affirming predilection sees these groups as more likely than either the Classical Pentecostals or Charismatics to affirm Seeker Sensitive or Emerging church ecclesial models. Broadly stated, Seeker and Emerging models are quick to jettison connections to church history, happy to establish localized and autonomous church polity, less stringent concerning teaching about both sin and the need to submit to Jesus' Lordship/Kingship, more intentionally shaped to address congregants' felt needs (however defined), and increasingly more willing to define the Gospel as social justice than as personal transformation by the Lord Jesus.

The State of the Matter

Above I have delineated the outstanding differences between these three major American Pentecostal trajectories. The fact of the matter today is that there is a great deal of cross-pollination that typifies all three of these, especially at the local church level. Perhaps the most immediate form of this transference is music. Any one of these three, on any given Sunday, may sing one another's hymns or choruses. Last year I stood smiling amid a Roman Catholic mass when I heard the congregants singing a Vineyard worship chorus. Many Classical Pentecostals, for their part, have learned from the Charismatics and Neo-Charismatics that there are sincere believers who also emphasize the role and presence of the Holy Spirit in Christian living, but in their own respective ways; this is having its own ecumenical impact as stereotypical barriers are pulled down, but it is also causing Pentecostals to look and sound like their Charismatic siblings. Charismatics have learned to value both eschatology and populist ecclesial expressions as means to invigorate their congregations. So blurred are the older ecclesial boundaries that parishioners in any one of these trajectories may have no idea how their own church or pastor is any different from the others. Having myself visited many of churches within each of these trajectories, I can attest to how much the ethos is growing similar.

The above noted dynamic of cross-pollination raises what I believe is the fundamental challenge confronting the Classical Pentecostals: will they uncritically accommodate to the forces of American culture? Perhaps the most immediate historical example of the dynamic I see transpiring among Classical Pentecostals can be paralleled to the Methodist movement. In the nineteenth century the Methodists were the largest group of Protestants in the United States. However, only a century later the Methodist movement was dwindling, both in terms of numbers and Christian influence. What happened? Methodist pastors, leaders and educators had largely accommodated to the spirit of the age. First, the Methodists succumbed at a philosophical-theological level. Modernism, the broadly constructed package of knowing that emphasized rationality, quantifiable measurement, and cause-and-effect verifiability so seduced many Methodists that they compromised their commitments to both the divinity and Lordship of Christ and the authority of Scripture. The logic was simple: if Jesus was just one of many ways to salvation or meaning then why would anyone particularly choose to follow him? If the Bible was just one more history book, as some modernist scholars were reasoning, why should one orient one's life to its teachings? And so the numeric ranks of the Methodists shrank. Second, many Methodists succumbed at a socio-cultural level. Amid their newfound respectability in American culture, their former emphasis that their members be somehow different from the world was ameliorated. At that level, the logic ran that if there was little to no difference between being Methodist or not, then why so be? Together, then, the philosophical-theological and socio-cultural dynamics eventually deteriorated the Methodist movement's vibrancy and impact.

While I was still engaged to the woman who is today my wife, my father-in-law, Dennis McNutt, told me that he did not so much have concerns for my Christian identity in light of any future failures. Instead, he said, he was more concerned about what would happen to me if I were to become successful. That kind of concern also can be applied at the corporate level. Unlike their many Methodist forebears, Classical Pentecostals are not so much succumbing to philosophic or theological liberalism; they seem to have learned from the historical lesson of Methodism and are holding to theological conservatism. However, like too many Methodists earlier in American history, the Classical Pentecostals are now subject to the forces of socio-cultural respectability which may in turn lead to a co-optation of their former identity. Twenty-first century Pentecostals are not publicly disparaged by either the vast sweeps of Christendom or the American society like they were many decades ago. As was noted above, there are over 20 million Pentecostals in the United States. By numeric force alone they are taken seriously by both politicians and the Wall Street marketers. They have established scores of colleges and universities. It is their very success that is threatening their future. The result is that they are becoming something that I've come to describe as an "American Evangelical pot of goo." Let me explain.

By "Evangelical" I mean such standard emphases as the Lordship of Christ, the authority of Scripture, universal human sinfulness, and the need for salvation;[17] all of this unnecessarily manifests with an over-emphasis on a conversion experience in the local church.[18] By "American" I intend to convey contemporary conservative American Protestant church features such as an emphasis on the nuclear family in sermons, the destiny of the United States as God's favored nation, a form of corporate worship that turns the focus from the Triune God to the individual Christian, and alarming measures of therapeutic sermonizing that borrow variously from pop-psychology, positive-thinking schools of thought, and success-for-living business strategizing that are all routinely passed off as serious pastoral counsel. This may seem unfair. After all, these latter features may not have their roots in historic American Evangelicalism. Nevertheless, these latter features have come to characterize American Evangelicalism, in its most ignoble forms, through and through. With the exception of the nuclear family emphasis, itself a traditional Christian teaching, these are all expressions of a popular kind of Americana which emphasizes pragmatism and individualism. In all of this, cultural conservatism is casually equated with, or understood to be part and parcel of, theological conservatism.

By "pot of goo" I mean to convey the vapid, indistinct, and prophetically fainthearted amalgam that is, unfortunately, only too characteristic of both Evangelical and Classical Pentecostal churches. Sadly, the aforenoted positive ecumenical impact of Christian cross-pollination is also seeing the erosion of historic distinctives, and that for many denominations. For Classical Pentecostal churches in the United States an increasing ownership of the "American Evangelical pot of goo" is causing a decreasing emphasis upon several inter-related historic features. The first concerns the Classical Pentecostal *sine qua non*: baptism in the Holy Spirit. For many reasons, not least of which concerns pragmatism (pastors ask themselves, will visitors return to a church wherein people speak in tongues?) Classical Pentecostal pastors are teaching less and less about Spirit-baptism.[19] Furthermore, in Pentecostal thinking it is broadly assumed that where the Holy Spirit is authentically present the church will flourish. So, if a church is not flourishing along the lines of the *charismata* it is not merely a matter deserving thoughtful reflection or concern, it is a perceived spiritual problem that too readily moves toward unnecessary spiritual castigation and ensuing embarrassment; better the matter be left alone by all concerned than go down that path.

While Classical Pentecostal accommodation to the "American Evangelical pot of goo" is hindering local church teaching and practice concerning Spirit baptism and the *charismata*, the same is true concerning other historic sermon staples such as eschatology and prophetic critiques of culture. Wanting to promote a positive ethos, and thus see visitors return, pastors may be slow to mention the after life or hell; as a result a necessary Christian quality of prophetic challenge is evacuated. First generation Pentecostals may have unnecessarily railed against the things they couldn't afford,[20] but at least they weren't afraid to challenge the value system of the world-spirit. That is no longer the case in too much of American Pentecostalism.

Lastly, accommodation to the "pot of goo" is having a deleterious effect on the older egalitarian character of Classical Pentecostalism. Scholars are divided as to how much gender equality actually characterized the early Pentecostals, but it seems fair to say they embraced egalitarianism more than occurs today. In my own denomination, the Assemblies of God, not one woman serves as an official of the highest power or influence at either the local district (state, state-section) or national level. In the Southern California District of the Assemblies of God there are 1,332 ministers. Of these 228 (about 17% of the total) are women, 85 of whom are minister's wives. One is a head pastor. That same head pastor is also the only female sectional presbyter in this district, presumably one of the more progressive districts in the denomination.[21] After 100 years of a movement that says it values the charisms of women, even to the extent that they were head pastors in the first generations, one would expect that there would be more women in positions of leadership, not less. This diminishment is directly related to Classical Pentecostals having been impacted by the Evangelical "pot of goo" that I am describing herein.

A Necessary Remedial Step

What can be done? It is one thing to delineate the problem, but what can be done to remedy this? First, to be fair to the Tradition to which I owe so much, I must say that the historical processes I described above may simply be unavoidable. Maybe it's nobody's fault. Perhaps it's simply impossible to transfer the vibrancy of an encounter with the living God from generation to generation. Maybe the charismatic season cannot be sustained by human means. Certainly the charismatic season cannot be coerced; we Pentecostals have thought for too long that all we need is just one more big revival. (I'm not at all against revival. I just believe that for too long we have prescribed for God what His revival must be like!) However, even if the charismatic season of Pentecostalism cannot be sustained by human means alone, is it accurate to maintain that Classical Pentecostalism chiefly has been a charismatic or revivalistic season? The answer is surely no. What then of the Pentecostal ethos? How then can we be involved in preserving that?

As a theologian I wonder whether that is the wrong question. If believers are to live not for themselves but for Christ, who himself came for the world, is it fair to muse whether self-preservation is the goal? What if the Pentecostal movement was raised up, not for itself, but for the purpose of re-introducing the global Church to the dynamic presence of the Holy Spirit? What if the Lord has used the Pentecostal movement for the sake of the salvation of hundreds of millions in the world? It may be that we Classical Pentecostals may find our purpose and future in serving the whole Church, for the glory of Christ and the transformation of the world.

As a historian, however, I find it unsatisfying to think our day is done. I refuse to believe that the same Lord who works in and through cultural contexts, even to the point that the Gospel becomes characterized by those very cultural contexts, has simply deigned to now forsake our American context. All of the great Christian Traditions have found ways to preserve themselves. Because I believe we have so much to offer, we must do the same even if the doing of that will not be easy. Unlike the Eastern Orthodox or the Roman Catholics we do not have a regular or prescribed liturgy that holds us together. Unlike the Lutherans or the Reformed we do not have a theological system that helps to unify us. Unlike the great historic Christian Traditions, we do not have a vast ecclesial institution that can convene synods for reflection and planning. What we do have is an historic openness to and reliance upon the leading of the Holy Spirit; I've not always known how much of that is just good old American ingenuity or how much of it is surrender to the Holy Spirit, or both. Nevertheless, we need to ask ourselves aloud, where do we go from here? This is not a question simply for scholars or even pastors in their local churches. It is a question that lay people, educators, pastors, church elders, and denominational officials must find a way to address, and that together. Unless all of these corporately begin to openly, frankly, and humbly assess their movement, to critically reflect upon—without the hollow and neurotic impulses to preserve either the status quo or the extant political machinery—what it means to be Pentecostal, and what about that is worth preserving for future generations, the movement in the United States will wither and die. Oh, to be sure it will not cease to exist numerically, but it will continue to morph itself away from the eschatological-irrupting beauty it once embodied and become a vapid and vanilla pot of goo.

Confronted with a not dissimilar dilemma in the 1960s Roman Catholicism called for an *aggiornamento*, an opening of the windows so fresh breezes could blow inward. In short, the Roman Catholics took up the brutally painful but necessary task of re-examining themselves and their identity. Despite the fact that the Roman Catholic Church is today exploding around the globe,[22] not all Catholics will agree with the results of Vatican II. Nevertheless, I am suggesting that their method was the right one for Classical Pentecostals. Admittedly, compared to the Roman Catholics we are handicapped. We do not have a centrally located hierarchy. We do not have centuries of tradition that we can assume and then build upon. We do not have the structures and avenues for dialogue already in place. We aren't even good at thinking critically. Nevertheless, unless a Classical Pentecostal *aggiornamento* both results and is received the movement will die.[23] Nobody will be to blame, and something precious will be lost to the forces of history.

Overview of the Book

This book is written to celebrate the centenary anniversary of the Azusa Street mission. My editorial colleague, Eric Patterson, and I are in important ways products of the ministries of William Seymour and those who followed in his footsteps. Because we both love our Pentecostal Tradition, each of us sees this book as a call for *aggiornamento*. The scholars who have contributed chapters each raise their own challenges and suggestions for the movement.

Frank Macchia suggests that baptism in the Holy Spirit, something he denotes as the movement's "crown jewel," be understood not merely as a one-time experience, but as an inclusive rubric for shaping a Pentecostal theology. Macchia rightly recognizes that bereft a thoroughgoing theological frame the Pentecostal movement cannot survive. Pentecostalism, if it is only understood to be an experience and not a worldview, will have no place to "hang its hat," so to speak.

Earl Creps and Calvin Johansson both examine Pentecostalism in its postmodern milieu, each with different assessments, conclusions, and predictions for the future. Creps makes some insightful categorizations for understanding different cultural types of Pentecostals. He sees a new and post-denominational kind of Pentecostalism emerging, one wherein the traditional core commitments are affirmed but where the older cultural package is being jettisoned. In his chapter on church music, Johansson describes and critiques the way postmodernism has transformed the theology within Pentecostalism. Both Creps and Johansson raise excellent grist for the mill of reflection.

Arlene Sanchez Walsh and Eric Patterson offer an overview of Pentecostalism among Latinos and address some of the following questions. Is it true, as some scholars are saying, that Latinos will be the hope of Pentecostalism in the United States? Will Latinos blend into the cultural ethos of the United States? What will be the impact of the Prosperity Gospel among Latino Pentecostals? How will Latino Pentecostals make use of the themes of Social Justice and Liberation? Will there be forces or currents that bring together the many kinds of Latino Pentecostals?

Jeff Hittenberger charts how the Scylla and Charybdis of higher education might be employed in light of Pentecostalism's historic and rather simple intellectualism; readers may be surprised to learn therein the vast reaches of Pentecostal institutions of higher education. Will Pentecostals opt for the allurement of secular academic respectability? If not, what will their schools look like? What will motivate their philosophy of education?

For her part Margaret Poloma explores the role of ritual—Pentecostals are ritualistic, despite their traditional claims to the contrary—and how that both reflects and shapes Pentecostalism. Her statistical studies of Assemblies of God pastors and churches are meant to be suggestive of the currents at work in other white Pentecostal denominations. Like many revival movements of Christian history, Pentecostals struggle with the problem of the sociological routinization of the charismatic moment. How Assemblies of God leaders do so, Poloma suggests, will determine the future. Writing about African-American Pentecostalism, David Daniels reasons that the Church of God in Christ (COGIC) is uniquely characterized and situated within American Pentecostalism. It may be that the COGIC has the capacity to be more flexible and creative with respect to the new challenges and opportunities at hand in the twenty-first century.

Oneness Pentecostals are examined regarding the future in David Bernard's chapter. Bernard notes what is unique about the Oneness folks and suggests fascinating reasons as to why that segment of the Pentecostal movement will flourish in the United States in years to come. He believes Oneness adherents will be able to variously integrate heart and head, belief and practice, success and enduring group motivation.

The Church of God (Cleveland, Tennessee) and its unique issues are noted and critiqued in Kimberly Alexander's chapter. She variously explores the tensions between experience and doctrine, the Holy Spirit and missions, and denominational political machinery and the role and place of women. Alexander urges her constituents to look to their own past in order to gain vision for their future.

The dialectical tensions latent within the Open Bible Churches are examined in David Cole's chapter. How will a denomination that values local church leadership continue to hold together when pressure is being exerted to decentralize? How will the Open Bible denomination, a group that has produced many important leaders, continue to exist when those same leaders leave for bigger ponds of influence? How will a denomination that values ecumenical activity function in light of its own inherent struggles over geographic territorialism?

Each of these Classical Pentecostal organizations faces its own unique issues, and we are quite pleased to have each one represented by scholars who know well each respective group's idiosyncrasies and strengths.

Notes

1. Vinson Synan, *Holiness-Pentecostal Tradition*, (Grand Rapids, Michigan: Eerdmans Publishing Company), 109.

2. Frank Bartleman, *Azusa Street,* (Plainfield, New Jersey: Logos International, 1980), xviii.

3. This would be characterized in terms of clapping, waving, and raising hands; dancing, marching, and falling in the Spirit, shouting; a call-and-response form of preaching and a general sense of spontaneity. A study involving Pentecostal kinesiology is Daniel Albrecht, "Pentecostal Spirituality: Looking through the Lens of Ritual," *Pneuma: The Journal of the Society for Pentecostal Studies* 14, no. 2 (Fall 1992): 107–125.

4. Classical Pentecostals (defined more carefully in the text below) have traditionally argued that the sign of baptism in the Holy Spirit is accompanied by speaking in tongues, if said baptism is to have authentically occurred. Seymour, by way of contrast, taught that the signs were being "flooded with the love of God and power for service." Cecil M. Robeck, Jr., "Azusa Street Revival," in *The New International Dictionary of Pentecostal and Charismatic Movements*, revised and expanded, ed. Stanley Burgess (Grand Rapids, Michigan: Zondervan, 2002), 349. Hereafter this dictionary will be identified as *NIDPCM*.

5. Cecil Robeck, Jr., "Azusa Street Revival," *NIDPCM*, 344–50. The Church of God, Cleveland, Tennessee, holds that its members comprise the earliest group of Pentecostals because there was a revival with speaking in tongues at Coker Creek, North Carolina, in 1896. Cf. Synan, *The Holiness-Pentecostal Movement*, 81. Others make the case that prior to the revival at Azusa Street there was a revival in Wales, led by a pastor named Evan Roberts, that witnessed speaking in tongues. Pastors in America began to seek a similar phenomenon. Cf. David D. Bundy, "Welsh Revival," *NIDPCM*, 1187–1188.

6. Cecil Robeck, Jr., "A Pentecostal Witness in an Eastern Context," Address given to the "Building Bridges, Breaking Walls" Conference in Prague, September 12, 1997, 1–4.

7. For a missiological overview see Gary B. McGee, "Overseas Missions (N. American Pentecostal)" in *NIDPCM*, 885–901.

8. David B. Barrett and Todd M. Johnson, "Global Statistics," *NIDPCM*, 284–302.

9. Scholars are divided about whether the Pentecostal movement caused or influenced the later Charismatic movement. We know that there were Pentecostal pastors, evangelists, and healers who, as early as the 1940s, reached beyond the pale of Classical Pentecostalism and into established Christian circles. Moreover, it seems self-evident that the Roman Catholic charismatic outpouring that followed Vatican II (1962–5) only happened as it did some 60 years after the Pentecostal movement took root and became notable in the United States. In 1967 Catholic leaders at Duquesne University, the earliest location for the Catholic charismatic movement, were reading *The Cross and the Switchblade* (1963), a book written by the Pentecostal David Wilkerson, an Assemblies of God minister, while they sought to experience the vibrancy of ancient Christendom. In other words, it may be that the Charismatic movement was not immediately caused by Pentecostalism, but clearly it was influenced by it. Cf. Peter D. Hocken," Charismatic Movement," *NIDPCM*, 477–519; T. Paul Thigpen, "Catholic Charismatic Renewal," *NIDPCM*, 460.

10. See Gary McGee, ed., *Initial Evidence: Historical and Biblical Perspectives on the Pentecostal Doctrine of Spirit Baptism* (Hendrickson, 1991) for explanations of the Pentecostal hermeneutic.

11. The a-rational would include elements that may not be opposed to the rational or intellectual, but which are neither immediately located in the more cognitive dimensions of being human. For brevity's sake, these would include dreams and visions, God's speaking in one's heart or soul, a playfulness an affective orientation to being both Christian and human.

12. To be fair, the populist character and influence of Pentecostalism both accompanies and is driven by a general global yearning for democratic forms of governance. For further study on Pentecostalism's populist and adaptive character see *The Globalization of Pentecostalism: A Religion Made To Travel*, eds. Murray W. Dempster, Byron D. Klaus, and Douglas Petersen (Irvine, California: Regnum Books International, 1999), especially Section II.

13. Many scholars of the movement would prefer to describe the early Pentecostals as Premodern. Postmodernism is defined here chiefly in terms of knowing. Whereas Modernism emphasized reason and intellect as the superior faculties for knowing and organizing life, Postmodernism is open to dynamics like intuition, experience, emotions, aesthetics, and relationships as means to authentic knowing. Indeed, Pentecostals utilized intuition, experience, emotions, kinesthetics, and relationships as they sought to know both God and life.

14. This broadly sectarian characteristic began to ameliorate somewhat in 1942 when several Pentecostal denominations joined the National Association of Evangelicals. This organization, formed to counter the more liberal Federal Council of Churches of Christ in America (today reorganized as the National Council of Churches) put the Pentecostals in touch with other conservative Protestants. These contacts and relationships have been influential in helping the Classical Pentecostals move toward societal respectability and theological maturity, but that has also come with its own costs: Pentecostals have been "Evangelicalized" on such issues as ecumenism, pacifism as a respectable option, women in the ministry, and biblical hermeneutics. Cf. Robeck, Jr., "National Association of Evangelicals," *NIDPCM*, 922–25.

15. A Pew Forum on Religion and Public Life study, published 10/5/06, puts the Pentecostal percentage of the U.S. population at 5%. This conservatively converts to more than 20 million. http://pewforum.org/surveys/pentecostal/

16. This is because socio-culturally and theologically they are more like Charismatics than Classical Pentecostals.

17. Evangelicals would traditionally include the sovereignty of God in this list; Classical Pentecostals are consistently more committed to Arminian notions of human free-willing.

18. See my, *Beyond Salvation: Eastern Orthodoxy and Classical Pentecostalism on Becoming Like Christ* (Great Britain: Paternoster Press, 2004), 205–10, for a fuller discussion of the impact this conversion emphasis is having on the historic Classical Pentecostal emphasis upon discipleship and sanctification.

19. Margaret Poloma, *Assemblies of God at the Crossroads: Charisma and Institutional Dilemmas* (Knoxville, Tennessee: The University of Tennessee Press, 1989), first began to take note of this dynamic. For my part I have not heard such a message from the pulpit in some twenty years.

20. Robert Mapes Anderson, *Vision of the Disinherited: The Making of American Pentecostalism* (Peabody, Massachusetts: Hendrickson Publishers, 1979), 195. Anderson's argument on this point is unduly narrow.

21. 2006–2007 Yearbook of the Southern California District Assemblies of God, 20–21.

22. Philip Jenkins, *The Next Christendom: The Coming of Global Christianity* (Oxford University, 2002).

23. Obviously, the mere holding of a meeting or even many meetings is not the answer. Rather, such gatherings need to be taken back to the local districts and churches and implemented in and as the process of reception: owning and becoming what the corporate gatherings have owned and espoused.

Chapter 2

Baptized in the Spirit:
A Reflection on the Future of Pentecostal Theology

Frank D. Macchia

Where is Pentecostal theology going? What are the creative possibilities for Pentecostal theology as it confronts new global and ecumenical challenges? No single essay can answer such questions adequately given the broad range of theological nuances prevalent throughout global Pentecostalism. So, I have chosen to begin a conversation about the future of Pentecostal theology using the baptism in the Holy Spirit as my focus of interest. I refer here to the most popular understanding of this metaphor among Pentecostals, namely, as an empowerment for service distinct from faith and water baptism and characterized by a heightened participation in extraordinary gifts of the Spirit. Not all Pentecostals globally view Spirit baptism in this way, but enough do to make this understanding of the metaphor most characteristically Pentecostal.

I focus in my essay on Spirit baptism because, traditionally, this metaphor has been honored as the "crown jewel" of Pentecostal spirituality and theology. The extent to which Spirit baptism no longer holds this place of honor among a number of the movement's most prolific theologians is highly significant for our understanding of the present state and future possibilities of Pentecostal theology. But it is my conviction that the future of Pentecostal theology will proceed in ways most fruitful to its unique ecumenical calling as a global movement of Christian faith if it seeks to take up its central distinctive again with renewed interest and theological creativity. Before proceeding with future possibilities, however, let us look at the present state of Pentecostal theology in relation to its most outstanding distinctive.

Spirit Baptism as the Unfinished Business of Pentecostal Theology

With some qualification, I think it is fair to say that the doctrine of the baptism in the Holy Spirit has been globally the most characteristic distinctive of Pentecostal theology. A survey of popular Pentecostal literature over the decades would reveal a dominant interest in this topic. Simon Chan is thus correct in noting that Pentecostals are not in agreement over all of their distinctives but that "what comes through over and over again in their discussions and writings is a certain kind of spiritual experience of an intense, direct, and overwhelming nature centering on the person of Christ which they schematize as 'baptism in the Holy Spirit.'"[1] There are prominent Pentecostal theologians from Africa and Latin America who would say the same.[2]

Spirit baptism, however, has declined in significance more recently among the most prolific Pentecostal theologians. Not since Harold Hunter's and Howard Ervin's theologies of Spirit baptism published nearly two decades ago has there been a similar effort written by a Pentecostal theologian.[3] Steven Land's seminal effort at writing a Pentecostal theology, *Pentecostal Spirituality: A Passion for the Kingdom*, devotes no more than a few pages to the doctrine. He explicitly takes issue with Dale Bruner's description of Pentecostal theology as "pneumatobaptistocentric" (Spirit baptism centered). Land regards Bruner's description as "missing the point altogether" concerning what is really distinctive about Pentecostal theology, which Land considers to be the sanctification of the affections as passions for the Kingdom of God.[4] The fact that a major Pentecostal theology can be written without much attention devoted to Spirit baptism is a remarkable shift in focus for Pentecostal theologians.

Russell P. Spittler has even written that the most popular Pentecostal understanding of Spirit baptism as "subsequent" to regeneration or Christian initiation is a "non-issue," since Pentecostals were more concerned with spiritual renewal than with creating a new *ordo salutis*.[5] In the context of historical theology, a recent book written on Spirit baptism by Pentecostal theologian Koo Dong Yun presents the popular classical Pentecostal treatment of this doctrine as little more than a historical curiosity.[6] Even the significant efforts by New Testament scholars, Robert Menzies[7] and Roger Stronstad,[8] to focus on the unique charismatic pneumatology of Luke in order to open up fresh possibilities for viewing Spirit baptism as distinct from regeneration have received no significant response from the most prolific among Pentecostal theologians. Simon Chan, Steven Land, Amos Yong, Veli-Matti Kärkkäinen, Terry Cross, Juan Sepulveda, and others have nearly ignored the topic. Even if Menzies and Stronstad are correct about Luke's charismatic understanding of Spirit baptism, it is still possible to integrate Luke's focus with Paul's soteriological pneumatology without assuming a separation between them.

The problem with the early Pentecostal fragmentation of Spirit baptism from regeneration/sanctification, besides the elitist implications of limiting the experience to those who speak in tongues, is that it separates power from purity in the Christian life. This separation of power from purity creates a supernaturalism without substantial christological guidance. The result is an otherworldly spirituality guided mainly by pragmatic concerns (as Grant Wacker rightly described the Pentecostal ethos).[9] It seems clear that part of the unfinished business of Pentecostal theology will be to deal with the issue of relating Spirit baptism to regeneration/sanctification so that it is not limited to an experience of charismatic empowerment or speaking in tongues as a charismatic sign.

The decline of interest in Spirit baptism among a number of Pentecostal theologians has also to do with the diversity of Pentecostal belief discovered in the more recent research into the history of Pentecostal theology. Walter Hollenweger's research revealed a vast doctrinal diversity among Pentecostals worldwide and even within the United States both now and from the beginning of the movement. His classic, *The Pentecostals*, fell like a bombshell in the late sixties and early seventies upon geographically sheltered Pentecostal groups surprised by the doctrinal diversity of the movement globally.[10] A number of Pentecostals have agreed with Hollenweger, wondering if it would not be better to speak of various "Pentecostalisms" theologically in the world. Ronald N. Bueno, for example, writes:

> I'm a Pentecostal. I was born, reared and live in El Salvador. Many of the studies I have read on Pentecostalism do not accord with or reflect my experiences in El Salvador. Although that does not cause me to reject, at least initially, many of these works, it does prompt me to ask different questions of the literature in relation to my experiences. Is there a Pentecostal movement, or are there Pentecostalisms?[11]

More recently, Douglas Jacobsen published a celebrated description of key theologies of the Pentecostal movement in the first twenty-five years of the movement in which he showed a diversity of theological interests prominent then among Pentecostal leaders.[12] There is a diversity of views among Pentecostals over key doctrines as well. For example, some Pentecostals do not hold to a sharp distinction between Spirit baptism and regeneration.[13] Others (especially outside of the United States) do not agree that speaking in tongues must accompany the baptism in the Spirit.[14]

The diversity of doctrinal emphases among Pentecostals globally and differences of viewpoint as to the meaning of distinctive Pentecostal doctrines have caused Hollenweger to reject doctrine as the key to understanding what is most distinctive about Pentecostal theology. He wrote, "A description of these theologies cannot begin with their concepts. I have rather to choose another way and describe how they are conceived, carried and might finally be born."[15] Hollenweger focused not on doctrinal issues but on the oral and dramatic nature of how theology is conceived among Pentecostals.

This shift in focus made Spirit baptism seem like an accident of history, a holdover from the Holiness Movement that is not at all significant to what is most distinctive about Pentecostal theology. Harvey Cox, in his extremely popular *Fire from Heaven*, also locates the ecumenical significance of Pentecostalism in its emphasis on "primal" religious experience, speech, and hope.[16] The narrow and ecumenically irrelevant understanding of Pentecostalism as a revivalist "tongues movement" was replaced in Hollenweger's and Cox's work with a Pentecostalism that seemed ecumenically relevant, at the forefront of a way of doing theology that is not burdened with post-enlightenment standards of rational discourse.

While recognizing the value of Hollenweger's approach to Pentecostal theology, it is also important to note that doctrinal issues cannot be so easily detached from the symbolic framework that shapes how a movement experiences God and thinks theologically. Furthermore, Spirit baptism is not only a doctrine but a metaphor that can and does function imaginatively among Pentecostals in ways other than doctrinal conceptualization. Hollenweger's and Cox's work does not necessarily displace Spirit baptism as a powerful metaphor of our participation in the very breath of God. In fact, it calls for the kind of participatory understanding of the divine/human relationship, in which believers are "baptized" into God.

The significance of the newer accent on diversity, however, is that it implicitly raised the important question as to whether or not there was and is any coherence to Pentecostal theology. Of course, we cannot deny that there was doctrinal diversity early on and historically among Pentecostals globally. But this diversity does not mean that there was not some kind of coherent, distinctive theological vision among Pentecostals. Donald W. Dayton showed that early Pentecostal theology advocated a four-fold devotion to Jesus as Savior, Spirit Baptizer, Healer, and Coming King.[17] Most significantly, D. William Faupel highlighted the final element of this four-fold gospel as that which was decisive, namely, the eschatological element.[18] Pentecostalism was mainly about the latter rain of the Spirit to restore the gifts and power of Pentecost to the church in order to empower global mission before Christ's soon return. Pentecostals viewed the church as a "missionary fellowship" that was "riding the crest of the wave of history" (Grant Wacker) toward the end of the latter days of the Spirit. Steven Land agrees, arguing that Pentecostal theology has mainly to do with the sanctification of the affections as passions for the Kingdom of God in the world.[19] We have in Land's work the important convergence of sanctification and eschatology, the two issues most connected to Spirit baptism in the Pentecostal imagination. The interesting point is that Land does not develop the Pentecostal understanding of Spirit baptism in their light.

Land's neglect of Spirit baptism is unfortunate. I think the historical and theological research of the past few decades has done well to note the complexity and diversity of Pentecostal theology historically. Land has done well in raising the important issues of sanctification and eschatology as implicitly vital to discovering a coherent Pentecostal theology in the midst of the diversity. But this research in my view has tended to down play the dominance of Spirit baptism as a distinctive Pentecostal theological concern historically. The highly significant issues of sanctification and eschatology were connected in some way centrally to Spirit baptism in the Pentecostal theological imagination. Thus the trend to displace Spirit baptism from its central role in Pentecostal theology is unfortunate, since Spirit baptism reveals Pentecostalism's central pneumatological interest, and not just pneumatological interest, but interest in the *experiential* side of the life of the Spirit. After all, Spirit baptism is a participatory metaphor of the divine/human relationship that has served to bolster the distinctly Pentecostal focus on the relationship with God as a lived experience that is powerful, life changing, and sometimes overwhelming. If Pentecostal theology is to rediscover its vitality as a theological movement, it would be wise not to abandon its central distinctive.

So, what is the "unfinished business" of Pentecostal theology? The first is the relationship of Spirit baptism to regeneration/sanctification. Pentecostals originally borrowed Spirit baptism from the doctrine of sanctification prevalent in the American Holiness Movement inspired chiefly by John Wesley's younger associate, John Fletcher. Throughout the history of the movement, Pentecostals have attempted to distinguish Spirit baptism as a charismatic empowerment for witness from sanctification as consecration and purification from sin. This distinction did not prevent Pentecostals from speaking of Spirit baptism in terms reminiscent of Wesley's sanctification doctrine. Some, for example, referred to Spirit baptism as a "baptism of love."[20]

Furthermore, one can argue that consecration from sin and empowerment for charismatic service are two sides (inward and outward or negative and positive) of the sanctification experience. David Lim thus said provocatively that Pentecostal descriptions of Spirit baptism have tended at times to serve as the functional equivalent of "vocational sanctification."[21] It seems that the sharp separation between sanctification and Spirit baptism among Pentecostals in some cases was more semantic than substantial. If Spirit baptism is to emerge among Pentecostal theologians as a metaphor of central significance, the rift between Spirit baptism and regeneration/sanctification will need to be healed.

Secondly, Pentecostalism will need to relate Spirit baptism to its emphasis historically on eschatology. I think Faupel and Land have shown convincingly that Pentecostalism highlighted the latter rain of the Spirit needed to bring the work of God to a climax. In a sense, Christ's coming for Pentecostals was to be met by a rain of the Holy Spirit within history that results in the proliferation of diverse gifts of the Spirit. If Spirit baptism is anything for Pentecostals, it is the emerging field of God's Spirit in the proliferation and diversification of Christ's presence among us through multiple gifts of the Spirit. There are understandably several theologians that have seen eschatology as the new horizon for an invigoration of Spirit baptism as a charismatic experience among Pentecostal theologians.

In the remaining section of this essay, I want to draw out some general lines of inquiry for the future of Pentecostal theology with a particular focus on the unfinished business of a theology of Spirit baptism in view. It is my conviction that Spirit baptism can bring a fruitful focus to Pentecostal theology once more but only if the narrow understanding of the metaphor is abandoned in favor of a more expansive understanding. I will begin with a brief biblical reflection.

Spirit Baptism and the Future of Pentecostal Theology

The unfinished business of Pentecostal theology suggests an agenda for the future of Pentecostal theology. First, I do not believe that Pentecostals can avoid the metaphor of Spirit baptism. This metaphor has dominated Pentecostal literature over the decades and is connected to several tensions still present in Pentecostal theology. This metaphor has also functioned to give expression to our heavy emphasis on Christ as the Bestower of the Spirit and on life in the Spirit, especially through multiple spiritual gifts. There is no way ahead that ignores the past. As Pentecostal theologians go about the constructive task of writing Christian theologies nourished by Pentecostal experience and testimony, the chief metaphor for describing what is distinctive about Pentecostal theology and what has plagued us as problematic theologically will need to be at least a key component of our theological reflection.

Second, the new awareness of Pentecostalism's global and doctrinal diversity implies that a variety of Pentecostal theologies will beneficially arise from a variety of contexts. This variety does not necessitate an abandonment of Spirit baptism a dominant theological category but it does imply that more than one interpretation of its meaning will be placed on the table for discussion. The North American Assemblies of God will certainly not dominate the discussion. Occasions for dialogue will undoubtedly increase among Assemblies of God theologians who clearly distinguish Spirit baptism from Christian initiation, Chilean or German Pentecostals who might see Spirit baptism as involving regeneration, Chinese or Mexican Oneness Pentecostals who would view Spirit baptism as culminating a conversion complex involving repentance and baptism in Jesus name, and Holiness Pentecostals from the United States who view Spirit baptism as the empowerment of a life that has been cleansed by a dramatic sanctification experience.

They will all tend to see Spirit baptism as a powerful experience that orients the church toward fervent prayer, extraordinary gifts of the Spirit, and missionary zeal while awaiting the return of Christ. How this is nuanced or accented will vary, however, along with how it is joined with other themes. The Spirit baptism theme is well-suited for this diversity, since as a biblical metaphor it tends to function with a certain amount of fluidity and ambiguity, even within the pages of Scripture.

Third, Pentecostal theology will need to come to terms with the tensions that have occasioned the rise of this "Spirit baptism centered" message. I can think of three in particular. The first has to do with the relationship of purity and power or sanctification and Spirit baptism. There may be different ways emerging throughout Pentecostalism for pursuing this constructive task, but I sense a more integrationist direction as gaining strength over the past tendency to fragment these from each other as distinct stages of initiation. The second has to do with the relationship of tongues to Spirit baptism. I suspect that the connection between them will be enriched theologically but the necessity of the connection increasingly called into question. The third has to do with the christocentric nature of Pentecostal theology. Specifically, how to describe its trinitarian context will increase in importance as well as how this relates to the people of faith in other religions that Pentecostals will encounter on the mission field. The interest in a theology of religions from a trinitarian perspective will need to continue among us if our theology is to serve to enlighten our fervent missionary efforts.

Fourth, Pentecostal theology will need to seek to relate Spirit baptism to eschatology. I have become convinced that the intensity of our spiritual experience, our accent on the miraculous, and our missionary zeal are all effected historically by the fervency of our eschatological expectation. Not that all Pentecostal contexts will emphasize eschatology equally. Asian and African Pentecostals have tended not to stress it as much as North American, European, and Latin American Pentecostalism, and even in these latter locations there have been signs of its waning in significance. But I believe that eschatology has left its imprint on our theological imagination in a way that is most likely permanent.

A conscious integration of Spirit baptism and eschatology has a firm biblical base, since John the Baptist announced the coming of Jesus as the Spirit Baptizer in the context of John's message about the coming Kingdom of God (Matt 3:1–12). Relating Spirit baptism to eschatology will provide Pentecostals with a way of dealing with other problems such as how to connect various elements of spiritual experience, including sanctification and empowerment for witness. It will also provide an expansive setting for relating in dialogue various ways of construing the metaphor of Spirit baptism, thus facilitating rather than closing the door to dialogue even with non-Pentecostal traditions. If Spirit baptism inaugurates the Kingdom of God, it involves a great many theological accents.

The distinctly Pentecostal emphasis on the Spirit as an eschatological gift holds potential for some degree of freedom from the debates raging over the nature of Spirit baptism among theologians loyal to different understandings of Christian initiation and, by extension, the nature of the Church. Provoked largely by the Pentecostal emphasis on Spirit baptism, theologians such as James Dunn[22] (from non-sacramental traditions) and Kilian McDonnell and George Montague[23] (from sacramental traditions) have produced impressive treatises connecting Spirit baptism to regeneration by faith and the sacraments of initiation (especially water baptism) respectively. The non-sacramental view assumes a Word ecclesiology that regards the Church mainly as a fellowship of believers. Spirit baptism is primarily understood as regeneration through faith in the Christ proclaimed in the Gospel. The sacramental view assumes a sacramental ecclesiology in which the Church is the sacrament or mediator of grace. Spirit baptism is then the gift of the Spirit given in water baptism or the sacraments of initiation. The Pentecostal understanding of Spirit baptism advocates a charismatic ecclesiology in which the people of God are consecrated from the world and charismatically empowered for service in the world. We are only dealing with differences of emphasis among overlapping ecclesiologies and understandings of Christian initiation. But it seems clear to me that much of the current impasse over the doctrine of Spirit baptism has to do with a deeper impasse in the debate among different understandings of the Church and Christian initiation.

If Spirit baptism, however, is a metaphor coined by John the Baptist in reference to the Kingdom of God as inaugurated and fulfilled by the Messiah, then it can be viewed as prior to, involving, and transcending issues of Christian initiation and ecclesiology. An eschatological view of Spirit baptism connects it first with the coming of the Kingdom of God in power and only second with the birth of the Church and the initiation of the believer to the Christian life. Spirit baptism thus involves acceptance of the promise of the Gospel by faith (Acts 2:39), water baptism as sacramental signs following (Acts 2:38), and, especially, empowerment unto living witness with charismatic signs following (Acts 1:8; 2:4). Ultimately, it involves the baptism of the entire creation unto the resurrection of the dead and new heavens and new earth, with apocalyptic signs (Acts 2:17–21). Karl Barth (a la Oscar Cullmann) wrote of a general baptism of Jesus from death to life that involves Jesus' entire life, death, and resurrection and in which we and, I would add, the entire creation participate through Spirit baptism.[24] Spirit baptism cannot be exhausted by any notion of Christian initiation. It precedes, involves, and transcends them all.

Concluding Biblical Reflection

Allow me to suggest an example of how Spirit baptism can be read from Scripture in a way that starts us on the path toward future dialogue. Spirit baptism draws our attention to Matthew 3. John the Baptist saw himself standing on the edge of the end of the world announcing the Messiah's act of "baptizing in the Spirit" (only the verb form is used) as the final act of salvation. John knew that his water baptism did not have the power to bring down the Spirit and to end the age. The prophets of old said in effect, "We circumcise the foreskin but God will circumcise the heart." So John uses similar prophetic rhetoric to say in effect, "I can baptize in water unto repentance but the Messiah will baptize in the Spirit unto judgment and purgation/restoration." John's baptism was preparatory, namely, to gather the repentant together in preparation for the final judgment and restoration. But "apocalyptic transcendence" belonged to the Messiah alone. Only from him will the wind of the Spirit blow away the chaff and store the wheat into barns. The wind of the Spirit implies both judgment and purgation/restoration. The themes of sanctification and eschatology converge in John's description of the Messiah's act of baptizing in the Spirit.

That the Messiah will be anointed of the Spirit is foretold (Isaiah 11:1–3; 61:1–3). But insight into the Messiah's role to dispense and baptize in the Spirit is unique to John the Baptist. The Spirit was understood in ancient Judaism as the breath of God (Gen. 1:1–2). Matthew implies that the Messiah will give the Spirit also. In fact, John's Gospel even has Jesus after his resurrection breathing the very breath of God upon the disciples (20:22). Since Jesus is the Word that "was God" (1:1) he was able to impart the Spirit as a divine privilege.

Returning to Matthew 3 and remaining with our eschatological theme, the opening of the heaven at Jesus' baptism is a typical sign depicting an apocalyptic revelation.[25] The descending of the dove is reminiscent perhaps of the Spirit brooding upon the waters of creation and the sign of new creation in the story of Noah.[26] Jesus is being commissioned here to usher in the Kingdom of God in power to make all things new: "If I cast out demons by the Spirit of God, the Kingdom of God has come upon you" (Matt. 12:28). John's Spirit baptism metaphor is part of his message concerning the coming Kingdom of God through the ministry of the Messiah (Matt. 3:2).

It seems clear that Spirit baptism in the Gospels is granted broad redemptive and eschatological implications that cannot be exhausted in any version of Christian initiation or of the essence of the church. Interestingly, Donald Hagner notes insightfully that the church connected to the Gospel of Matthew saw parallels between its Christian baptism and Jesus' Jordan experience. But this church also recognized the unique eschatological undertones in the complex of events at the Jordan that await fulfillment at the end of salvation history.[27] I believe that Hagner's insight can be applied quite broadly. The vision of Spirit baptism foretold by John the Baptist and depicted in Jesus' Jordan experience pointed to final judgment and to the final sanctification of the entire creation.

Spirit baptism points to redemption through Christ as substantially pneumatological and eschatological. God certainly baptizes the disciples in the Spirit at Pentecost but Luke is quick to note as well the final apocalyptic horizon of this event (Acts 2:17–21). Since Spirit baptism inaugurates the Kingdom of God, it has an expansive reach, involving regeneration, baptism, and powerful charismatic empowerment. Spirit baptism is reaches for the very sanctification of creation as the final dwelling place of God.

This brief reflection raises possibilities for developing a global theology of Spirit baptism that cannot be discussed here. Let me just say that I believe Pentecostal theology is ripe to reconsider its central distinctive with fresh vigor in the light of those themes most intimately connected to the metaphor historically in Pentecostal theology. These themes, sanctification and eschatology (among others), also happen to be intimately connected to pneumatology in the Scripture. We face an invaluable opportunity to fashion a biblical theology of Spirit baptism that brings our pneumatological emphasis to the ecumenical table. There is "breathing room" in the future for a Pentecostal contribution to an ecumenical pneumatology that will bring Pentecostals from various contexts to the dialogue table and will hopefully bless other communions as they most certainly have blessed us.

Notes

1. Simon Chan, *Pentecostal Theology and the Christian Spiritual Tradition* (England: Sheffield Academic Press, 2003), 7.

2. Allan Anderson, *Zion and Pentecost: The Spirituality and Experience of Pentecostal and Zionist/Apostolic Churches in South Africa* (Pretoria: University of South Africa Press, 2000), 244; Miguel Alvarez, "The South and the Latin American paradigm of the Pentecostal Movement," *Asian Journal of Pentecostal Studies* 5, no.1 (2002): 141.

3. H. D. Hunter, *Spirit Baptism: A Pentecostal Alternative* (Lanham, MD: University Press of America, 1983), 10; H. M. Ervin, *Conversion-Initiation and the Baptism in the Holy Spirit: A Critique of James D. G. Dunn, Baptism in the Holy Spirit* (Peabody, MA: Hendrickson, 1984).

4. Steven J. Land, *Pentecostal Spirituality: A Passion for the Kingdom* (Sheffield Academic Press, 1993), 62–63.

5. Russell P. Spittler, "Suggested Areas for Further Research in Pentecostal Studies," *Pneuma: The Journal of the Society for Pentecostal Studies* 5 (1983): 43.

6. Koo Dong Yun, *Baptism in the Holy Spirit: An Ecumenical Theology of Spirit Baptism* (Lanham, MD: University Press of America, 2003), 23–44. Yun's constructive chapter at the end of the book does not take up the classical Pentecostal view, 147–162.

7. Roger Stronstad, *Charismatic Theology of St. Luke* (Peabody, MA: Hendrickson, 1984).

8. Robert Menzies, *Empowered for Witness: The Spirit in Luke-Acts* (England: Sheffield Academic Press, 1991).

9. Grant Wacker, *Heaven Below: Early Pentecostals and American Culture* (Cambridge, MA: Harvard University Press, 2003).

10. Walter J. Hollenweger, *The Pentecostals*, 2nd ed. (Peabody, MA: Hendrickson, 1988).

11. Ronald N. Bueno, "Listening to the Margins: Re-historicizing Pentecostal Experiences and Identities," in *The Globalization of Pentecostalism*, (Irvine, CA: Regnum Press, 1999), 269. I am grateful to Dale Irvin for directing me to this quote, Dale T. Irvin, "Pentecostal Historiography and Global Christianity: Rethinking the Question of Origins" in *Pneuma: The Journal of the Society for Pentecostal Studies* 27, no. 2 (Fall 2005): 45.

12. Douglas Jacobsen, *Thinking in the Spirit: Theologies of the Early Pentecostal Movement* (Bloomington, IN: Indiana University Press, 2003), 12.

13. There are Pentecostals in Germany and Chile, for example, who would identify Spirit baptism with regeneration. See Juan Sepulveda, "Born Again: Baptism and the Spirit: A Pentecostal Perspective," in eds. J_rgen Moltmann and Karl-Josef Kuschel, *Pentecostal Movements as an Ecumenical Challenge, Concilium,* 3 (1996): 104–109.

14. In the United States, Pentecostal leader, Jack Hayford, created a stir when he refused to make tongues a necessary sign of Spirit baptism. See Jack Hayford, The *Beauty of Spiritual Language: My Journey Toward the Heart of God* (Dallas: Word Pub., 1992), 89–107. There has always been a diversity of views in the history of Pentecostal theology over the relationship of tongues to Spirit baptism, though most Pentecostals in the United States would expect tongues to accompany the experience at some point in the Christian life. See, Cecil M. Robeck's insightful discussion of this entire issue, "An Emerging Magisterium: The Case of the Assemblies of God," *Pneuma: The Journal of the Society for Pentecostal Studies* 25, no. 2 (Fall 2003): 164–215.

15. Walter J. Hollenweger, "Theology of the New World," *The Expository Times* 87 (May 1976): 228.

16. Harvey Cox, *Fire From Heaven: The Rise of Pentecostal Spirituality and the Reshaping of Religion in the Twenty-First Century* (New York: Addison-Wesley Pub., 1995).

17. Donald W. Dayton, *Theological Roots of Pentecostalism* (Grand Rapids, MI: Zondervan, 1988).

18. D. William Faupel, *The Everlasting Gospel: The Significance of Eschatology in the Development of Pentecostal Thought* (Sheffield Academic Press, 1996).

19. Richard Land, *Pentecostal Spirituality: A Passion for the Kingdom* (Sheffield Academic Press, 1993).

20. As examples, note, "The Old Time Pentecost," *The Apostolic Faith* (Sept. 1906): 1 (author unknown); E. N. Bell, "Believers in Sanctification," *The Christian Evangel* (September 19, 1914): 3; Will Trotter, "A Revival of Love Needed," *The Weekly Evangel* (April 3, 1915): 1.

21. Shared with the author personally.

22. James D. G. Dunn, *The Baptism in the Holy Spirit: A Re-examination on the New Testament Teaching on the Gift of the Spirit in Relation to Pentecostalism Today* (London: SCM, 1970).

23. Kilian McDonnell and George T. Montague, *Christian Initiation and Baptism in the Holy Spirit: Evidence from the First Eight Centuries* (Collegeville, MN: Liturgical Press, 1991).

24. Karl Barth, *Church Dogmatics*, vol. IV, part 4, eds. G. W. Bromiley, T. F. Torrance (Edinborough: T & T Clark, 1969), 32.

25. John Nolland, *Luke 1-9:20, Word Biblical Commentary*, vol. 35A, eds. David A. Hubbard and Glen W. Barker (Dallas: Word Books, Pub., 1989), 162.

26. Donald A. Hagner, Matthew 1–13, *Word Biblical Commentary*, vol. 33A, eds. David A. Hubbard, Glen W. Barker (Dallas: Word Books, Pub., 1993), 58.

27. Hagner, 60.

Chapter 3

Postmodern Pentecostals? Emerging Subcultures Among Young Pentecostal Leaders

Earl Creps

North American Christianity is operating in a cultural setting very different from the one most church leaders have been trained to expect. The assumptions of modernity (individualism-scientism-optimism-monism) that underlay much of Western Christian spirituality are being alloyed by postmodern influences (communalism-experientialism-suspicion-pluralism) to create an environment of burgeoning complexity that morphs before our eyes. The struggle of Christian scholars and church leaders to come to terms with this evolving cultural landscape is indicated by the sheer volume of literature being generated about it.[1]

The object of this scholarly attention is the postmodern turn, a widespread rejection of modern technological rationalism. Postmoderns are turning away from what they perceive to be modernity's malevolent optimism, a force that is culturally bland at best and globally dominating at worst. As befits the term, postmodernism is in the eye of the beholder. For academics, it tends to refer to a critique of modern epistemology along with the idea of referential language, and absolutism of all kinds.[2] But outside the academy, it also describes movements within the arts and architecture, an attack on the imperialism that now disguises itself as globalization, and a general "mood" of skepticism.[3] One of the most influential forces stemming from postmodernism is a spiritual pluralism which regards personal spirituality as a replacement for organized religion. The two primary "sins" for this open architecture spirituality are injustice and intolerance. So long as these are avoided, the individual weaves a customized spirituality from a variety of strands which may be rearranged over time. Some of these elements might even be Christian.[4] This highly spiritual, but irreligious person is proving to be a daunting challenge to the Christian church.[5]

Debate rages over the nature and the scale of this shift. While Paul Elbert complains about "the unsubstantiated assumption that the world in which we evangelize is somehow delineated by 'postmodernism,'"[6] Craig Van Gelder blithely refers to postmodernism as "the cultural air we breath."[7] The one thing that almost everyone would agree upon, however, is that something has changed, and Pentecostals are caught in the middle of it.

Pentecostals understand themselves as a product of Christian revival movements that erupted in the early twentieth century, with the defining experience being a multi-year series of meetings beginning in 1906 at Azusa Street in Los Angeles.[8] All of what are termed the "classical Pentecostal" denominations, including the Assemblies of God, trace their origins to this event,[9] which they viewed as restoring the supernatural experiences of the New Testament Christians to the contemporary church.[10] Chief among these experiences was "the baptism in the Holy Spirit," which they viewed as an empowerment from God to bring the Christian message to the world supported by miraculous signs and wonders. Spirit baptism was always accompanied by the "initial physical evidence" of *glossolalia*, speaking in other tongues. Today, Spirit baptism and evidential tongues are regarded by many Pentecostals as the signature traits and distinctive doctrines of the movement.[11] Despite the historical prevalence of these teachings, however, being a Pentecostal has never been a completely static set of characteristics. Every generation has had to come to grips with its spiritual identity in its own way.

This essay is a preliminary report on the *Postmodern Pentecostals* research project undertaken in an attempt to tell the story of the younger leaders who will shape the future Pentecostal ministry in this emerging postmodern culture. With 22 percent of American Christians reporting in surveys that their church is "charismatic or Pentecostal," the potential influence of engaging these issues is significant.[12] The project's goal is both to reflect the struggle of Pentecostals in transition, and to provide a vehicle for further research endeavors aimed at understanding the nature of Pentecostal identity.

Methodology

The basic method of the research is the field interview. This preliminary account reflects a snowball sample of thirty-one individual interviews and three focus groups, composed of no more than six people each, developed by aleatory selection.[13] Most of the interview respondents come from within the Assemblies of God (AG) or from the margins of the denomination. They are virtually all in their twenties or early thirties, most are Anglos, with about one-third being female, and two-thirds male. The majority are AG ministers. The receptivity of the respondents to a qualitative research using a conversational interviewing style was quite positive, as indicated by the unanimous acceptance that my requests for interviews found across the country.[14] In fact, several respondents concluded our sessions by remarking that I was the first person with denominational ties who had ever listened to their views.

The final report on the research will integrate findings from 17 interview questions,[15] producing a map of how younger Pentecostal leaders are coming to terms with ministry in a marginalized Church. The objective of this essay, however, is to discern the ways in which these twenty-somethings understand their Pentecostal *identity*. Major subcultures discerned from listening to the interview respondents as a whole will be illustrated with representative quotations. In field interviews, then, to use sociologist Margaret Poloma's phrase, I have been "dancing between involvement and detachment"[16] in hopes of discerning the dynamics of the subcultures that young Pentecostal leaders call home,[17] and of suggesting agenda items for further quantitative and qualitative research on the future of U.S. Pentecostalism and its identity.[18]

Postmodern Pentecostals

Following Victor Turner, Alan Roxburgh refers to the Church's current experience as one of "liminality."[19] This marginalization began when modernity challenged the Church as the center of culture with the skeptical individual observer and attendant business/scientific enterprises. Postmodernism furthers the disestablishment of Christianity in the West by making it one of many, overlapping spiritual options in a culture that now has *no center* of any kind. Consequently, the "if you build it they will come" strategy of Christendom (which assumed a credible Church operating in a majority Christian culture) is losing viability. Christian denominations are scrambling to adapt their ministries to hit the moving target of emerging culture. [20]

Pentecostals are no exception. Being neither precisely Fundamentalists nor exactly Evangelicals, Pentecostal Christians have struggled to attain a sense of identity within late twentieth century modernism. Russell Spittler has noted otherworldliness, orality, and commitment to biblical authority as among the key values of the movement.[21] Stephen Land has described the emotional heart of Pentecostalism as "a passion for the Kingdom of God."[22] Taken together these attributes describe a Christian subculture that has never fit comfortably into either the liberal or conservative traditions, both of which are indebted to the scientific rationalism of modernity in their own way.

Thus, the postmodern turn could represent a fresh opportunity, and challenge, for Pentecostals to define themselves and their missionary endeavors. As Wonsuk Ma explains, "The great interest in spirituality that paradoxically exists in a 'post-modern' world opens a vast opportunity to Pentecostals."[23] This congruence of Pentecostalism's experiential identity and postmodernism's spirituality will involve many challenges of contextualization, requiring Pentecostals to reassess their worship forms, social attitudes, hermeneutic stance, and ethical notions. The movement will have to discern how to do its faith in fresh ways, bound by neither the domesticating influences of suburbia,[24] nor the stylized legalisms of another era.[25] Unlike some of their older peers, however, young Pentecostal leaders are simply not waiting for others to define their ministry models, theological insights, or, most importantly, the very nature of Pentecostal identity itself. The diversity that has always marked the movement is expressing itself among them in ways that will have profound implications for the future.

Emerging Pentecostalisms

In the interviews I heard multiple voices of emerging Pentecostalisms, at least within the AG. This presentation focuses on the subcultures identified during the interviews and discerned from transcripts. Future reports will deal with the variety of other issues also covered in the interviews. The point of the exercise is not to label people, which is offensive to postmoderns, but to discern the voices of various Pentecostal futures, as one would be able to pick out the individual harmonies in a piece of music.

While the interview respondents were diverse in some ways (most being pastors, some being students, and/or church members in the AG), from the outset it was clear that these mostly twenty-somethings were native to a culture different from my own.[26] Even those loyal to their denomination were not clones of their elders. One youth pastor described it to me this way: "I wouldn't go to the drycleaners because I have an iron at home. But my [senior] pastor would make a ton of Folgers at the office, but won't go to Starbucks. . . but I would go to 'Bucks for the environment.'"[27] I found that the cultural discrepancies run deeper than a preference for stronger coffee.

The voices heard in the project have a substantial range. One quite agitated AG pastor walked up to me in a hallway at Assemblies of God Theological Seminary and explained that he had done some reading on these issues and that, "I don't have any postmodern people in *my* church!" I concluded he was probably correct. On another occasion, a younger staff pastor from the Northwest confided: "If we don't get rid of all the Pentecostal stuff, we'll never hold on to the visitors." An email correspondent asked, "Can a postmodern church still be committed to the gifts of the spirit?" Another confessed that, "I feel as if my whole ministry is going through a transition and maybe a reconstruction." Thus, I have encountered a substantial group of people who are trying to work out their Pentecostalism in postmodern terms, some who are trying to work out their postmodernity in Pentecostal terms, and many combinations in between. Few seem willing to accept either emerging culture *or* their Pentecostal heritage uncritically.

The signature trait of these respondents was the "pause" that so often followed my opening question: "Are you a Pentecostal?" The fact that they needed a moment to compose a reply sometimes said more than the reply itself. The question is no longer simple, if it ever was.[28] At this point, I hear three voices emerge from the listening project with varying degrees of clarity: *loyalist, post-distinctive,* and *post-denominational.* The representativeness of each voice will have to be discovered by other researchers. The overlap between and among the subcultures will be obvious, perhaps because they speak to the future of the same movement. Numerous AG respondents expressed anxiety about their re-sponses being made public. Although none have asked for anonymity, the names used in the following sections are all pseudonyms.

Loyalist Pentecostals

Sometimes the "pause" did not happen. A significant number of respondents had absolutely no hesitation in answering my first question. For instance, Chuck, an undergraduate at an AG university, told me he was a Pentecostal, "with all my heart."[29] When asked how representative his views were of other students on campus, he surmised that the consensus would strongly support Pentecostal dis-tinctives such as initial physical evidence, but would question the amount of emphasis on tongues in the past, and would reject the tendency to make one gift an almost exclusive definition of the movement. However, even this condition was not meant to challenge the AG doctrinal statement. For Chuck, Pentecost is a known quantity which, perhaps with some small changes in spin, is essentially ready *as-is* for action in emerging culture. Further reflection will likely be con-fined to small refinements rather than paradigm shifts.

Clearly, much of this attitude is rooted in the tradition found in the move-ment. Interview respondents with this positive disposition often went immedi-ately to a discussion of their family's heritage in Pentecost, citing the number of generations involved, serving in ministry, or the like. For some, this *was* the answer to the question: *heritage = identity*. For others, family experiences were important, but represented only one phase of their identity formation. For exam-ple, Dan, a youth pastor from the Midwest commented that, "I used to describe myself as a Pentecostal growing up because that's what my parents were. But I came to that point where I looked into the Bible myself. . . and just realized that from out of the scripture and the Holy Spirit is real and that's a gift for all to have. And I've been filled with the Holy Spirit and therefore I am Pentecostal." When I asked how he knew he had been filled, he responded, "Well I began speaking in tongues and that's what I still believe today that that is the initial physical evidence of the Holy Spirit." Rather than being purely from heritage, then, this staff pastor's loyalty is *evolutionary*. He has qualms about the conser-vatism of the movement, and its ability to receive outsiders, but his core loyalty is in place.[30]

Gordon, a campus missionary on the West Coast came into the AG much later in life than did Chuck, and so did not refer to heritage. Perhaps for this rea-son, he pushed his response into an apologia for both Pentecostal experience and theology:

> I am indeed a Pentecostal. . . It's theologically accurate. By 'Pente-costal' I mean that I embrace the theology of the spiritual gifts oper-ating today, which would make me at least Charismatic. But in addi-tion, I believe there is a unique experience that people need to have

with the Holy Spirit called being filled with the Spirit, being baptized
in the Holy Spirit, whatever terminology you would like to use that is
marked by an outward manifestation of speaking in tongues when it
happens. The way I think about it is sort of like the Holy Spirit is doing a deep work inside of you, and his elbow kind of flares out and
hits this other lever that is somewhat connected and glossolalia,
tongues pours forth.

As is common in those who speak this "dialect" of Pentecost, Gordon also
strongly supports the notion that denominational structures, with all their limita-
tions, are extremely valuable. He cites pragmatic reasons such as raising missionary funds, but also contends that judicatories "are like firewalls in the body
of Christ. I think ministries need accountability. And I don't think that individual churches provide that effectively."[31] Coming from an "outsider" posture
then, he has built a case for being Pentecostal, and for being part of a larger organization. Lacking a heritage in the movement, Gordon is making his own.

Working as pastors and as missionaries to the arts community in a large
Eastern city, Mark and Lois answered my deceptively simple first questions
with, "big time," and then proceeded to sing me a line of a Spanish language
chorus which basically says, "I'm Pentecostal from my head to my shoes." For
these two leaders of a quite non-traditional AG ministry, the key issue is simple.
Lois put it this way, "Oh, man, that's the power. We need to have power. You
have to have power to minister in the city." Mark added, "So we see the church
or the AG as the gun. We see the Holy Spirit as the ammunition. It's the power
. . . and without that, we might a well just become, you know, Presbyterian or
some other denomination. . . but it's not about denominationalism or anything.
It's about power, pure and simple, the presence of God."[32] For these respondents, Pentecost deserves loyalty, not so much because of heritage, or theological argument, as simple necessity: *no power* = *no ministry*.

My general observation of the Loyalists is that the majority of them are the
children of Pentecostals (often ministers), most of them recall their Spirit baptism experience fondly from childhood or teen years, but that some of them have
had their convictions severely tested along the way. It is overly simplistic to
regard them simply as conservators of their parent's faith. Their loyalty has often been formed by walking through profound doubts, sometimes developed
from contact with other theologies, but often simply part of the struggle for self-
definition that occurs in late adolescence.

In fact, even with a generally positive experience with the AG, this personal
trial can be the defining season of their lives. Those who come through this season of doubt seem to be loyal in a more mature way than those who have known
nothing but comfort on the issue of identity. Speaking of the end of his struggle,
Dan recalled, "it was almost as if a voice was leading me that this is real, there's
no hiding this, no reason to be afraid of this, no reason to be ashamed of this."

Dan expressed a form of loyalty that is no longer naïve; he has considered the alternatives and chosen his heritage above them.

Post-distinctive Pentecostals

A group of AG pastors in a Midwestern district recently admitted to one of my respondents that not one of them is teaching the doctrines of Spirit baptism and initial evidence in public. Feeling a lack of solid theological support for these distinctives (known popularly as "7 and 8"),[33] their question was, "do young leaders have to commit intellectual suicide to believe this?" And their concern was that some are "falling on their swords on this one." Yet, "Not a single person here had any animosity toward the AG, only a deep affection and love." The goal of the discussion: "to better the movement."

While this form of loyalty does not regard Pentecost as a totally fixed quantity, neither does it counsel revolt or wholesale doctrinal revision. The post-distinctive Pentecostal seeks out dialogue on the critical identity issues and is perplexed by the perceived unwillingness of leadership to engage in this discussion.[34] Their question could be put very simply: if we cannot talk about these things openly, does that mean they cannot stand up to scrutiny?[35]

A number of respondents expressed this concern wistfully, obviously feeling torn between a spiritual community to which they wanted to belong and theological and cultural dilemmas that might make belonging impossible. No one in this subculture seemed happy about living with these tensions, with many AG interview respondents verbalizing their worries about the future of the denomination and their place in it. As Andrew, an AG church planter pleaded, "we love you guys, we want to be a part of this. . . give us the leeway to figure some things out. . . Don't be the Methodist pastors of 1901 that kicked all your forefathers out."[36]

A core concern of the post-distinctive sub-culture is the "routinization of the charismata,"[37] the tendency to reduce spontaneous religious experience to a predictable template that is more easily controlled. A young senior pastor from a large metropolitan area, Mack defines Pentecostalism as "being filled with the Spirit," but goes on to caution,

> I'm not sure it's that predictable, mechanical thing we turn it into. I think it's about allowing the wind of the Spirit to blow us wherever the wind in the Spirit wants to blow us, and it's about so much more than initial physical evidence. You know I read Acts two and I see young men dreaming dreams and old men seeing visions, and to me that's as much of a supernatural byproduct of being filled with the Spirit as speaking in tongues. And yet, just seems like there's an overemphasis or overkill on just one small dimension of what it means to be filled with the Spirit.[38]

Asked would you consider yourself a Pentecostal, he responds, "that's tough because I hate labels." Citing the potentially offensive nature of religious identifications in his hugely diverse city, Mack said,

> So I don't go around saying I'm 'Pentecostal' as much as just trying to emphasize the importance of, man, I want everything God has for me. I want to be filled with the Spirit of God, which to me means just being kind of immersed in the Spirit and allowing the Spirit just to have control of my life and where I'm headed. So I don't know. That's not a very good answer. . . I just steer clear of labels. It might be a generational thing too.

In a darker reflection he expressed his fears of a routinization of Spirit baptism:

> It just seems that we say that we believe in the power of the Spirit, and then we hijack it by having this formula—this is how it has to happen. And I just don't want to put God in that kind of box. . . I think you can hold to initial physical evidence, throw the formula out, but praying away for people, and encouraging them in a way that says, 'God's going to do it how God's going to do it'. . . if initial physical evidence is true, you don't have to worry about it because that's going to be what happens.

Mack's post-distinctiveness, then, is a both/and proposition. While not rejecting initial evidence outright, he certainly has no plans to emphasize it in his seeker-oriented, mid-town church. Moreover, he regards loyalists as promoting "labels" and "formulas" that both stereotype people, and confine the Spirit to one, narrowly defined standard operating procedure. Mack's flexibility on these issues places him on collision course with other AG leaders who regard the absolute connection between Spirit baptism and tongues as essential, not just to the movement's identity, but to its survival. He avoids this collision, as many AG post-distinctives do, by keeping his views relatively private.

Tom, a senior pastor from the West Coast took an even stronger stand, describing the whole issue as "a tender spot in my conscience."[39] A phrase he used early in our talk was illuminating, "I certainly *believe that I believe* in the Pentecostal distinctive." Clearly, Tom is still working out what he believes his beliefs are, and so is standing back from them by one level. Throughout our dialog, he referred to himself often as "conflicted," despite his very positive feelings about having grown up with parents who were AG ministers and whom he greatly admires.

> For me I don't see why that initial physical evidence couldn't you know. . . manifest itself in other areas of giftedness; leadership, teaching, the gift of hospitality. . . Do I believe the gifts, the power gifts, the third wave gifts or whatever, do I believe that they are

available to the body at large? Absolutely. Do I believe that every believer has to possess those gifts or that distinctive in order to be fruitful or effective in life and ministry? Absolutely not.

Obviously, these are views Tom holds with reluctance, but with a strong level of
conviction. I sensed that he felt a lack of credible alternatives, largely due to
very negative personal experiences with extremism in Pentecost in the past, and
the success of non-Pentecostal churches in his area in the present. His reasoning
was simple: if Christian ministries can have highly visible success without Pentecostal distinctives, then why bother with them and run the risk of alienating
outsiders and cultivating religious extremism among insiders?

Our talk revealed what would become a common pattern in those on the doctrinal fringes of the AG: the implication in childhood that those outside the Pentecostal fold were spiritually inferior, and a really terrible experience at youth
camp, generally regarding prayer for Spirit baptism. Tom described the former:
"But in my growing up. . . my perception was I wasn't sure if anybody could
really understand salvation apart from a Pentecostal experience."

The latter issue related to a best friend who did not received Spirit baptism in
a summer youth camp.

> I remember going to camp with my best friend, we were best friends
> growing up. Junior high camp, eighth year. It still bothers me how
> they wear you down, they wear them down with games, they wear
> you down with a speaker, they wear you down, wear you down, wear
> you down. And now stand up here I've got a guy on each side of me
> holding my arms up and one guy in front of me just saying, 'hallelu-
> jah, hallelujah,'. . . 'just let it come, let it come.' I'm exhausted. I'm
> in eighth grade, I'm a teenager. This is the same practice they use in
> brain washing. Say the same thing over and over again. It's hot.
> There's people shouting all around me. All of the sudden I have this
> baptism experience. Okay now my buddy is right by me. Best friends.
> He doesn't get it. He's even been praying for it more diligently than I
> have. He believes in it more passionately than I do. To this day he has
> not been baptized in the Holy Spirit. Now am I better than him? Why
> hasn't he had that experience? Is he less than a believer?[40]

This memory seems to have become an icon for everything Tom perceives to be
wrong with an emphasis on distinctives. For him, they are out of bounds when
they create division in the body of Christ for the sole purpose of establishing one
"separatist" group's preferred identity at the expense of other believers.

Bob, a young minister in a very postmodern Western city, grew up in a conservative AG church and echoed some of Tom's complaints. He referred to distinctives as "the sacred cow," seeing them as associated with a "showy" form of
Pentecost in which "every form of worship, to prayer, to living out faith became
when we were at church."[41]

However, the core of Bob's qualms about the official AG view of distinctives centers on what they do *not* explain. His ministry's leadership team involves believers from a variety of denominations. "Some don't speak in tongues but I see them move in the gifts of the Spirit more than those who do speak in tongues. And it's kind of challenged me in a lot of ways like what is the initial evidence? I always struggled with the fact that we have made a doctrine out of a manifestation. . . . But I've seen Lutherans with the gift of prophecy over someone and it's kind of challenged my paradigm in a sense."

Like other speakers of the post-distinctive dialect, Bob seems to be searching for a pneumatology with more explanatory power than he perceives in the current notion of initial evidence. Oddly, with one exception, the only other doctrinal issue to appear in my interviews has been the nature of Spirit baptism itself.[42] And yet, with regard to the evidences issue, I have found a subculture that wants to remain within denominational ranks, but has no intention of giving distinctives the emphasis received from their predecessors, or from loyalists of their own age. Their position is what I would call one of *soft distinctives*, desirable experiences that should not be reduced to formulas or contended for in a rigid way. Their priority is to be filled with God more than to do so within a specified pattern, at least until better explanations of the doctrines are forthcoming.

This subculture continues to sign off on AG distinctives at ministerial credential renewal time, but does not do so without pangs of conscience. They seem to handle the dilemma by demoting these issues to a secondary status in their minds that does not require a rigorous interpretation,[43] or by cleverly redefining the words in the doctrinal statement.[44] They are developing definitions of Pentecost with a "third wave" accent, defining the movement in ways that advocate Spirit baptism, but include distinctives more as recommendations than as obligations.[45] However, the process of forging this definition leaves these leaders "conflicted," a condition which is also true of the fellowships that are dealing with them. They do not treat this conflict lightly. In fact, I had the distinct impression that they think about it all the time. What troubles them most is the lack of "safe" environments in which to voice their doubts and have their issues addressed.

Post-denominational Pentecostals

A third subculture also answers with an unflinching "yes" when asked if they are Pentecostal, but means this affirmation in a very different way. This group resembles their Loyalist peers in a devotion to Spirit fullness, and shares the Post-distinctive suspicion of rigidly defining doctrines. However, unlike the other varieties, post-denominational Pentecostals reject the idea of being formally affiliated with a judicatory structure.[46] This position is quite reminiscent of the early days of the AG when even the notion of forming a national organization was extremely controversial.[47] The fear at the time was that a religious bureaucracy would soon develop into a Spirit-quenching behemoth. Post-denominationals have simply revived this issue and applied it in postmodern times.[48]

For example, Mitchell (who described himself as being "in the Assemblies of God from 1991, '92 or so 'till '96") exclaimed his surprise at my research interests in an email: "You're an Assembly of God man and you're all into the emerging church. . . how odd is that?"[49] Dale expressed the same astonishment when he wrote that, "I had to blink a few times when I saw AGTS."[50] He went on to describe how he migrated out of the AG to a staff position at "a non-denominational-charismatic-lite-seeker-boomer-mega-church."

> While at Bible college. . . my mantra to other students was "we have to change it from within. . . " When I discovered grace and reflected on the abusive churches I had been a part of (and a perpetrator in), I chucked the AG and dismissed looking into any church with "AG" attachments. Imagine trying to find a spirit-filled church accepting women in ministry that also understood the postmodern transition that WASN'T AG affiliated. Talk about shrinking your pool. . .

Like others interviewed from this group, Dale tells a story of pain and regret stemming from what he perceives as authoritarian pastoral leadership, plus a personal reluctance to participate in spiritual extremes. Interestingly, Dale's wife still has AG ministry credentials, holding the door open for the possibility of a return. In fact, some young AG leaders have maintained respect for the move-ment's credentialing of women for the ministry.[51] This egalitarian stance could be a starting point for eventual reconciliation.

Other post-denominationals are technically still part of the fellowship by ministerial credential or church membership, yet are philosophically absent, or at least highly critical. In a recent blog, for example, Todd referred to the AG as "my stodgy, often overly fundamental denomination. . . " These *soft post-denominationals* take issue as much with the culture of the movement as with its beliefs and practices. Without some form of intervention many of them could become exiles from the denomination in the next few years. Some already have. My sense is that, when more of their significant peer relationships are outside the AG than inside, they begin emigrating to a non-denominational status. Af-filiating with another formal group seems to hold little appeal.

Mitchell left an AG church after suffering under a pastor with a "large per-sonality." "Relationships led my family into the AG," he recalls, "the forcible closure of those relationships led us out." He now worships in a house church setting in a large Southern city. His house church is part of a small international network, most of which is "post-Pentecostal in one form or another."[52] Although he defines Pentecostalism as denominations that arose from Azusa Street, Mitchell noted wistfully that, "Surely there must be a center that holds us all together."[53] Being firmly post-distinctive in outlook, many of Mitchell's Pentecostal peers also are turning to the house church in an attempt to define that "center" as communal relationships, rather than charismatic practice. These home groups seem to be a major refuge for AG exiles.

My sense of the post-denominational tribe is that they have made three discoveries: (1) history—they no longer view as credible the idea that Christianity was devoid of virtue before Azusa Street;[54] (2) culture—they are aware of the ways in which modernity has shaped the faith,[55] and; (3) variety—they are unable to see Christian worship as confined to any one pattern forever.[56] These "discoveries" have made it more difficult to see any one polity or doctrinal statement as defining Pentecost for all time. Consequently, post-denominationals seem to be using these discoveries to create a three-dimension intellectual space in which they are developing their revision of Pentecostalism. While loyalists consider distinctives and formal membership as fixed points (or targets) which we are obligated to approximate (the closer to the target, the more loyal), post-denominationals desire the freedom of exploring the new territory opened up by discovery. In truth, even many post-distinctives share this ethos, frequently using terms such as "journey" and "conversation" to describe their quest.

Citing Paul's critique of factions in Corinth, Mitchell contends that, "any movement that is actually alive doesn't even have a name yet. . . I consider myself post-Pentecostal, but not anti-Pentecostal, taking my Pentecostal heritage and moving beyond that." He envisions the whole church as going post-denominational, and the AG with it. For this subculture, then, the best way to be truly Pentecostal is to be free of mandatory distinctives and denominational ties.

Conclusion: Pentecostal—Finally

The interviewing phase of the *Postmodern Pentecostals* project felt on many occasions as if I had walked into a room where a conversation was already taking place. In an email contact, Nick confessed that "You have caught me in the middle of a season of evaluating Pentecostal issues."[57] As a guest, then, I am listening only to one segment of a dialog that precedes me and will continue long after I am gone. This report represents a summary of what I have heard so far in my role as a "visitor" on the issue of Pentecostal identity.

Loyalist, post-distinctive, and post-denominational voices can all be heard in various combinations. I suspect that future research will yield not just refinements to this understanding, but whole new ways of thinking about these subcultures among young Pentecostal leadership. Hopefully, this essay will serve to catalyze such thinking.

There appears to be one major concept which ties together much of the dialog among emerging Pentecostal leaders: the desire to move from a narrow, particularistic Pentecost defended from a *disciplinary* posture, to a broader, more holistic understanding that reflects a *dialogic* posture. As Mack puts it, "by narrowly defining the baptism we might have actually boxed God in as opposed to allowing him in the fullness of what the Holy Spirit is all about."[58] Bob supplies a more specific example:

> Well, my definition of Pentecostalism has been I guess changing over maybe the last year. I think especially in our context of ministry which is full-on postmodernism. It's just it's being Spirit-led. . . Pentecostalism is to me today is being in the marketplace and being Spirit-led in the market place. Getting a word of knowledge isn't just for Bessie Lou at the altar call but it's for John at Starbucks.

Younger leaders are, in many ways, simply doing what Pentecostals have done since Azusa Street, trying to sort out how the beliefs and practices of the movement make the journey from the church to the sidewalk. For them, a Pentecost that does not function at Starbucks is no Pentecost at all.

The strategic choices for Pentecostal denominations in dealing with these young leaders might be summarized as disengagement, discipline, or dialogue. The passive route of disengagement assumes that their questions are a product of youth, and that they will eventually grow into the views of their elders if given time and kept out of positions of influence. The disciplinary stance regards Pentecostal distinctives as so essential they must be defended immediately by the exercise of power (e.g., the revocation of ministerial credentials) on the part of denominational authorities. The dialogic route would seek to engage young leaders in open discussion of both the strengths and weaknesses of the movement and its beliefs. The balance achieved between these three approaches, will almost certainly play a vital role in defining the relationship of Pentecostal denominations to their younger leaders. The first question of my first interview revealed this dynamic, when I asked David, a theology student from an AG background, "are you a Pentecostal?" After the "pause" he said, "yes—finally."

APPENDIX A

Postmodern Pentecostals Field Interview Questions

1. Are you a "Pentecostal?"

2. What does that word mean to you?

3. What role do Spirit baptism and Initial Physical Evidence play in your current understanding of Pentecostalism? [Tell me about your own Spirit baptism experience.]

4. Have you ever had a time when your Pentecostal convictions were seriously in doubt in your own mind?

5. How do you handle the issue of Spirit baptism in your ministry context?

6. How do you handle the gifts of the Spirit in your ministry context?

7. When thinking about the future of Pentecostalism in the United States, are you more of an optimist or a pessimist? Why?

8. What would the "ideal" Pentecostal church/ministry look like to you?

9. Let me ask you to play consultant: what advice would you give the national leaders of Pentecostal denominations in the United States?

10. What have you read that has been most influential in shaping your perspective on Pentecostalism?

11. How has the idea of "postmodernism" been significant to you in ministry and/or your understanding of Pentecostalism—if it has?

12. Tell me your favorite story about a Pentecostal experience, either from your own life or something powerful you have seen God do for someone else?

13. Who else should I interview?

14. If you were doing these interviews, what questions would you ask, or ask differently, that I have not covered?

15. How representative do you feel your views on Pentecostalism are among your peers?

16. Any parting shots?

17. May I have your permission to quote from your remarks? If so what level of anonymity, if any, do you prefer?

Notes

1. See my "Emerging Culture/Emerging Church: A Select Resource List." Available online at: http://www.agts.edu/faculty/faculty_publications/bibliographies/creps_bibliogr aphy/index.html. The 1700 sources catalogued in this ever-growing bibliography are one indication of the sheer scale of the scholarly and popular analysis of these issues.

2. Jean-Francois Lyotard describes postmodernism as "incredulity toward meta-narratives," a rejection of any totalizing account of reality, in his seminal work, *The Postmodern Condition: A Report on Knowledge* (Minneapolis, MN: University of Minnesota Press, 1999), xxiv; Richard J. Mouw, "Pentecostal Evangelism," *Word and World* 16 no. 3 (1996): 354–357.

3. Stanley Grenz refers to this "postmodern mood" or "postmodern ethos" as one in which, "For the first time in recent history, the emerging generation does not share the conviction of their parents that the world is becoming a better place in which to live. . . They believe that the survival of humankind is now at stake." *A Primer on Postmodernism* (Grand Rapids: Eerdmans, 1996), 7–8, 13, 83.

4. See Robert C. Fuller, *Spiritual, but Not Religious: Understanding Unchurched America* (Cambridge: Oxford University Press, 2001). Alan Wolfe frames the issue of religion being conformed to culture, and contends that, "American religion has been so transformed that we have reached the end of religion as we know it. This does not mean religion no longer has meaning. It means we will have to know it in new ways." *The Transformation of American Religion: How We Actually Live Our Faith* (New York: Free Press, 2003), 264. In a major interview study, Robert Wuthnow describes this religious transition as a shift of metaphor from a spirituality of "dwelling" in the 1950s to a spirituality of "seeking" today. *After Heaven: Spirituality in American Since the 1950's* (Berkley, CA: University of California Press, 1998), 3, 198. He describes the essence of the change: "Many Americans struggle to invent new languages to describe their faith. As they do, their beliefs are becoming more eclectic, and their commitments are often becoming more private. . . fewer people live within spiritual enclaves that they can take for granted and. . . more options are available from which to piece together a spiritual life."

5. Craig Van Gelder, "Postmodernism and Evangelicals: A Unique Missiological Challenge at the Beginning of the 21st Century," *Missiology* (October 2002): 495. Italics mine.

6. Paul Elbert, "Book Review" *Asian Journal of Pentecostal Studies* 4, no. 2 (2001): 332. For an example of this debate among practitioners see: "Great Debate: Is Postmodernism in the Church Overblown?" *Leadership Weekly*. Available online: http://www.christianity today.com/leaders/special/postmodernsim.html

7. Van Gelder, 492.

8. The reference here is primarily to American Pentecostals, the subject of the present study. In contrast to the popular notion of Azusa as sole wellspring of the movement, Douglas Jacobsen, argues that Pentecostalism has been diverse from its earliest days,

with origins he terms "scattered and fluid." See his *Thinking in the Spirit: Theologies of the Early Pentecostal Movement* (Bloomington, IN.: Indiana University Press, 2003), 10.

9. McGee, 25–26, 58–63, 585.

10. Acts 1-2 are the New Testament passage most often cited by Pentecostals to interpret and defend their experiences as legitimate. See Byron D. Klaus, "Pentecostalism," *Encyclopedia of Religious Freedom*, ed. Catharine Cookson (New York: Routledge, 2003), 330–35.

11. With regard to the (U.S.) Assemblies of God, Margaret Poloma's survey research has found general agreement with this statement, with clergy reporting higher levels of support than congregants. See *The Assemblies of God at the Crossroads: Charisma and Institutional Dilemmas* (Knoxville: University of Tennessee Press, 1989), 40.

12. Surprisingly, one survey found that "both the churched and the unchurched were equally likely to brand themselves as 'charismatic or Pentecostal.'" [21%] George Barna, *Re-Churching the Unchurched* (Ventura, CA: Issachar Resources, 2000), 42. "29% of Protestant Senior Pastors label themselves 'charismatic or Pentecostal.'" Other surveys place the percentage of Pentecostals in the population significantly lower. Margaret Poloma notes that "Results of surveys place the size of the Pentecostal population of America from 5% to 12% depending on the measurement used. According to Smidt, Green, Kellstedt and Goth (1996), 3.6% of the adult population belongs to a classic Pentecostal church. When non-denominational charismatics are added, the figure increases to 5%. Smidt, et al. (1996: 223) have made an interesting observation about this seeming small figure, noting that the only Protestant denominational families to exceed this size are Baptists, Methodists, and Lutherans, with Lutherans only a fraction larger. . . .When respondents were asked if they spoke in tongues, a classic litmus test for Pentecostal Spirit Baptism, the figure rose to 8.7%." "The Spirit Bade Me Go: Pentecostalism and Global Religion." Paper Prepared for Presentation at the Association for the Sociology of Religion Annual Meetings, August 11-13, 2000. Washington, D.C., 2. Available online. http://hirr.hartsem.edu/research/Pente.%20and%20Global%20Religion.doc] Some sense of the international scope of the movement is found in Somini Sengupta and Larry Rohter, "Where Faith Grows, Fired by Pentecostalism," *New York Times*, October 14, 2003.

13. This report is "preliminary," in two ways: (1) since interviewing was still underway when this article was drafted, only the first third of the interviews are considered; and, (2) the conclusions largely reflect the answers to questions concerning Pentecostal identity, items 1–4, of a 17-item questionnaire (See footnotes 8 and 9, and Appendix A). The final project will reflect approximately 85 interviews, 7 internet bulletin boards, and almost 700 messages from a bulletin board devoted expressly to this topic. Interviewing and internet communication were supplemented by three closed-door listening sessions held in three different states with groups of younger leaders ranging in size from half a dozen to twenty, and by 20 site visits to non-traditional churches and ministries that define themselves as "Pentecostal" in some way and also conceive of themselves as engaging emerging culture. This experience allows me to consider issues that concern individuals (such as how to define "Pentecostal"), and those that occupy the attention of congregations (such as what to do about that definition). Pencil and paper surveys of Assembly of God undergraduates, and a nominal group study of an Assemblies of God District will round out the final version of this report. I am deeply grateful for the financial support of the Louisville Institute that made this project possible, and for the able counsel of

Donald Miller (USC) and Richard Flory (BIOLA), who have consulted with me throughout.

14. All interviews were audio and/or videotaped and transcribed. The first several interviews were conducted with only one planned question: "Are you a Pentecostal?" This query was suggested by many hours spent in background research both with discussion groups and individuals, all of whom I found largely by accident. Free-form sessions gradually gave rise to about seventeen items that were formulated into a standard set of questions asked to all subsequent interview respondents. Each interview began with a recording of the respondent's age, spiritual background, education and ministry.

15. See Appendix, Postmodern Pentecostals Field Interview Questions.

16. Margaret M. Poloma, *Main Street Mystics: The Toronto Blessing and Reviving Pentecostalism* (Lanham, MD: AltaMira Press, 2003), 248.

17. All quotations from field interviews are presented in their original form, sometimes edited for brevity. This approach seemed more conducive to the readability of the essay than inserting "sic" many dozens of times, since the grammatical errors will be obvious to the reader as those common to conversational speech.

18. Wolfgang Vondey, "Christian Amnesia: Who in the World Are Pentecostals?" *Asian Journal of Pentecostal Theology* 4, no. 1 (2001): 21–39. "Since the rise of modern classical Pentecostalism in the early twentieth century, the majority of approaches to the identity of the movement in North America have focused on its most distinctive feature: the practice of speaking in tongues. . . Charismatic renewal forced classical Pentecostals to deal with issues of their identity in more depth. . . The visible outcome is a large amount of literature dealing with the theological, historical, or sociological themes distinctive to the movement. A unifying and ordering principle of identity, however, is still missing." (30–1) Douglas Petersen concurs: "Further, it must be recognized that an interpretive consensus on the nature of Pentecostalism does not exist even from within the movement." Douglas Petersen, "Pentecostals: Who Are They?" in *Mission as Transformation: A Theology of the Whole Gospel,* eds. Vinay Samuel and Chris Sugden (Oxford: Regnum, 1999), 77.

19. Alan J. Roxburgh, *The Missionary Congregation: Leadership and Liminality* (Harrisburg, PA: Trinity Press International, 1997).

20. Mike Regele and Mark Schulz, *Death of the Church* (Grand Rapids, MI: Zondervan, 1996); R.R. Reno, *In the Ruins of the Church: Sustaining Faith in an Age of Diminished Christianity* (Grand Rapids: Brazos, 2002); Douglas John Hall, *The End of Christendom and the Future of Christianity* (London: Wipf & Stock, 2002); Thomas G. Bandy, *Fragile Hope: Your Church in 2020* (New York: Easum-Bandy Associates, 2002); David Jacoby Bosch and Alan Neely, eds. *Believing in the Future: Toward A Missiology of Western Culture* (Harrisburg, PA: Trinity Press International, 1995).

21. Russell P. Spittler, "Implicit Values in Pentecostal Missions," *Missiology: An International Review* 16 no. 4 (1988): 409–424.

22. Steven J. Land, *Pentecostal Spirituality: A Passion for the Kingdom* (Sheffield, UK: Sheffield Academic Press, 1997).

23. Wonsuk Ma, "Biblical Studies in the Pentecostal Tradition: Yesterday, Today, and Tomorrow," in *The Globalization of Pentecostalism,* 63.

24. Frank D. Macchia, "God Present in a Confused Situation: The Mixed Influence of the Charismatic Movement on Classical Pentecostalism in the United States," *Pneuma* 18, no. 1 (Spring 1996): 34. Macchia notes that, "North American, particularly white,

Pentecostalism has lost a degree of its eschatological fervor as it has gradually abandoned the urban poor for the suburban middle class. Storefront and tent meetings that tended to function as eschatological 'colonies' of enthusiastic believers were soon replaced by mega churches and ministries that focused attention on success for middle class Christians in the here-and-now."

25. Macchia states the reliance on strict holiness codes as an aspect of Pentecostal identity: "Holiness taboos, though sometimes trivial and hypocritical were also part of the Pentecostal attempt to identify an ecclesiastical subculture that resisted and criticized the spirit of the age" (45).

26. Leonard Sweet describes younger people as "natives" and older people as "immigrants" to postmodernity. Leonard I. Sweet, *Carpe Manana: Is Your Church Ready to Seize Tomorrow?* (Grand Rapids, MI: Zondervan, 2001). Interestingly, a small 2003 survey of faculty, students, and administration at an Assemblies of God bible college found that those over 35 reporting "distinctives" as the biggest challenge for the church ahead, while those under 35 said that the relevance of doctrine, family breakdown, and integrity were the major issues.

27. Mike, interview with author, Dallas, Texas, January 3, 2004.

28. Douglas Jacobsen concludes: "First generation Pentecostals were divided by a host of practical and doctrinal differences, and the boundaries of the Pentecostal movement as a whole were ragged and to some degree flexible. Even the core idea of the baptism in the Spirit was debated. . . All in all, the question of who was and who was not a Pentecostal Christian was at least as difficult to answer in the early years of the twentieth century *as it is today*. . . All this means that there is no meta-model of Pentecostalism—no essence of Pentecostalism or normative archetype—that can provide an infallible rule against which to judge all the various particular renditions of Pentecostal faith and theology to determine precisely which is the most Pentecostal and/or the least Pentecostal." He contrasts this view with the "clear-boundary-line vision of the movement." Jacobsen, 10, 12, 286 (italics added).

29. Chuck, interview with author November 21, 2003.

30. Dan's case is reminiscent of Margaret Poloma's finding that, "Survey analysis results /from 447 AG pastors in 1999/ placed within this theoretical context /Lewis Coser & Thomas O'Dea/ can be succinctly summarized as follows: *the Assemblies of God has a solid core around which there are varying levels of ambiguity.* The ambiguity that exists on peripheral issues appears to function as a safety-valve mechanism feeding the ongoing dialectical interrelationship between charisma and institution building." Margaret Poloma, "Charisma and Structure in the Assemblies of God," Draft paper for the Organizing Religious Work Project, Hartford Institute for Religion Research (2002), 5.

31. Gordon, interview with author, July 2003.

32. Mark and Lois, interview with author, July 2003.

33. *The Statement of Fundamental Truths* (http://ag.org/top/beliefs/truths.cfm) contains the sixteen basic doctrines of the (U.S.) Assemblies of God. At the popular level, this list is sometimes referred to as "the sixteen," within which the doctrines of "the Baptism in the Holy Ghost" and "the Initial Physical Evidence of the Baptism in the Holy Ghost" occupy the seventh and eighth positions, lending themselves to the designation. "7 and 8." Having heard this expression hundreds of times in field research, I never once witnessed a young Pentecostal offer a definition. It appears that the meaning of the phrase is simply assumed within their subcultures, perhaps indicating how closely these two doctrines are associated and how much attention they receive. However, it is important to

note that the phrase seems to be reserved largely for private settings, and seems to be used rarely in public or official communication. I have heard the phrase among older leaders as well, meaning that it is not the exclusive possession of the young. However, in my observation, even elder leaders use "7 and 8" almost exclusively in private settings. The observance of this protocol may indicate that the level of tension attached to these two doctrines engenders a respectful, official wording for public discussions, and a casual, unofficial shorthand for private settings.

34. For a discussion of the role of distinctives see Russell P. Spittler, "Maintaining Distinctives: The Future of Pentecostalism," in *Pentecostals from the Inside Out: A Candid Look at One of America's Fastest Growing Religious Movements*, Ed. Harold B. Smith (Wheaton, Ill.: Victor Books, 1990), 121–134.

35. Some post-distinctives, for example, perceived the exclusion of doctrinal issues (specifically "7 and 8") from some of the *Vision for Transformation* regional meetings held by the Assemblies of God in 2002 and 2003 as an example of their concern, interpreting this boundary on the discussion as defensive, an attempt to deny the existence of the proverbial elephant in the living room. Ironically, scholarly discussion of "7 and 8" abounds. See, for example, the "Initial Evidence, Again" issue of the *Asian Journal of Pentecostal Studies* 2, no. 2 (July 1999). However, Cecil M. Robeck, Jr. points out the controversy that can attach to such discussions within the Assemblies of God domestically in "An Emerging Magisterium? The Case of the Assemblies of God," *Pneuma* 25, no. 2 (Fall 2003): 164-215. See also, Poloma's discussion of "The Price of Theological Dissent," in *The Assemblies of God at the Crossroads*, 169–172.

36. Andrew, interview with author, 10 June 2004.

37. Poloma, "Pentecostalism in a Postmodern Age," 6; Donald E. Miller, "Routinizing Charismata: The Vineyard Christian Fellowship in the Post-Wimber Era," *Pneuma* 25, no. 2 (Fall 2003): 216–239.

38. Mack, interview with author, July 12, 2003.

39. Tom, interview with author, September 30, 2003.

40. For a poignant depiction of the "chronic seeker" phenomenon and its personal impact see Sam Rima's account in *Overcoming the Dark Side of Leadership : The Paradox of Personal Dysfunction* (Grand Rapids: Baker Books, 1997), 24–26. He describes a Pentecostal upbringing in which Spirit baptism evidenced by tongues was "God's ultimate stamp of approval for a job well done."

41. Bob, telephone interview with author, September 5, 2003.

42. One interview respondent did take issue with the AG view of eschatology.

43. Vondey suggests the notion of a "hierarchy of truths" as one way of resolving Pentecostal identity issues in a globalized context. Vondey, 22.

44. For example, several respondents emphasized the word "physical" as implying that other, *non*-physical evidences might exist along with tongues, effectively expanding the borders on evidence beyond glossolalia. Another told me that he signs off on "7 and 8" by thinking of the doctrines as products of the historical era in which they were developed.

45. The "third wave" refers to the notion common among Charismatic Christians that a first "wave" of the Holy Spirit arrived in the Pentecostal revivals of the early twentieth century, a second "wave" following in mid-century in the form of the Charismatic Renewal within both Protestant and Catholic congregations, and a third wave now is restoring the gifts of the Holy Spirit more fully to the Church, especially those related to prophecy, healing, and apostolic leadership. The Vineyard Christian Fellowship is often

cited as an example of a third wave group, set apart from classical Pentecostal denominations by a variety of factors, including a rejection of the initial evidence doctrine. See C. Peter Wagner, *The Third Wave of the Holy Spirit: Encountering the Power of Signs and Wonders Today* (New York: Servant Publications, 1988); Charles H. Kraft. *Christianity with Power: Your Worldview and Your Experience of the Supernatural* (New York: Vine Books, 1989).

46. Alister McGrath notes that "both individual churches and Christians in America are showing an increasing reluctance to define themselves denominationally." *The Future of Christianity* (Malden, Mass.: Blackwell Publishers, 2002): 44. See also, Elmer Towns, *Is the Day of the Denomination Dead?*[Elmer Towns Online Library] (Nashville, TN.: Thomas Nelson, nd). Available online: http://64.233.161.104/search?q=cache:SsdWI PQbDMkJ:www.elmetowns.com/books/online/denom_dead/Is_the_Day_of_the_Denomi ntion_Dead%255BETowns%255D.PDF+%22denominational+loyalty%22+AND+Pentec ostals&hl=en Accessed July 10, 2004.

47. Some recent survey research among Protestant clergy has found their denominational loyalties to be fairly strong, with Pentecostal/Charismatic ministers being "particularly likely to be committed to their denominations. . . and particularly like to feel that their denomination is an important part of their church's identity. . . /and/ among the least likely to have this worry. . . that their denomination is headed in the wrong way." However, this general consensus conceals a generational divide: "Older pastors were over twice as likely to agree strongly with this statement. . . that their denomination is an important part of their church's identity. . . than were young ministers (55% among those 60 and older, 36% among those 45 to 59, and 26% among those under 45)." Ellison Research, "Study Shows Ministers Want More Cooperation Among Denominations, but Are often Frustrated at a Lack of Agreement within their Own Denomination," Available online: http://www.ellisonresearch.com/ERPS%20II/release%207%20denominations.htm Accessed July 10, 2004. "Pentecostal and charismatic ministers are the ones most likely to see things the same way their denomination does; 82% say their theology is pretty much in line with their denomination's." Ellison Research, "Study Shows Four out of Ten Protestant Ministers Are Not on the Same Page as their Denomination Politically or Theologically," Available online: http://www.ellisonresearch.com/ERPS%20II/Release %205%20 Denominational%20Match.htm Accessed 10 July 2004.

48. An insightful interview study of EPC (Evangelical, Charismatic, and Pentecostal) "church leavers" is offered by Alan Jamieson in *Churchless Faith: Faith Journeys Beyond the Churches* (London: Society for the Preservation of Christian Knowledge, 2002). While his interview population is drawn largely from New Zealanders, Jamieson's differentiation of leavers into various subcultures tied to faith development stages (i.e., disillusioned followers, reflective exiles, transitional explorers, and integrated wayfinders) suggests that the condition of the post-denominational Pentecostals in the present study is significantly more complex than the label implies. Jamieson cites (9) Dave Tomlinson's *The Post-Evangelical* [Revised North American Edition] (El Cajon, CA: emergentYS Books, 2003) as pointing to "a growing dissatisfaction with evangelicalism among many immersed in our increasingly postmodern culture. Tomlinson's insight and analysis have greatly helped our understanding of the issues behind many people's decision to leave and provided an understanding of the increasing mismatch between popular forms of church and a postmodern social context."

49. Mitchell, email communication with the author, January 14 and 17, 2004.

50. Dale, email communication with the author, May 31, 2003.

51. Tim Bednar, Blog: "Women in Ministry: The Emerging Church Has Not Gone Far Enough," Moxy Turtle: About the Church in the World." Available online [http://www.e-church.com/Blog-detail.asp?EntryID=517&BloggerID=1] Accessed January 30, 2004.

52. Wolfe notes that "home churching has not been widely studied by social scientists /but/ has a strong appeal to certain kinds of religious believers for whom authenticity of experience is more important than congregational affiliation, which they are likely to dismiss as mere 'churchianity'. . . The House church movement aims to practice what one believer, Glenn Heller calls 'relational Christianity' rather than 'accomplishment Christianity.'" Wolfe compares house church members to home-schoolers, both being conservative subcultures "distrustful of public worlds from which they feel alienated." *The Transformation of American Religion: How We Actually Live Our Faith* (New York: Free Press, 2003), 50, 51.

53. Mitchell, telephone interview with the author, January 23, 2004.

54. Especially influential in this regard have been Robert E. Webber, Ancient-Future Evangelism: Making Your Church a Faith-Forming Community (Grand Rapids: Baker, 2003); *Ancient-Future Faith: Rethinking Evangelism for a Postmodern World* (Grand Rapids: Baker, 1999); and, George G. Hunter, III, *The Celtic Way of Evangelism: How Christianity Can Reach the West. . . Again* (Nashville: Abingdon, 2000).

55. Leonard Sweet and Brian McLaren are perhaps the most influential writers on this issue for younger practitioners, in addition to a huge number of internet resources. See, for example, Sites Unseen at http://geocities.com/redwookie/ for the largest compilation of internet links on the emerging church of which I am aware.

56. See Paul Basden, *The Worship Maze: Finding a Style to Fit Your Church* (Downers Grove, IL: InterVarsity, 1999), and Robert Wuthnow, *All in Sync: How Music and Art Are Revitalizing American Religion* (University of California Press, 2003).

57. Nick, email communication with the author, August 18, 2003.

58. Mack, interview with author, December 9, 2003.

Chapter 4

Music in the Pentecostal Movement

Calvin M. Johansson

The arts influence as well as reflect the values of a culture. They also influence and reflect the values of religious institutions. This is so because all arts are built upon philosophical worldview assumptions which encode value systems. Such assumptions may vary from society to society, group to group, and person to person. But they cannot be avoided. All human activity, including the arts, is based upon presuppositions, acknowledged or not. Everyone, including believers, has a worldview which regulates artistic choice.

Historically, the primary art form used by the fledgling Pentecostal movement in its meetings was music. Painting, sculpture, architecture, and stained glass were largely ignored. The fellowship's musical usage was based on a worldview aesthetic which was predominantly unstated and unacknowledged. This did not lessen the fact that the worldview was there. It was just that the attention of these early Pentecostals was riveted elsewhere. Nevertheless, the foundational worldview assumptions which drove the new movement's use of music had a profound and lasting effect on Pentecostal development through the years. In addition, its musical aesthetic eventually influenced many older established denominations.

What were the foundational presuppositions which governed the Pentecostal pioneers' use of music? How have the aesthetics of Pentecostal musical usage fit in with the worldview of the prevailing wider culture? Have the foundational tenets of Pentecostal aesthetics changed as the movement has expanded? Will these tenets be adequate for the future? Can such a worldview framework serve as a foundation for the movement's musical and spiritual maturation? These and other related topics will be considered in this chapter.

To reflect on the future of Pentecostalism and have one's reflection be something more than pure conjecture requires an analysis based on observable evidence. The author has followed the movement's progress first-hand for most of its history. Taking a cue from Heinrich Schenker's method of musical analysis,[1] we will look at three time periods roughly corresponding to Schenker's three analytical structural levels: background (Hintergrund), middleground (Mittelgrund), and foreground (Vordergrund). For purposes of this essay, a chronology beginning with the background will be used: Hintergrund—ca 1900 to 1945 (the end of World War II); Mittelgrund—1945 to 2000; and Vordergrund—2000 to the present. While the division between background and middleground is fairly clear (World War II), the sectioning between middleground and foreground is less so. Societal changes underway in the years following World War II were dramatic and notable. But between the twentieth and twenty-first centuries they were not as obvious. Change continued to accelerate unabated but without marked boundaries. That does not make the changes any less important, merely less conspicuous.

Hintergrund (ca 1900–1945)

The Hintergrund or background of Pentecostal musical usage specifically begins with the outbreak of the Pentecostal revival in the early years of the twentieth century. Focused as they were on receiving the Pentecostal experience, the founders had little time or inclination to draw up a carefully thought through church music aesthetic. They simply used readily available music which fit their purpose. They also joined (unbeknownst to them) an existing musical tradition which harkened back to the Reformation: congregational participation.

Participation

Of the many sixteenth century reforms which touched upon music in worship only one became a foundational tenet of Pentecostalism—that had to do with congregational musical participation. Others, such as Luther's strong belief in the need for excellence in musical composition or Calvin's unshakable view that the Psalms, being of divine composure, should be the church's primary song, were not of import to the Pentecostal founders.

But the crucial, even critical, change wrought by Luther, Calvin, and all other reformers was adopted by Pentecostals—the absolute necessity of full congregational involvement in worship. The priesthood of all believers demanded that individuals within the worshiping community eschew spectatorship and fully and consciously employ their hearts, minds, and bodies in acts of worship. One did not go to church to view worship. One went to *do* worship. Corporate worship meant a body of believers with each person engaged in worshiping together. This was accomplished during the Reformation primarily through congregational singing: chorales in Lutheran churches, metrical psalmody in Reformed churches. Everyone was encouraged and expected to sing.

Likewise in early Pentecostalism, believer participation was practiced with Reformation zeal. They followed the New Testament practice noted by St. Paul that "When you come together, each one has a hymn, a lesson, a revelation, a tongue, or an interpretation," (1 Corinthians 14:26) and again, "addressing one another in psalms and hymns and spiritual songs, singing and making melody to the Lord with all your heart" (Ephesians 5:19).[2] There was freedom to initiate a song or chorus from within the gathered body of believers. One of the vivid memories of my childhood was my grandmother with her tremulous voice starting a song "all by herself." After a few words, the assembly "caught on" and joined her. It was not an uncommon practice. Whether initiated by a song leader, pastor, or individual seated in the congregation, the entire body sang. With a reputation for wholehearted, even boisterous, music making, these early Pentecostals practiced a New Testament worship involvement which would please the most ardent 16th century reformer. Making worship participatory and singing a primary way to participate, congregations literally became true worshiping communities. Strong individual participation in corporate singing became a signature trait of the early Pentecostal movement. It is the first presupposition on which the early Pentecostal pioneers based their musical usage.

Pragmatism

Attitude

Four constituent elements form the second foundational presupposition of Pentecostalism: pragmatism.[3] The first was attitudinal—an emotional rejection of anything that smacked of institutional religion. If mainstream Protestants favored pipe organs, Pentecostals disfavored them. If Psalmody or hymnody were the custom, Pentecostals preferred something else. If high art was the normative fare for pre-service music and offertories, Pentecostals turned to low art. If mainline churches drew upon formal liturgy, Pentecostals adopted spontaneity. This reflexive reaction against denominationalism's musical practices was, generally speaking, associative. Because these church bodies were seen as cold, spiritually dead tombs of religious decay, everything that reminded Pentecostal believers of what they had come from tended to be rejected. The possibility that the baby could be thrown out with the bath water was never seriously contemplated. Their impassioned Pentecostal fervor, a new-found relationship with Jesus, a profound love for God along with the infilling of the Holy Spirit, left precious little tolerance for contemplating, let alone using, "the old way." The instinctive emotional abhorrence they had for nominal Christianity was as involuntary as it was impassioned. It was a reactionary emotional revulsion expressed at a primal emotional level.

Functionality

Second, the early Pentecostals tended to base their choices on functionality. If something worked, it was adopted. Music was employed which gave a desired result; no other criterion need be considered. It must be remembered that the attention of these Pentecostal believers was on supernatural signs and wonders. By and large, they were not musically sophisticated. Even if they had been (and a few were), aesthetic beliefs would have been suspended in favor of a music which better fit emerging Pentecostal practice.

This predisposition to use music on the basis of its achieving predetermined results was a telling mark of the new movement. Music for praying, rejoicing, enjoying, clapping, or background was believed to have merit only as it satisfactorily fulfilled its function. This was not particularly unusual. Church music is a functional art form. But in this case, little or no thought was given to the aesthetic worth of the art form itself. As a result, a practice emerged which stripped church music of objective musical standards. A theistic worldview which was so meticulously attuned to Pentecostal theology and practice was never applied to the arts. Cast adrift from the need for musical integrity, music's only criterion for use was that it fulfill the purpose of those employing it. Functionality became everything.

Revival/Holiness Tradition

Third, the new movement inherited the music of an established revival tradition. With antecedents in the First Great Awakening of the 1730s–1740s,[4] the Second Great Awakening of 1795–1840 developed a song type whose style influenced the music Pentecostals would embrace. The camp meeting hymn, as it became known, evolved in the revival meetings of the south and west. Texts were individualistic and evangelistic. The music was crude, emotional, rhythmic, simplistic, and repetitive—much like the secular popular songs and ballads of the day. Its most enduring feature, other than its rather frivolous character, was its refrain. For instance, the American Sunday School Union, established in 1817, utilized songs in a style influenced by the camp meeting song; ". . . catchy, easily remembered melody, simple harmony and rhythm, and an inevitable refrain."[5] Though few of these songs are sung today, their musical aesthetic profoundly shaped the development of religious popular song in the second half of the nineteenth century.

In the revivalist tradition, Pentecostals were at the forefront of musically conforming to the wider culture. They did not attempt to utilize the historic psalmody of the reformed tradition or the established hymnody of the ecclesiastical church. Rather, they appropriated the popular religious music of common folk as their music. It is noteworthy that the gospel song stylistically copied the light music of the time: music hall tunes, Stephen Foster songs, ballads, and the ever popular tunes of the frontier. Consumed as they were with the imminent return of Jesus and the need to evangelize the lost, their concern was to reach as many people for Christ as possible. Since the musical taste of those they tended to reach was that of low art, the founders fostered a philosophical attitude of musically accommodating the gospel to the current musical vernacular.[6] It did not seem unusual to them that their cultural accommodation did not extend to fashion, morals, ethics, or amusements. Music (not text) for the founders was presumed to be in a category in which holiness standards did not apply. Given that belief, it is not inconsistent that the music they chose was a music "not very different from the entertainment music of that day, except for the lyrics!"[7]

Accommodation

Accommodation came naturally to the Pentecostal movement, coming as it did from within the Wesleyan revival/holiness tradition. Adapting to the contextual cultural conditions of people was an important part of making the gospel relevant to believers and non-believers alike. This unwritten accommodative understanding was stronger than any written document could ever have been. The enduring legacy of early accommodative measures was to make the result of that accommodation into a Pentecostal "way of doing things." Musically, that way was to follow most carefully the changing style of music that most adherents enjoyed: popular music. This accommodative policy, unwritten though it was, served to make Pentecostal music accommodatively dynamic.

Once the accommodative die was cast, the founders were quick to develop any musical usage which helped their cause: spontaneous singing initiated by members of the congregation, the use of repetition, the singing of choruses excerpted from gospel songs, background music at altar services, tongues singing, the use of band or orchestral instruments played by church volunteers for accompanying congregational singing, and in some cases, for playing preludes or offertories.

Mittlegrund (1945–2000)

Participation

Popular music as it evolved after World War II turned out to be "listener music"—music not made to be sung by the people but listened to by the people. Sheet music on the parlor organ or piano gave way to recordings stacked beside a playback machine. Radio disk jockeys, as well as TV programs such as *American Bandstand* and MTV channels, were dedicated to creating and satisfying the demand for musical product. Moreover, acting in its role as a shaper of culture, post World War II popular music (rock) took on the task of revamping the nation's value system. Through sound and text, it sowed the seeds of a worldview which eventually yielded fruit beyond the wildest expectations of musicians.[8] Though some railed against the form, the young were not listening. Their ears were filled with the popular music of their day, just as the older generation's ears had been attuned to the popular music of theirs. Pop music of one sort or another was fast becoming the principal music of the nation.

The result was 50 years of continually lessening amateur music-making, especially in the vocal area. Think about it. There were few places in society (if any) where a person regularly sang on a daily basis. On the other hand, there were very few places one could go to avoid being force-fed recorded music. Even being put on hold on the telephone required one to listen to background music. By the year 2000, it was clear that music had emerged as a commodity—recorded, packaged, and ready for the play button.

The first Pentecostal presupposition of strong worshiper participation in congregational singing waned as the years of the Mittelgrund advanced. One reason for this was the changing face of musical culture. If one did not sing in everyday life, how realistic was it to expect singing in Sunday worship? A huge difference existed between the activity of singing and the passivity of listening. Coupled with a shift in congregational perception, music-making began to rely less on the person in the pew and more on leaders and electronic gadgetry.

In 1945, the passion and viability of worship was in direct proportion to the vitality with which the congregation sang, among other things. But by the end of the century, it was apparent that most people's best honest-to-goodness musical efforts had been abandoned. Mirroring the secular musical scene, one watched and listened to an amplified band in church, while parishioners sang less and less except for a few dedicated souls. Even if one did sing full voice, it would not have made one iota of difference in the amount or quality of the congregational sound. The decibel level of the amplified praise team saw to that. In smaller churches which had no vocal band, recordings (often with the screening of an accompanying video) were sometimes used to fill the church with the impression of substantial, albeit illusory, "congregational" music.

In this period, Pentecostals discarded a significant measure of personal responsibility for pursuing an impassioned corporate praise. Going to church became an activity in which one sat back lost in the crowd to watch worship unfold. Pentecostal singing evolved from being hearty to being half-hearted. Yes, some still sang, but less so. On the whole, the decline in earnest and meaningful congregational singing changed the practice of strong participation in worship to something the founders would have found abhorrent: spectatorship. The Mittelgrund transformed congregations into fans.

Pragmatism

Pragmatism, the second foundational pillar on which Pentecostals built their church music polity, flourished during the Mittelgrund years. Each component of pragmatism morphed into a module which further buttressed a "Pentecostal" approach to ministry. It was a worldview position that, hardened by success, became intractable.

Attitude

As World War II drew to a close, Pentecostals began to reach out to other Christian groups. In 1943, a beginning was made with a number of Pentecostal bodies joining with Evangelicals to found the National Association of Evangelicals. Such widening of perspective eventually extended to mainline non-evangelical churches. In the '50s and '60s many adherents of Roman Catholicism, Anglicanism, and other denominations accepted and received the Baptism in the Holy Spirit with the initial evidence of speaking in tongues. These Pentecostal experiences appeared to validate as authentic the Christianity of the more liberal traditions. Many of these Spirit-filled believers formed loose alliances known as Charismatics, groups which would exert a powerful influence over the original or "classical" Pentecostals in the last quarter of the century.

All of this was not lost on the musicians of the movement. The severe knee-jerk reaction against historic denominationalism was reduced to a mere twitch. This more open attitude resulted in the publishing of hymnals that actually contained enough hymns to warrant being called hymnals. Choirs with formal vestments were developed, organs restored, and graded church music programs added to the list of activities offered by larger churches. Church musicians read methods books by non-Pentecostals, studied in dedicated music schools, attempted to emulate techniques and procedures learned from observation, and sang more hymns in worship services. National Pentecostal church music conferences were organized. As the movement grew, church musicians began to be hired as part of a church's staff and became known as music ministers. It appeared that Pentecostal music was coming of age.

Yet having inherited a 50-year-old birthright of singing religious popular music as found in the gospel song tradition, Pentecostals were wary of going too far afield from their roots. Other than a slight increase in the use of hymns, acceptance of denominational church music largely was limited to methods and techniques. An upgrading of compositional standards did not make it past first base. Other than a passing nod to the three Bs (Bach, Beethoven, and Brahms), Pentecostals never felt comfortable using the best in church music. They may have acknowledged the great masters intellectually, but emotionally they were not ready to make "classical" music, as it was called, a regular normative part of worship. There seemed to be inbred in Pentecostalism an unwritten rule, an emotional predilection for pop art that, even during this period of rapprochement with denominationalism, kept them welded to popular style and opposed to and repulsed by compositional excellence.

As the century continued, the Pentecostal attitude toward musical populism never wavered. When rock music spawned a religious counterpart in the form of Contemporary Christian Music (CCM), Pentecostals, after some hesitation, embraced the new form. The popular old-line gospel song and choruses were gradually replaced in the '80s and '90s by the newer popular style. It became the premier music of progressive Pentecostalism. In fact, by the year 2000, CCM not only was embedded in every corner of Pentecostalism, it had migrated to the very denominations whose model music programs had served to inspire Pentecostals in the early years of the Mittelgrund.

Functionality

If a Pentecostal musician were asked, "What is the function of music in worship?" the likely answer would be, "Music is a vehicle through which we praise God." But further answers would be sure to follow: "It can cover up noise, fill silence, create atmosphere, be a means of service, accompany singing, and manipulate and control people." Church music, functional art that it is, is pliable. It has the ability to do many things.

It did not take long for Pentecostals to realize the uses to which church music might be put. Not only was it useful to facilitate praise through song, music was used early on as atmosphere-maker. I recall one evangelist in the '50s who, during his sermonizing, implored the organist, "Keep playing; it keeps the Spirit of God on me." Mood music at the altar service has, of course, a long history in Pentecostalism. It has been endorsed at the highest levels of Pentecostal leadership. With such background, it is not surprising that the functional uses of music were extended to their limit in the Mittelgrund. Musicians were asked to play before the service, during interludes between songs, during prayers, Scripture readings, offerings, announcements, almost everything except for the sermon. The other exception was generally during a message in tongues and interpretation. Here the congregation paid careful attention. No musically induced atmosphere was needed.

Spontaneity dried up. The founders' choice of songs had tended to be impromptu, varying with what the leader and congregation were moved to choose at any given moment. This rather loose methodology gave way in the Mittelgrund to a more structured one, though the song leader would still, on occasion, ask the congregation for favorites chosen on the spot. This worked well as long as there were few musicians involved: a pianist, an organist, and perhaps a few instruments. But when larger numbers of people (such as praise teams and bands or large orchestras) became involved in leading the singing, the free-wheeling approach to congregational song was dropped. Nevertheless, the appearance of spontaneity remained because the congregation generally did not have the song menu. As far as they were concerned not all that much had changed. By the end of the century, congregational song became tightly controlled by the music director. Although some unplanned variety could be achieved by those proficient in the use of hand signals, in general, Pentecostal singing became less spontaneous and more prescriptive during the Mittelgrund.

The traditional Pentecostal song service was eventually consolidated into one continuous string of songs. Standing, people were admonished to praise and clap their hands along with rhythmic body swaying and whatever singing might take place prompted by an ever-present video screen. The song service's function was to make people *feel*, which music is readily capable of doing. Objective theological biblical connections (as found in hymns, for example) were abandoned for the emotionalistic euphoria engendered by endless repetitions of CCM songs. Part of the technique for accomplishing this had to do with the raw psychological manipulative power that extremely loud rhythmic music has over the nervous system. As the century progressed, trap set and microphone teamed up to make Pentecostal music an overt exercise in congregational control.

This evolution should not surprise us. The nineteenth century musical tradition from which the Pentecostal movement sprang was a light church music tradition. But it was a musical tradition closer in style to western musical values than that initiated by the rock revolution of the '50s. The music of rock was entertainment music, pure and simple. It had no redeeming qualities of edification or aesthetic enrichment—qualities that the better gospel songs shared in to some degree. Rock was in every sense an anti-music, light years removed from western artistic norms. Nevertheless, for Pentecostals, being in a popular music track, the die was cast. CCM, the religious counterpart to secular contemporary popular music, won the day by the '80s and came to full fruition by the end of the Mittelgrund. Putting religious words to a music of rebellion, frivolity, or amusement did not change the music's basic ethos. Entertainment music used in worship transformed worship into entertainment. This metamorphosis was probably the most significant change of the Mittelgrund period. Pleasuring the self became one of church music's functions.

Revival/Holiness Tradition

The movement's concern for purity of life in the early twentieth century was due to the incredible love Pentecostals had for Jesus. They believed His return was imminent and lived life with an expectancy which colored everything they did. Their focus, or tunnel vision if you will, was on Christ. Consequently, they developed a consuming passion for fulfilling the Great Commission at home and abroad. Jesus was coming any day.

At the beginning of the Mittelgrund, all Pentecostals, regardless of differences in holiness doctrine, practiced a substantial social separatism. Though the prohibition against life insurance, Coca-Cola, professional sports, doctors, and medicine had been dropped by 1945, the prohibition against makeup, movies, gambling, dancing, tobacco, card playing, and liquor was retained. Less unanimity existed concerning mixed bathing, skating rinks, bowling, and women's trousers. Whatever precise regional standard may have developed, Pentecostalism as a whole emerged from World War II with a traditional holiness attitude toward the world: touch not, taste not, handle not.

Curiously, music was absent from the catalog of sins. Behavior associated with certain musics such as dance halls, cocktail lounges, night clubs, and bar rooms was forbidden. But the music itself was never banned. Consequently, Pentecostals were just as familiar as anyone else with the latest and greatest from the hit parade. By the '70s vocal solos performed in church were invariably sung using the vocal techniques of popular music. And by the end of the Mittelgrund, the most bizarre of pop music practices from secular culture could be found in some churches on occasion: gyrating musicians, strobe lights, smoke, and pounding, pulsating, beat-driven music.

The dichotomization, then, between music and behavior lessened during the Mittelgrund, and the sharp contrast between Pentecostals and the general culture faded significantly. Perspectives toward items in the aforementioned list (makeup, movies, gambling, dancing, tobacco, card playing, and liquor) were revised. By the end of the century, Pentecostal assimilation of pop music, movies, TV shows, and magazine articles caused them to identify with popular culture to such a degree that Pentecostalism as a whole could no longer be considered a practicing holiness movement by any stretch of the imagination. One Pentecostal pastor so identified with pop culture he purchased for his automobile special license plates which read "007," a movie icon and egregious example of immorality. Many leaders kept up with the latest popular singers and bands, movie stars, and TV shows and personalities. Profanity in the media and sexual sins on the screen were tolerated.

Musically, Pentecostals never had a true holiness praxis. But in the Mittelgrund, Pentecostals' value-neutral musical understanding was extended to the broad sweep of culture. It affirmed the revivalist tradition with further forays into contemporized religious music. By the end of the century, little of the old holiness separatism remained, having been replaced by a new inclusion and tolerance. From the musical seed sown in its infancy, Pentecostalism had finally reaped a crop of societal weeds. Much of culture's worldview outlook had become part of the Pentecostal vision.

Accommodation

Historically, the accommodation of the gospel to culture is one of the thorniest problems with which the church has had to contend. How far does the church go in making the good news of Jesus Christ culturally relevant? Does the form of communicating the gospel affect the content of the message? Can the battery case be separated from its electrical charge?

Pentecostals have taken the clear position that form and content can be separated. Their position has been consistent and unwavering: "We change the method, not the message." This philosophy is the pragmatic cornerstone on which all Pentecostal evangelism efforts and worship services are built. Judged by the rapid growth of the movement, it has been enormously successful.

The '60s' and '70s' experiment to improve the depth of congregational song by the regular singing of a wider selection of hymns (other than "All Hail the Power of Jesus' Name" and "Holy, Holy, Holy!") was abandoned in the '80s and early '90s. The problem was that such musical fare was not felt to be sustainable in the face of a popular culture moving in the opposite direction. And if Pentecostal music was in agreement on any one thing it was that music, being a matter of personal taste, was free to become whatever was necessary to please taste.

This is not to say that all was smooth sailing. Pentecostals, like other church bodies, had their worship wars in the last decade of the century. The older generation with its musical taste crystallized was loath to accept the younger generation's choices. Conflict arose. The problem was, of course, the basic premise of Pentecostal church music: musical relativism. Controlled by the subjective vagaries of personal/postmodern taste rather than by the objective analysis of musical/theological value, church music was held hostage to a Mittelgrund culture increasingly out of touch with Christian theism.

It is difficult to imagine what happened to the musical psyche of the general public during the Mittelgrund. This was no ordinary period. Change, rapid change, even revolutionary change, in every corner of society was its essence. Music, whose changes were more apparent than that of many areas, mutated almost beyond recognition in some cases. The unrelenting march of pop music becoming constantly harsher and more brutal changed our aesthetic sensibilities. As it evolved into ever ungracious sounds, people, unable to escape it, began to adjust to it little by little: ears hardened, sensitivity withered, artistic consciousness deadened. Like an addictive drug, it took increasingly strong jolts to achieve the desired affect. People first became tolerant, then attached, to such a diet. To provide a church music accommodative to such a musical environment, Pentecostals gave in to it. Pragmatists that they were, they split message (text) from medium (music). For Pentecostals in the Mittelgrund, words spoke louder than actions.

As rock-style vocal and instrumental bands became the norm, Pentecostalism turned to the religious version: the so-called "CCM praise team." Taking hold in the late '80s, these groupings of drums, guitars, electronic keyboard, obligato instruments, and several microphoned singers were universally used in Pentecostal circles. Such ensembles functioned as song leader, worship leader, soloist, and choir. In fact, they also musically replaced the congregation in many instances. The ensemble was generally so loud and dominating that people tended to mumble rather than sing, listen rather than participate.

The Mittelgrund shows Pentecostalism's accommodative philosophy with more clarity than that shown in the Hintergrund. The extremes of cultural metamorphoses were relatively minimal in 1900–1945 compared to 1945–2000. At century's end, every church body was struggling with the Mittelgrund's rapid remake of culture. But Pentecostals were ahead of the game. Committed to a pragmatic accommodative philosophy, they had few misgivings concerning musical accommodation; they were experienced shape-shifters.

Technology

Additional structures were added to the Hintergrund frame during the Mittelgrund. Of these, electronic technology has come to be a permanent and indispensable part of Pentecostal convention. While not doctrinal, it has become as basic as the Trinity. Indeed, Pentecostal pulpiteers discovered the rush given by powerful amplification. Intoxicated with their discovery, their love affair with massive speaker systems had, not surprisingly, a pragmatic root: amplification was one way to exert power over a congregation.

Both the content and quality of congregational song changed dramatically with the advent of projected words on large movie screens. Chorus singing, a hallmark of Pentecostals from the very beginning, originated with the singing of gospel song refrains apart from their stanzas. From this practice, a dedicated chorus genre arose during the last years of the Hintergrund and the first years of the Mittelgrund. Though some few congregations still used them, it took only a few years at the end of the Mittelgrund for most churches to discard this most useful body of memorized song. Not only did Pentecostals lose a whole memorized chorus genre, they lost the hymn and gospel song genres as well. As worship leaders and music directors programmed only that for which they had visual images, over 600 years of sung theology was abandoned. Then too with the hymnal's demise, people had no source to hone their music reading skills because screen projection did not include the music. The dumbing-down of the movement's musical proficiency did nothing to enhance the spirituality and maturation of its adherents.

Technology took Pentecostal church music prisoner in the Mittelgrund. It perpetrated major shifts in what was sung and how it was sung. The electronics industry flourished as sales of sound equipment soared. Succumbing to the bent of popular culture, the church put technology over music, the cart before the horse. While technology was a boon in some areas of church life, its overall influence on music proved detrimental. At the end of this period, Pentecostal music had become as dependent on electronics as a parasite on its host.

Blended Worship

Blended worship (also referred to as convergence worship) came about as an obvious answer to the '90s' so-called "worship wars." Following the drift of popular culture, the programming of CCM type songs with their heavy dependence on technology came to be known as "contemporary style," as opposed to "traditional style." The preference for one over the other was passionately and hotly debated within Pentecostalism as it was in other communions. So contentious was the fight that churches split over the issue. Others gained or lost members according to their ability or inability to please their attendees. When everything was said and done, the worship wars clearly were fought over one thing—music.

Pentecostal leaders in the Mittelgrund tended to treat style without reference to an objective referent. Text was the objective analyzable part of the equation, music the subjective value-neutral part. Therefore, believing that style was not a matter of theological consequence but a matter of preference, the worship wars were thought to be an emotional hot-button issue over relatively inconsequential matters. The division over musical style often separated young from old, musical from less musical, pragmatists from idealists, scholars from workers, theists from postmodernists, high art enthusiasts from low art buffs. The impassioned, heart-felt fervor with which these battles were fought was significant. This was not a war simply over musical preference. This was a war for church music's soul.

With such a divisive issue and with no ready answer to deal with the problem, Pentecostals fell back on their well-used worldview philosophy—pragmatism. Unable to satisfy both sides of the debate, pastors and musicians compromised. They turned to what was being touted in the broader Christian community as blended or convergence worship—a combination of both traditional and contemporary music. Blended worship made perfect sense—something for everyone. Worship had become a supermarket and worshipers consumers—Pentecostal connoisseurs of musical preference.

Praise and Worship

A significant attachment to the Mittelgrund frame was the fragmentation of the worship service. For much of the century, Pentecostal worship was considered a gestalt made up of prayer, singing, sermon, the operation of the gifts of the Spirit, altar intercession, offering, announcements, testimonies, musical specials, Scripture reading, and occasionally the Lord's supper. With the mid-period explosive growth of Charismatics, their practice of spending extremely large blocks of time singing (1/2 to 1 1/2 hours) impressed Pentecostals to follow suit. In emulating them, Pentecostals eventually adopted a new nomenclature along with a changed definition of worship. The narrowly focused purpose of lengthy Charismatic times of song was the praise and worship of God. Hence it was natural for them to think of praise and worship as a matter essentially tied to, and eventually limited to, song. This way of using the word "worship" caused popular religion to change its perception of worship's content: worship came to mean singing.

The religious popular music industry also latched on to the word. It was to their advantage to have customers think of certain music as "worship." Linking their wares to as revered a tradition as the worship of Almighty God was a word-connection stroke of genius. A category of popular music emerged labeled "praise and worship" which served to connect the praise and worship product with all that worship meant to the buyer. People purchased praise and worship recordings, "put on some praise and worship" in their CD players, preferred the praise and worship style, composed praise and worship music, and did praise and worship in church. To "lead the worship" meant to "lead the singing," and to stay for the worship meant to stay for the song service.

In conclusion, though certainly more tumultuous than the Hintergrund, church music in the Mittelgrund was no more strife-ridden than that found during the transition from psalmody to hymnody in the eighteenth and nineteenth centuries. However, that fact shows with particular lucidity the radical revolutionary nature of the Mittelgrund. Never before in any historical period had church music changed so utterly, yet, for the changes engendered, caused so little conflict. The reason the Mittelgrund era was less fractious than might have been expected was that Pentecostal church music and the wider societal culture moved, more or less, in lock step. There was not that much contrast between the two. The fact that any hostility occurred at all is surprising because Pentecostalism had swallowed (hook, line, and sinker) culture's postmodern and postchristian aesthetic: music (not text) is essentially value-neutral and worldview free.

The first basic presupposition of Pentecostal musical philosophy (participation) became weaker in the Mittelgrund. On the other hand, pragmatism, the second basic presupposition of Pentecostal music ministry, expanded mightily in this period. Committed to doing whatever appeared to bring results, the Mittelgrund's accommodative efforts were extended through technology, a blended yet restrictive musical choice, and a compartmentalized concept of worship. Among the various motivations for strengthening the pragmatic bent is the feeling that pragmatism has served the movement well. Pentecostalism has grown phenomenally and its constituents have achieved a certain respectability. Moreover its musical philosophy is being appropriated by almost all denominations to an increasing degree. One cannot argue with success so "if it ain't broke, don't fix it."

Vordergrund (2000–   )

The Likely Future: The Next Fifty Years

Tracing the broad sweep of a century of Pentecostal music-making reveals one undeniable, noteworthy fact: consistency. From top to bottom, left to right, inside and out, through thick and thin, Pentecostalism has stayed the course of its founders. Though the first foundational presupposition of energetic and responsible congregational musical participation declined in the last two decades of the Mittelgrund, it was nonetheless a manifest Pentecostal trait for most of the century, especially when compared to other church bodies. The coming years will, no doubt, see a further erosion of conscientious and indefatigable congregational singing as technology, spectatorship, and the decline in musical amateurism take their toll.

The second foundational presupposition, pragmatism, gained in strength throughout the Mittelgrund. In the future, Pentecostals will, true to form, ingest whatever culture brings. With an enthusiastic pragmatism born of tried and true experience, Pentecostals (who have a history of readily assimilating the latest trends in popular music) will continue to adapt to the changing tastes of society. Evangelizing the unsaved will oblige Pentecostals to select music that unbelievers prefer, given that musical likability is believed to be a prerequisite for relevant communication. They will also be guided by such entities as para-church organizations, megachurches, market strategists, and statistical research. The one thing Pentecostals will not do is to carve out a "Pentecostal musical niche" and then exist to resist altering it. Fluctuating as regularly as the top 40, the name of the game will be musical change.

It goes without saying that the Pentecostal church music of tomorrow will be based on the secular pop music of tomorrow (with, of course, the compulsory time lag for familiarization and musical adaptation). The use of popular music as a model for church music is a tradition as old as the Pentecostal movement itself. While the founders would never accept the music used today, they would agree that its use was proper if it brought the desired result. They would, however, be dismayed at its deleterious effect upon truly great congregational singing. Since pop is more passive than participatory, the church music of the future will be largely performer-driven. In addition, the fact that all popular music, sacred or secular, is entertainment music, it must be assumed that entertainment will make further forays into Pentecostal worship. There will be a concerted effort to rationalize entertainment worship as a legitimate worship "style," just as entertainment evangelism became generally accepted in the Mittelgrund.

Pentecostals will write off all past musical expressions of the faith. Their attitude of indifference toward historic denominational usage will (except for a small minority) become once again prejudicial against all church music except that which has the ambience of popular appeal. They will note that denominational churches that grow are those that have adopted religious popular expression. Pentecostals will continue to maintain that they are following the practice of Martin Luther and others who appropriated "pop music" for their church music needs—a common, but fallacious, argument because the type of pop music Pentecostals now use has no historic precedent (being a purely twentieth century phenomenon).

Music will continue to be used functionally. It will be as prevalent as wall-to-wall carpeting. Monetary resources permitting, worshipers, cradled in an environment of sound from arrival in the parking lot to departure, will find no place for silence and reflection—not even in the restrooms. Chosen carefully to produce a predetermined atmosphere for a particular time and place, the music will be as seamless as a new-age loop.

In the coming years, some Pentecostal fellowships will overtly begin to pattern their music after particular secular bands. This has already happened in the wider church growth movement where the attempt to closely emulate the everyday listening preferences of people dictate Sunday's musical style. Each treated autonomously, there will be little or no connection made between the texts of popular music and the music itself. This disconnect between text and music will allow the church to use any musical style as long as it has conspicuously religious texts. The effort will be to style a church's music for a specific audience. Each church will have its distinct ambience within the pop genre for the pleasure of its particular market target.

The present thinking is that music is the single most important determiner of who attends a particular church and who stays away. Its importance both in evangelism and in the maintenance of a viable congregation cannot be overemphasized. The facts tend to bear this out. The worship wars of the '90s were about musical style. The churches that have grown the fastest—the megachurches—invariably use religious pop music. There are few exceptions. Pop music is part of the market strategy used to attract the pop generation.

In all of this, the legitimacy of accommodating the gospel to culture via the popular music of secular culture will be of no concern. That issue has been laid to rest by breaking down the musical walls between the world and the church. Radical accommodation will give Pentecostals an identification with culture which will eliminate any suspicion of the old churchly rigidity. Worldly standards will be embraced as a way to reach the world with biblical standards. The difference between the two will lessen, and musically the two will merge.

Pentecostal worship will become an electronic media event, particularly in the larger churches. Video clips, complete sound board control of all music, the use of musical recordings of one kind or another, recorded videos of members' personal testimonies complete with professionally produced musical and visual background, video advertisements of church activities, as well as appeals for workers, funds, and solicitations for prayer, will be normative. Live music will be retained only if it is star-studded or if it is to the church's advantage to give members musical leadership responsibilities. The tendency toward individual spiritual experience will encourage technology to produce a church version of virtual reality.

There will be an increasing abundance of specific worship styles—a worship service to fit every taste. Worship will be thought of as a commodity to fit the needs (tastes) of the "audience." In all probability the word "worship" will recover its comprehensive meaning. Word, prayer, offering, and music will be considered once again as part of the total worship service experience.

Conclusion: An Alternative Vision for Pentecostal Music

A Prophetic Summation

Several things are apparent in this Schenkarian-like look at the past, present, and future of Pentecostalism's musical usage. First, based on the historical observations made in these pages, it is apparent that the central pillars on which all Pentecostal music ministry is established are not equally fitting for a movement which purports to practice the "full gospel." Participation is a meritorious key necessity for Pentecostals. It cannot be dispensed with without changing the essential nature of Pentecostal worship. Pragmatism, on the other hand is problematical. Though it has appeared to serve the movement well, it has exacted a high price. It has induced Pentecostals to embrace the non-theistic worldview philosophies of relativism and extreme subjectivism and to countenance aspects of postmodernism. It has also made the movement compromise-prone toward the full authority of Scripture over all areas of life. Pragmatism is a worldview philosophy quite out of step with Christian theism. A Christian worldview does have standards with which to contend. No Pentecostal would say that an immoral act was right even if it appeared to be the means of bringing a soul to saving grace. What Pentecostalism did was to practice a theism which utilized an objective worldview regarding morality and ethics, but embraced a subjective worldview when considering the aesthetic realm. Such a fragmented worldview compartmentalized faith. Theology was focused narrowly in certain areas of life but omitted in others. Music was thought to be a subjective entity quite on its own. Pentecostals had to make choices on music, but things other than objective biblical precepts were the criteria by which they chose.

It is true that the basic underlying presupposition on which most of the musical house of Pentecostalism was built is pragmatism. But under the scrutiny of Scripture, it is a philosophy which comes up wanting. Or to put it more bluntly, pragmatism is an anti-biblical philosophy. Scripture does not teach that good ends justify poor means. Rather, Scripture is clearly a book about very particular means. Musical means (works) should be disciplined by and determined by standards of the gospel. Good scriptural ends need good scriptural means.

Second, Pentecostal music ministry is based on taste—individual taste. The incurvature of designing musical worship around subjective desire rather than objective value ultimately inclines worship toward idolatry. In actuality, the self is worshiped. The First Commandment is broken.

Third, the accommodative understanding of Pentecostalism is fatally flawed. To believe that music and text are mutually exclusive is to completely misunderstand the nature of form and content. In reality, the message is bound into the warp and woof of the medium. The gospel is a unified whole—gospel belief/gospel action. Thinking of the gospel as propositional statements cut off from "delivery systems" is dangerous. To believe that the message of a song text is unaffected by the quality, style, or ambience of the music reveals a misconception of the way art works. When the gospel is put to a music whose form repudiates what the gospel stands for (as is the case with all pop music), the result is a different gospel no matter how sincere the effort.[9]

Fourth, the Pentecostal movement has consistently been a popular music movement. The Hintergrund use of the popular gospel song is understandable, but the movement's eventual assimilation of rock music in the Mittelgrund has taken Pentecostal music ministry to radical extremes. The entire rock revolution was just that—a revolution. Twentieth-century popular music of any stripe is not equal to being the gospel in musical action. Incompatible and counterproductive, it is hazardous to one's spiritual health. Like a malignancy, this music degrades far more than musical aesthetics. It will eventually infect one's total value system: moral, social, ethical, theological, as well as musical.

Fifth, the value neutrality of relativism and postmodernism (musical worldview traits adopted by Pentecostals) are fraught with danger. I am skeptical of the claim that one can embrace postmodernism and be a Christian. Christians do believe in absolutes, in objectivity, and in truth as revealed in Scripture. How much of postmodern thought and practice can Pentecostals embrace without losing their distinctive scriptural belief system? Adopting the values of postmodernism, whether musical, ethical, social, moral, or philosophical, in the belief that successful evangelism requires it, changes the core value system of Pentecostalism. The acceptance of musical value-neutrality is antipathetic to basic Christian theism. At the least it is inconsistent; at most it is heretical. Musical value is part of the complex of values which make up Christian theism. To remove it for the sake of accommodation is to preach louder than any sermon that values are expendable.

A New Direction

To live up to their potential, Pentecostals must take a new musical direction. Biblical, Holy Spirit yielded and guided reorientation will necessitate a major turnaround—change that is sure to be excruciatingly painful and require sacrifices of many kinds. Undergirding the whole enterprise will be a more fitting definition of success. Success will be redefined as faithfulness and fidelity to Scripture.

Wholehearted, responsible congregational singing will be reinstated. There will be an honesty put into effect which precludes using electronic methods to give the illusion of hearty group participation. Any predilection for entertainment will be dampened by corporate worship involvement and scriptural musical choice. Worshiper spectatorship will be discouraged and services will be planned that encourage people to take part.

Pentecostal music ought not to be modeled after popular music. Rather, it should be based upon musical and spiritual value. Musical goodness and integrity, rather than taste, will be the arbiter of value. Music will be understandable to worshipers with an ethos commensurate with scriptural norms. A Pentecostal theistic worldview, coherent, comprehensive, and creative, will impact all phases of church music from composition to selection to rehearsal to execution. Will musical quality be carefully evaluated, because heretofore that has not been a scriptural part of the selection process?

Pragmatism will be jettisoned. In its place, an accommodative paradigm will be embraced based on the Incarnation. Incarnational accommodation affirms the necessity of relevancy but does not split message from medium, content from form. Rather, forms are used which affirm gospel standards and which are apprehensible within the contextual conditions of people. Can such music be found? The clear and unequivocal answer is "yes." Music ought not be employed based on preference, but upon its aesthetic quality, its comprehensibility, its ability to disciple, and its capacity for facilitating worship.[10]

Finally, a new understanding of what it means to be Pentecostal in a culture out of touch with biblical Christianity must be found.[11] In a society which rejects absolutes, values, and truth, Pentecostals must practice them tirelessly in their music. Yes, that will make Pentecostals different from society—pilgrims on a holy mission. To be "in the world" does not mean becoming like it. Scripture pointedly rejects being "of the world," an injunction to disavow the world system and all that it finds desirable. A new Pentecostal holiness separatism in the matter of musical values in and out of church is very much needed. Not only ought we to get our own musical house in order but we must salt the wider culture with sound biblical musical values. Pentecostal musicians must begin to discipline their music scripturally, and with pastoral concern and evangelistic fervor, begin the new century with as much fidelity to incarnational methodology as that which was afforded pragmatism in the last century. Music ministry based on the Incarnation will make Pentecostals distinct from Evangelicalism, as most Evangelicals have now embraced pragmatism as intensely as Pentecostals did in the twentieth century. Jesus, in the Great Commission, said to baptize all nations and to teach "them to observe all things whatsoever I have commanded you." The gospel is replete with church music implications. Pentecostals must move on to a higher level where the gospel is worked out in good musical action—good music, the show and tell of the good news.

Notes

1. Heinrich Schenker, Austrian music theorist, developed a method of musical analysis based on three levels of comprehension. First, the foreground (the musical work complete in every detail) yields insight into the second, the middleground. Here the piece with its complexity simplified leads to the third level, the background, a further reduction of detail which finally reveals the work's basic foundational structure.

The Schenkerian system attempts to expose the organic relatedness of a musical work. In other words, the art work's final shape is an outworking of its fundamental design. The basic structure permeates a worthy composition in a manner which gives cohesion to the work. The final version of the piece is the product of the artistic workings-out of the underlying frame. It is this frame which, in the most basic sense, contains the potential of the work. This background is the music's underlying governance.

Though a Schenkerian analysis of an actual piece of music begins with the foreground moving through the middleground to arrive at the background, it seems advantageous to reverse the order when studying the historic use of music. In our case, understanding the theological, philosophical, and aesthetic bent of the Pentecostal founders (background) will shed significant light on the development (middleground) of, and present (foreground) use of music in Pentecostal circles. The initial frame upon which Pentecostal musical usage was built may be the most important single assemblage of information necessary to understanding its present musical usage and, more importantly, for establishing a prophetic footing for the future.

2. All references in this chapter are taken from the Revised Standard Version.

3. Pragmatism is a philosophy which looks at results to justify means. That is to say, methods are scrutinized only in light of achievement. Hence any means, any method, any material, and any course of action is possible if it eventually brings the desired result. There are no right or wrong methods or materials in themselves. Pragmatism allows and admits anything. If it appears to work as intended, whatever was done is fully justified.

4. The revivals of the 18th and 19th centuries each had their preferred congregational music. The grasp that metrical psalmody had on church song was gradually relinquished as the hymns of Isaac Watts, the father of English hymnody, took hold. Though the *Bay Psalm Book* of 1640, the first book printed in the Colonies, held sway in New England for more than a century, the versifications of Watts, which gradually became less literal, more literary, and more in tune with New Testament experience, led to the eventual domination of hymnody.

5. Donald P. Hustad, *Jubilate II: Church Music in Worship and Renewal* (Carol Stream, Illinois: Hope Publishing Co., 1993), 232.

6. The employment of a secular non-churchly attitude toward music is clearly revealed not only by Pentecost's choice of musical material but by the instrumentation used to accompany that material. While evangelistic meetings had generally tended to use the pipe organ or reed organ whenever possible, Reuben Torrey's (an associate of Dwight L. Moody) song leader, Charles Alexander, opted for the piano. He "found that the percussive piano was more helpful in leading the livelier songs of his day." Pentecostals followed suit. Instruments of all types were employed in the manner of the Salvation Army. Hand-clapping enhanced the toe-tapping bounce of this lively and rhythmic congregational music.

7. Hustad, *Jubilate! Church Music in the Evangelical Tradition* (Carol Stream, Illinois: Hope Publishing Co., 1981), 21.

8. The rock and roll revolution of the 1950s was arguably the most influential musical metamorphosis in history. With its dozens of stylistic permutations, rock became the most popular music in the world and has been at the cutting edge of societal transformation for half a century. All that we became morally, socially, ethically, spiritually, and aesthetically was due in large measure to the systematic assimilation of the values advanced in popular music. Ideas popularized through this music replaced many of the basic core values common to our national life. Introduced first by popular music, a decade

or two later they began to be adopted by society. Whether sexual promiscuity, aesthetic hardening, breakdown of the family, clerical powerlessness, class discomfiture, or what have you, popular music broke the trail. Pentecostals, hardly knowing what to make of this new music, ignored it at first. But the strength and scope of the rock revolt caused some to stand against it. Such action is noted by David Wilkerson's publication of *The Devil's Heartbeat: Rock and Roll!* in which sixteen sins caused by rock music were listed. Other Pentecostals such as Bob Larson (*Hippies, Hindus and Rock & Roll,* 1970) and numerous other evangelicals followed suit. It did little good. Being chauffeured by a teenager, evangelist Bob Larson wrote: "After just walking out of the solemnity of a worship service, I wasn't quite prepared to hear my driver's favorite rock group sing of smoking pot and sleeping with groupies. In fact, I probably would have said something if it hadn't been for my wife's elbow in my ribs."

9. In another couple of decades, religious rock (CCM) became normative in most Pentecostal churches. See: John Makujina, *Measuring the Music: Another Look at the Contemporary Christian Music Debate* (Salem, Ohio: Schmul Publishing Co., 2000); Dan Lucarini, *Why I Left the Contemporary Christian Music Movement* (Darlington, England: Evangelical Press, 2002); Karl Tsatalbasidis, *Drums, Rock, and Worship* (Roseville, California: Amazing Facts, Inc., 2003); Samuel Bacchiocchi, ed., *The Christian & Rock Music* (Berrien Springs, Michigan: Biblical Perspectives, 2000).

10. For a fuller treatment of this and other related topics see Calvin M. Johansson: *Music & Ministry: a Biblical Counterpoint,* second edition (Peabody, Massachusetts: Hendrickson Publisher, 1998), chapter five. Also Johansson: *Discipling Music Ministry: Twenty-first Century Directions* (Peabody, Massachusetts: Hendrickson, 1992).

11. A description of incarnational methodology may be found in chapter four and an application in chapter nine of my *Music & Ministry: a Biblical Counterpoint,* second edition.

Chapter 5

Latino Pentecostalism:
Globalized Christianity and the United States

Arlene M. Sánchez Walsh and Eric Dean Patterson

The question of the future of Pentecostalism in the United States raises several issues that require reframing, particularly framed within a Latino perspective. The most prominent one is the geographical specificity of the scope of this book: American Pentecostalism. Latinos, particularly immigrants, tend not to see the Americas as an issue of North or South, but often as a seamless whole, where crossing borders, working, raising families, and worshipping are done on both sides of political boundaries. The historical and geographical fluidity of Latino Pentecostalism is a transnational or globalized phenomenon, making the story of Latinos an integral part of the future of Pentecostalism in the United States.

This chapter argues that Latinos were present at the beginning of the last century's Pentecostal "outpouring" at Azusa Street, and that in many ways the challenges that they faced then and now parallel challenges that other Pentecostals, particularly those of color, face and have faced. Moreover, as citizens of multiple communities, Latino Pentecostals have numerous voices competing for their attention, from the prosperity gospel of neo-Pentecostals to the social justice message of liberationists. Finally, I evaluate whether Latino Pentecostal communities will continue to function as cultural enclaves that reinforce Latino identity within the larger dominant culture or if Latino Pentecostalism will "evangelicalize" and go mainstream as most Pentecostal denominations in the United States have.

Latino Pentecostals in the United States: The Early Years

When one considers that the Azusa Street revival which kicked off twentieth century Pentecostalism was located in Los Angeles, it should be no surprise that Latinos, primarily of Mexican ancestry, were present. Some were remnants of the old California elite (*Californios*), others were part of an immigrant working class—miners, laborers, and railroad workers escaping from the authoritar-

ian regime of Porfirio Díaz and the conditions which led in just a few years to
the bloody Mexican Revolution. These individuals were almost entirely Catholic, and Spanish was their primary language. By the turn of the century some
local Protestant congregations began reaching out to the Latino community, but
religious education was often a masked attempt at Americanization.

Thus the religious "marketplace" offered few choices: either to remain
within the Catholic Church which wielded tremendous hegemony over one's life
and family, or seek another religious venue, but one that often implicitly (or
explicitly) demanded assimilation.[1] The Azusa Street revival of 1906–1909
seemed to offer a third way—a religious movement that embraced diversity, the
poor, the powerless, and the person of color. Azusa Street's leader, Brother
Seymour, said, "It is noticeable how free all nationalities feel. If a Mexican or
German cannot speak English, he gets up and speaks in his own tongue and feels
quite at home for the spirit interprets through the face and people say amen."[2]
Frank Bartleman, a participant at Azusa Street, wrote, "Pentecost has come to
Los Angeles, the American Jerusalem. Every sect, creed, and doctrine under
heaven. . . . as well as every nation is represented."[3] The key manifestation of
Azusa Street, *glossolalia* or speaking in tongues, was seen as a gift of God
bridging the barriers of language and race. In many cases the manifestation was
"missionary tongues," which provided an individual with a language hitherto
unknown (Spanish) with which to evangelize in the plaza or the fields to people
who did not speak English.[4]

We have a few written accounts from Mexicans who participated in the
Azusa Street revival, such as A.C. Valdez, Abundio and Rosa López, Luís
López, and Romanita Valenzuela.[5] A few general observations about the experience of early Latino Pentecostals are worth noting. First, conversions took
place in the haunts of the poor—homes, social missions, plazas, and jails—sites
where a marginal population might find themselves in early twentieth century
Los Angeles. Second, spiritual conversion often occurred in tandem with other
forms of deliverance, such as divine healing and restoration of relationships
within the home.

Third, Azusa Street initiated the Mexican population into the evangelical
world of Pentecostals as well as the fissiparous theological environment that
marked American Protestantism. Mexican converts split among themselves over
the Trinitarian/Oneness issue and established churches that spread the Oneness
message independently of Euro-American Oneness congregations in Los Angeles in 1909 and into Mexico by 1912.[6]

Finally, there remains the question of Pentecostalism and culture. Was, and
is, preaching Pentecostalism anti-Catholic, and by extension, anti-Latino? We
argue that Latino Pentecostals developed a historical memory and religious identity separate from Catholicism, and that by maintaining certain faith traditions
these Pentecostal identities continue to this day as important cultural markers,

operating separately from Catholicism's historical memory and religious identity.

Religious Marginalization and Exclusion

As noted above, one feature of early Latino Pentecostals in the United States is their general marginalization in society. The dominant religion was mainline Protestant, Latinos were Catholic or new Pentecostals. The dominant language was English, they spoke Spanish. The dominant culture was the confident Yankee triumphalism of the period associated with conquering the frontier, innovations in science and technology, and feelings of Anglo-Saxon superiority. Most Latinos were immigrants of the working class with little of the heady optimism associated with Anglos who passed them on the street.

Although the Azusa Street revival was initially "color blind," this quickly changed. Within the first decade of the movement the racial barriers that were characteristic of American society, especially between whites and blacks, were institutionalized in Pentecostal denominations: the black Church of God in Christ and various Apostolic Faith churches versus the white Assemblies of God and parallel white denominations. In the case of Latinos, the language barrier reinforced segregation of Pentecostal denominations. When outreach to Latinos in the United States was promoted by white Pentecostals, it was seen as (foreign) missionary activity not as (home) evangelism. Today many Pentecostal denominations in the United States, for various reasons including pragmatic attempts to deal with language differences, have Latino or Hispanic organizational structures that are separate from and run parallel to their English-speaking counterparts.

However, Pentecostal Latinos were doubly marginalized. Not only were they disenfranchised from the dominant culture, their decision to pursue Pentecostalism immediately thrust them out of their Catholic community. Traditional Catholicism permeated every part of community life and the decision to leave the Catholic Church could result in broken relationships, limits to economic opportunity, and social ostracism. As Allen Figueroa Deck writes,

> The thoughtful Hispanic will view evangelical efforts to convert Hispanics as a particularly vicious attack on his or her cultural identity. Even though the Hispanic American may not be active in practicing the Catholic faith, he or she perceives that the culture is permeated by a kind of Catholic ethos and symbols that revolves around a rich collection of rites and symbols. Many of these rites and symbols are imbued with a certain Catholic spirit. The evangelical penchant for reducing the mediation between God and humanity to the Scriptures is antithetical to the Hispanic Catholic tendency to multiple mediations...Hispanics have often experienced serious family divisions when a members becomes Protestant. In Hispanic culture, this is not

just a religious matter. It is a profound cultural, social, and familial rupture.[7]

Thus, over time perhaps the most important religious contribution of Latino Pentecostalism has nothing to do with integration with Anglo Pentecostalism but its position as an alternative to the dominance of the Roman Catholic Church. As Pentecostalism has grown it has competed for "market share" with the Roman Catholic Church. In the religious and cultural marketplace of ideas, Pentecostalism enlivens religious life by making a once stagnant monopoly compete for the faithful. It has also energized non-Pentecostal Protestants who have incorporated much of Pentecostalism's vibrancy into their own worship. This is true of countless Latino Protestant churches today: Pentecostal styles of worship attenuated to Pentecostal theology that allow for upraised hands, emotional prayer, and is some cases prayer for healing and speaking in tongues. Latino Pentecostalism has also changed the dynamics of the Roman Catholic Church as the charismatic movement of the 1960s and 1970s demonstrates. Moreover, the hegemony of the Catholic Church among American Latinos is slipping. Whereas over ninety percent of Latinos in the United States reported themselves to be Catholic in the 1970s, today approximately one third of Latinos consider themselves to be "non-Catholic," including millions of Latino Pentecostals.[8]

In sum, it seems likely that for the foreseeable future, Latino Pentecostalism will continue to compete, not only in the urban and southwestern United States, but throughout the Western hemisphere, with the Roman Catholic Church. It will continue to be a religious movement of the numerical minority and likely have its greatest appeal among the marginalized in society: women, immigrants, and those who are poor, sick, and needy. And in the United States, many Latino Pentecostals will feel more at home in their own congregations and communities than in "blended" or assimilated congregations.

Latino Pentecostalism as Cultural Identity

For many reasons, ethnic Pentecostals often have maintained a distinct, ethnically-specific religious identity, infused with cultural and social signifiers that make them Latino and Pentecostal without having to abandon one in favor of the other. Whereas much of the historic experiential fervency has diminished in white middle-class Pentecostal circles, that fervency still flourishes in Latino Pentecostal communities where the communal bonds of families and shared experiences sustain and promote an experience-based religion.

However, it is unclear if twenty-first century Latino Pentecostalism will reify old cultural norms or acculturate, as immigrant cultures often do, within the larger evangelical and American cultural landscapes. On the one hand there are scholars who argue for the distinctiveness of Latino Pentecostalism. For instance Samuel Solivan says that in contrast to the dominant, English-speaking American "culture of association," Latino culture is the "community of being."

The community of being is the community of shared identity, an identity that is communal, linguistically Spanish, family-oriented, and in contrast to the individualistic ethos of mass culture. Solivan says that Latinos "bridge both worlds, culturally and linguistically. [They] must do what they do best: be a community that can function on the boundary between both worlds, speaking both Spanish and English well, managing both cultures, yet firmly rooted in their own."[9] Solivan asserts that a unique "Hispanic Pentecostal Theology," based on spiritual experience combined with the pathos and marginalization many Latinos have dealt with, is the course that Latino churches should pursue.

The Solivan position seems to believe that there is a single Latino identity in the United States. However, as Ruiz points out, "Immigrants and their children pick, borrow, retain, and create distinctive cultural forms. There is not a single hermetic Mexican or Mexican American culture but rather permeable cultures rooted in generation, region, class and personal experience"[10] If there is no single culture, then presumably there is no single religious heritage informing the faith lives of Latinos. Consequently, assumptions anchoring scholarship about Latinos and religion need reconceptualization. This is especially true for second- and third-generation immigrants. Sociologists Ruben Rumbault and Alejandro Portes suggest that a host of factors, not simply ethnicity, determine how second-generation immigrants, in particular, acculturate effectively into American society.[11] Moreover, when one considers that Pentecostalism by its very nature is pragmatic and adaptive in social contexts, it seems likely that Latino Pentecostals would be the first to engage and evolve in the context of the larger American culture.

Although it seems likely that there will continue to be Latino Pentecostal "communities of being" based on language and ethnicity, it seems also likely that many Latino Pentecostals will build bridges to the larger evangelical and American cultures. This is especially true for the children and grandchildren of immigrants who acculturate within the larger American context. The real question for twenty-first century Latino Pentecostalism is whether it will have an independent national and international theological voice that is based on its contributions to global Pentecostalism rather than on preserving culture and language.

Immigration and Reverse Missions

Scholars have known for quite a few years that Pentecostalism's future is in the developing world, and that we in North America are recipients of Pentecostalism's latest guises through the migration of peoples from the developing world. For instance, recent works by Philip Jenkins, David Martin, Eric Patterson, and Karla Poewe are but a few of the many volumes that have attempted to make sense of Pentecostal growth in the developing world.[12] For our part, we will speculate on the crucial question of how Latin American Pentecostal immigration changes North American Pentecostalism, since this immigration stream will be one of the most important streams that revitalizes Pentecostal churches throughout the United States and Canada. According to the U.S. census bureau (2003), Latinos represent about one-seventh of the U.S. population (forty million people). Moreover, in any given year the number of legal and undocumented immigrants in or to the United States is estimated in the millions.

North American Pentecostalism will continue to be a religion of immigrants whose fluid movements across borders shape and reshape the nature of their Pentecostal experience. Latino immigrants for example, not only continue the process identified some years ago as "reverse missions," but the vast borderlands between the United States and Mexico continues to provide North American Pentecostalism with the vitality of new members and a diversity of new movements. Asian and African immigration will also continue to add to the diversity among Pentecostals.

The international face of Pentecostalism means that we cannot look at Pentecostalism as simply defined by theologically rigid doctrines that demarcate strict denominational boundaries. One way to think of the increasingly globalized Pentecostalism is as a style, comprised partially of worship and a diffuse set of spiritual practices, that evangelical Christians accept and utilize to revitalize their own particularly denominations. Consequently, globalized Pentecostalism is a particular way of expressing one's Christian faith that crosses denominational lines and in effect creates a charismatic Christianity that all manner of people partake in, whether they call themselves Pentecostals or not.

An intriguing case of this globalized Pentecostalism is the growth of imported Pentecostal and neo-Pentecostal entities that often espouse the prosperity gospel such as the Brazilian church, *Iglesia Universal Reino de Dios* (Universal Church of the Reign of God; UCRG). There are high levels of coordination between the Brazilian headquarters and its churches worldwide. For example, there are "Parar de Sufrir" ("Stop the Suffering") banners that announce the weekly schedule of UCRG churches in every major Latino urban community in the United States. Rather than U.S. missionaries traveling to Brazil, the UCRG practices "reverse missions:" exporting Brazilian missionaries to the United States. This results in U.S. congregations mimicking their Brazilian counterparts, including a leadership style that it is authoritarian and strictly hierarchical.

Other religious immigrants and imports occur daily. Whether it is the worker who crosses illegally into the United States to seek wages and brings his Pentecostal identity with him from Guatemala, the Portuguese-speaking missionary from Rio de Janeiro to Brazilian émigrés in San Diego, or the back and forth flow of Pentecostal immigrants from Puerto Rico and Mexico to the United States, religion travels easily. In the end, Latino Pentecostals certainly will benefit from being plugged into the globalization of world Pentecostalism. In contrast, Anglo Pentecostal denominations still seem to be frozen in a foreign missions model and unable to realize that, numerically speaking, they are junior partners in the world's fastest growing religious enterprise.

The Gospel of Prosperity

Some scholars have recognized the existence within Pentecostalism of a strand, often associated with post-war "neo-Pentecostalism," that focuses less on the believer's responsibility for ethical conduct and more on economic entitlement. This has been characterized as "name it and claim it," "health and wealth," or the "prosperity gospel." In the United States, this position has long been associated with the Word of Faith movement of Kenneth Hagin, as well as the ministries of Kenneth Copeland and independent charismatics like Oral Roberts.[13]

Numerous scholars have argued that seekers come to Pentecostalism to gain material benefits and physical healing (Annis, 1987; Glazier, 1980; Chesnutt, 1997; Cox, 1995; Martin, 1991, 2002). However, scholars such as Swatos (1994) says that there is a new trend in (neo-)Pentecostalism that focuses on the results (economic fruits) of faith instead of the methods (frugality) of the ascetic "Protestant Ethic." As Simon Coleman writes, the gospel of prosperity is one trend in "the globalization of charismatic Christianity."[14]

Because Latino Pentecostalism has never existed in spiritual isolation from social and cultural forces, one key distinction to watch for in the coming years will be how this prosperity gospel has begun to and will continue to influence Latino churches. One may ask what the attraction might be for Latinos, who are disproportionately living in at or near the poverty line, in adopting a theology of prosperity? On the surface, the answer seems to be that Latinos have adopted much of the prosperity gospel because they have come to believe that there is a correlation between faithfulness and economic gain. By way of contrast, suffering, long a staple of Roman Catholic and Latino religiosity, is now understood within the prosperity gospel as something that can and should be erased. So great is the shift that within the constructs of the prosperity gospel suffering is often even understood to be a sign of spiritual weakness.

One of the best known examples of the prosperity gospel was introduced above: the Pentecostal church from Brazil, the *Iglesia Universal Reino de Dios* (UCRG). This Brazilian church import not only focuses heavily on the health and wealth gospel but also on deliverance ministries. It has compartmentalized its services to the point that every day of the week is dedicated to a different spiritual gift. For example, every Monday is a day of spiritual cleansing, Tuesday is set aside for healing, and Friday might be a day for prayer for debt reduction and financial prosperity. Not only is this church very controversial inside Brazil, Pentecostals across Latin America view UCRG as too focused on deliverance ministries; they too often blend their brand of Christianity with syncretistic ephemera such as Florida water (used by Spiritualists) and utilize prayers that seem more like incantations for health, wealth, and deliverance from demonic possession.

There are other smaller and more localized prosperity gospel imports from Guatemala and Puerto Rico in places like Chicago and Los Angeles which are now branching out in the United States. Since the prosperity gospel tends to find homes outside classical Pentecostal denominations, in independent congregations or nondenominational settings, it may also follow that Latinos, seeking that theological home, will move further and further away from classical denominations and become increasingly cross- or post-denominational like their white evangelical counterparts.

Social Justice and Liberation

When it comes to theologizing about money, three vectors are possible for Latino Pentecostals. The first takes its cue from Roman Catholicism and the experience of many classical Pentecostals: accept poverty as part of a life of suffering in this world just as Christ did. A second path is that of the prosperity gospel discussed above, which claims that faith can yield both spiritual and economic breakthroughs. A third possibility is a Pentecostal liberation theology.

Since Vatican II, liberation themes have resounded throughout the Spanish-speaking world. Liberation theology, a mixture of popular theology with a political message of empowerment and social justice, seemed to explode within some sectors of the developing world, particularly Latin American Catholicism, in the 1970s and 1980s. Denigrated by many in the Catholic hierarchy as well as by most Protestants for its Marxist, redistributionist overtones and overt challenge to the political status quo, the practical effects of liberation theology were felt in many parishes from about 1970–1985. Perhaps most importantly, liberation theology called for the involvement of parishioners in ecclesial base communities (CEBs)—self-help communities led by priests that were supposed to focus on education and social action.

Interestingly, there are voices such as Eldin Villafañe and Samuel Solivan within contemporary Latino Pentecostalism who are using the liberation lexicon in advocating for social justice and progressive political action, calling their program a "Hispanic Pentecostal Ethic."[15] This ethical concern seeks to blend liberation theology with focused attention on the healing power of the Holy Spirit and the active work that the Spirit does in terms of delivering people from life-controlling problems. They call for a radical reorientation of one's faith life away from the rigorous piety characteristic of Pentecostals to an outward focus on a systematic prophetic voice for their communities. Such calls are reminiscent of the prophetic legacy that many Pentecostals promote as part of an idyllic first fifteen years of the movement. For instance, Samuel Solivan extends Gustavo Gutierrez's *Theology of Liberation* to the outreach programs already characteristic of Pentecostal churches: "For Pentecostals, reaching out to the unwed mother, the homeless, the poor and the alcoholic is as political important as electing a local official. From a Pentecostal perspective, the preaching of the gospel is the most political and socially radical activity the world has known. *Although this is true, it is a half truth"* (italics added). Solivan goes on to call for a holistic or "orthopathic" leading of the Spirit that would result in social activism for "better housing, education, and healthcare."[16]

Nonetheless, it seems unlikely that a Pentecostal liberationism will be the hallmark of twenty-first century Latino congregations. For numerous reasons liberation theology has largely declined in the Third World.[17] In the United States, these calls have been taken up only by a minority of Pentecostals, Anglo or Latino, many of whom are academically oriented rather than focused on pastoral efforts, and therefore have not resulted in the wholesale restructuring of churches, pastors, and community life that some have wanted to see.

Conclusion

This essay has suggested certain trends that can be identified as Latino Pentecostalism(s) enter the twenty-first century. Latino Pentecostalism has been the nexus of Pentecostal spiritual experience and Latino ethnic and community identity, and for some this will continue. However, in the United States there is no single Latino community nor is there a single Pentecostal identity: both are dynamic and evolving in relationship to trends in immigration, globalization, evangelicalism, and world charismatic Christianity. Certainly many Latinos in the United States will continue to be among the poorer segments of society and perhaps liberationist themes, particularly if tied to existing political programs, may attract some. However, such attempts are more likely to succeed among academics than among pastors and parishioners. In contrast, it seems likely that the popularity of the prosperity gospel will continue to increase among charismatics and Pentecostals in the United States and worldwide.

A concluding question has to do with the relationship of Pentecostalism, both Latino and other forms, to American Christianity. What will Latino Pentecostalism's relation to American Christianity be? What will that relationship reveal about Latino Pentecostals and their position in the larger body of Christianity? We think these two questions are intertwined, since, for many Pentecostal denominations, specifically groups like the Assemblies of God and Church of God (Cleveland, Tennessee), much of their growth over the past two decades has come from Latinos. The Assemblies of God, without new Latino membership supporting its infrastructure, would actually be losing members. The larger question might be, what will Pentecostalism look like to the larger American context? And if the growth of African American bodies, like the Church of God in Christ, and the inclusion of Asian Pentecostals in various denominations continue, will classical Pentecostalism be able to represent the multicultural nature of its demographics? Will American Christianity be able to make sense of an evangelical movement that will be largely comprised of people of color?

These are intriguing questions. If one wants to examine history for some clues, the answer to these questions may disappoint as well as enlighten. In fact, Pentecostalism's relationship with broader American Christianity has never been comfortable. From the beginning, when early Pentecostals were forced from their churches and pulpits for having received the baptism of the Holy Spirit, to recent times, when churches of certain denominations that eschew charismatic practice have been asked to withdraw or have been disfellowshipped, being Pentecostal in American religious society has not been an easy call. Pentecostalism's touchy relationship with Roman Catholicism, especially over issues involving Latinos, has been marked by a suspicion that Pentecostals were bent on "stealing sheep," so that they have been viewed historically in a paradoxical way. Firstly, they have been viewed as poor country cousins to the more refined, theologically sophisticated mainline brethren; as overly emotional and possible unstable; and, as not exhibiting the proper amount of schooling for some denominations. At the same time, Pentecostals have been viewed as crafty master evangelists, stealing unassuming flocks away from their shepherds with their appeal to the emotional, the fanatical, and the unsound doctrines of spiritual gifts. Pentecostalism's relationship with mainline Protestants, like other evangelicals, continues to be icy, and the new volleys on "moral values," gay and lesbian clergy, and especially gay marriage, will not dissuade mainline Protestants that Pentecostals really are no different than their stereotypical portrayals as those poor country cousins. Conversely, mainline Protestants' views on such issues will not dissuade Pentecostals that there can be legitimate disagreement on such divisive issues within Christianity without descending to judgments on who is truly Christian and who is not.

These fissures that have dominated American Christian discourse since its beginnings will not change, but become more complicated as the collective face that many American Christians see representing Pentecostalism will be Latino, African American, and Asian. For that matter, the same may be said of American Catholicism: in the next generation nearly one third of its members will be people of color. It is our estimation that the issue of the diversity of American Christianity—Pentecostal, Evangelical, Catholic, Episcopal or other—will demonstrate to others either its greatest weakness or its greatest strength. One wonders whether those faces, those different faces, will be able to lead their denominations, preside over their colleges and universities, and learn the most basic premise that has escaped us so far: Christianity will be known by the way it treats its own.

Notes

1. Finke and Starke utilize a market analogy to describe the competition between religious groups. A free society provides a "marketplace" where religious "entrepreneurs" can market their wares. Pentecostals are often media-savvy, utilizing contemporary music and promotional campaigns in addition to testimonies of healing and deliverance to "sell" their message. Traditional Catholic leaders have been much less adept at such competition, particularly because they have had a historical "monopoly" among Latinos and Latin Americans. Rodney Stark and Roger Finke, *The Churching of America, 1776–1900* (New Brunswick, NJ: Princeton University Press, 1992). For the "marketplace" analogy applied to Latin America, see Anthony J. Gill, "Rendering unto Caesar? Religious Competition and Catholic Political Strategy in Latin America, 1962–1979" in *American Journal of Political Science*, 38, no. 2 (May, 1994).

2. William Seymour, "Missionary Notes," *Apostolic Faith* 1, no. 3 (November 1906), 1.

3. Frank Bartleman, quoted in Cecil M. Robeck Jr., ed. *Witness to Pentecost: The Life of Frank Bartleman* (New York: Garland, 1985). 25.

4. Grant Wacker, *Heaven Below* (Cambridge, MA: Harvard University Press, 2001). 48.

5. For more on these early Mexican Pentecostal pioneers, see Arlene M. Sanchez Walsh, *Latino Pentecostal Identity: Evangelical Faith, Self, and Society* (New York: Columbia University Press, 2003), chapter 1.

6. Walsh, 19.

7. Allen Figueroa Deck, *The Challenge of Evangelical/Pentecostal Christianity to Hispanic Catholicism in the U.S.* (Working Paper Series: Cushwa Center for the Study of American Catholicism, 1992), 14.

8. See "Latino Pentecostals in the United States" in *Newsweek*, March 21, 2005, 30–31.

9. Solivan, 121.

10. Vicki Ruiz, "Dead Ends or Gold Mines? Using Missionary Records in Mexican American Women's History" in *Unequal Sisters*, ed. Vicki L. Ruiz and Ellen Carol Dubois, 2nd ed., (New York: Routledge, 1994), 304.

11. Alejandro Portes and Ruben G. Rumbaut, *Legacies: The Story of the Immigrant Second Generation* (Berkeley: University of California Press, 2001), 45–46.

12. Philip Jenkins, *The Next Christendom: The Coming of Global Christianity* (Oxford: Oxford University Press, 2003); David Martin, *Pentecostalism: The World, Their Parish* (Oxford: Blackwell, 2001); Eric Patterson, *Latin America's Neo-Reformation: Religion's Influence on Contemporary Politics* (New York: Routledge, 2005); Karla Poewe, ed., *Charismatic Christianity as a Global Culture* (Columbia, SC: University of South Carolina Press, 1994).

13. For a discussion that clearly links the U.S. "Word of Faith" and allied movements to global neo-Pentecostalism, see Simon Coleman, *The Globalisation of Charismatic Christianity: Spreading the Gospel of Prosperity* (Cambridge: Cambridge University Press, 2000).

14. Coleman, 4.

15. For instance, see Eldin Villafane, *The Liberating Spirit* (Grand Rapids, MI: Eerdmans, 1997).

16. Samuel Solivan, *The Spirit, Pathos, and Liberation: Toward a Hispanic Pentecostal Theology* (Sheffield, UK: Sheffield Academic Press, 1998), 145.

17. For a discussion of the rise and fall of liberation theology, see Eric Patterson, *Latin America's Neo-Reformation* (New York: Routledge, 2005), chapter 2.

Chapter 6

The Future of Pentecostal Higher Education: the Ring, the Shire, or the Redemption of Middle Earth?

Jeff Hittenberger

In J.R.R. Tolkien's epic trilogy, *The Lord of the Rings*, Frodo Baggins faces a dilemma. He has inherited a ring of extraordinary power, but a ring with links to a rising evil that threatens all of Middle Earth, including his beloved home, the idyllic Shire. What should he do? He might follow the way of others who possessed the ring and yielded to its powers. He might choose to bury the ring, remain in the comfort of his Shire and hope the evil stays away. There is, however, a third choice. Frodo might choose to set out on a journey in fellowship with his hobbit brothers, accompanied by an elf, a dwarf, a wizard, and a king in disguise. He might choose to challenge the dark powers beyond the boundaries of the Shire and take part in the redemption of Middle Earth.[1]

Pentecostal educators are likewise faced with difficult choices and divergent paths. This chapter examines key issues for Pentecostal higher education in the United States in the twenty-first century, addressing the following questions:

- How did Pentecostal higher education emerge in the United States and what is its current status?
- What are the visions of faculty and administrators within Pentecostal institutions of higher education (IHEs) and what challenges do they face?
- What might Pentecostal educators learn from the experience of other Christian IHEs, and from their own history, about the challenges they are likely to face in years to come?
- What are some key questions that Pentecostal educators will need to attend to in the coming generation if their IHEs are to achieve their missions and fulfill their visions?

This chapter draws on a review of relevant literature, collection and analysis of data from universities and denominations, analysis of IHE histories, mission statements, and vision statements, and interviews with 39 faculty members and administrators (including 11 Presidents) from Pentecostal IHEs.[2] The majority of these interviewees work within Assemblies of God (AG) institutions.

The Emergence and Current Status of Pentecostal Higher Education

As the twentieth century opened, the United States was emerging as a global power, expanding its markets, and mobilizing its workers for industrial production. College and university education was becoming accessible to larger numbers of Americans, often in technical and scientific fields recognized as crucial to industrial growth and international influence.

The religious emphasis of nineteenth century American higher education was losing its attraction as modernization promised to create heaven on earth through scientific means. Modern conceptions of knowledge (mechanistic, empirical, and quantitative) undermined the credibility of religious epistemologies rooted in revelation. Modernism was even winning adherents among many Christians in higher education, who believed that general Christian values could be integrated with modern scientific methods (and ideas such as Darwinian evolution) to bring about a "Christian century" of social and intellectual progress.[3] Such optimism was soon to be shattered by World War I.

In the midst of this era of dramatic change, the Pentecostal movement in the United States was born. While American colleges and universities were embracing increasingly empirical and rationalistic modes of knowledge, participants in the Pentecostal revival were experiencing, first hand, divine revelation, physical healing, and "gifts of the Holy Spirit," such as had been experienced by the first century followers of Jesus Christ.

These early Pentecostals were non-participants in the religion vs. science culture wars within the early twentieth century colleges and universities, not because they had abandoned the universities, but because they had never been there. As people of few means and limited schooling, Pentecostals did not believe that education, science, progress, or governments were the keys to the Kingdom of God on earth. Rather, these early Pentecostals believed that God alone could redeem a desperately sinful and broken world. They saw themselves as participants in the outpouring of the Holy Spirit, spoken of by the prophet Joel,[4] which would usher in salvation, healing, and the Second Coming of Christ.

Though their faith was not *in* education, the early Pentecostals were not opposed to education, particularly Bible study and pastoral training, as a means to an end. The twentieth century Pentecostal revival in the United States began in a short-term Bible school in 1901. The revival produced and was sustained by many such schools that functioned as training centers for Pentecostal church workers. Bible training during the day was often complemented by evangelistic services in the evening.

Scores of Pentecostal institutions of higher education of various types have since been established in the United States. They can be categorized as follows:

Type 1: Bible schools and church-based Bible institutes (CBBIs) focus on practical ministry training, many of which are "proto-IHEs" not requiring completion of secondary education. Dozens of Type 1 Pentecostal institutions are functioning in the United States.

Type 2: Bible colleges (typically residential) with accreditation from the Association for Biblical Higher Education (ABHE, which until June 2004 was the Accrediting Association of Bible Colleges, formerly AABIBC), or similar, offering two-, three-, or four-year training programs for pastors, evangelists, and missionaries. A survey of the membership of the Pentecostal and Charismatic Churches of North America (PCCNA), the fellowship of classical Pentecostal denominations, yielded a list of eight Type 2 Pentecostal institutions in the United States.[5]

Type 3: Christian colleges with regional accreditation associated with one of the six regional accrediting bodies in the United States, offering an expanded array of courses and majors in addition to church ministry or theology.[6] A number of these Pentecostal institutions are members of the evangelical grouping known as the Council of Christian Colleges and Universities (CCCU). Many of these have become Type 5 institutions (see below), but a survey of PCCNA members yielded a list of five regionally-accredited Pentecostal Christian colleges.[7]

Type 4: Regionally-accredited seminaries offering graduate degree programs. Only three such institutions were identified by a search of PCCNA members (Assemblies of God Theological Seminary; Church of God Theological Seminary; and Charles H. Mason Theological Seminary affiliated with the Church of God in Christ[8]), but others, such as the School of Divinity at Regent University, and the School of Theology and Missions at Oral Roberts University function within the framework of a Type 5 Pentecostal university.

Type 5: Regionally-accredited Christian comprehensive universities offering both undergraduate degrees in a variety of majors and graduate programs in various professional fields, twelve of which are now functioning within the Pentecostal movement in the United States and most of which are CCCU members.[9]

Recently, Global University of the AG has emerged as potentially a new type of Pentecostal IHE. Global is an expression of the theological-education-by-extension (TEE) movement, specifically the product of the merger of the AG's International Correspondence Institute (ICI-offering international correspondence courses) and Berean (offering domestic correspondence courses). While other Pentecostal IHEs offer online degree programs (e.g., Regent University and Oral Roberts University [ORU]), they do so as Type 5 institutions, regionally-accredited universities with a strong campus-based center. Global's decision to seek regional accreditation from the North Central Association (it currently has Candidate status), the fact that it does not have a campus offering in-person programs, and the fact that it is a theological-education-by-extension program puts it in a unique position and may signal the emergence of a new kind of Pentecostal IHE that falls outside the typology above.

Overall enrollment growth in Pentecostal IHEs in the United States is strong. In the AG, for example, while enrollments of traditional students in denominationally-endorsed institutions have grown by about 20 percent over the past decade, non-traditional enrollments, encompassing extension programs, degree completion programs, distance education, correspondence courses, or study centers, have doubled. Enrollment trends favor Type 4, and, especially, Type 5 institutions (as well as CBBIs).[10] Type 2 Bible colleges have had difficulty sustaining enrollments and many (including the AG flagship institution Central Bible College) are now seeking regional accreditation. The number of Type 3 institutions has diminished greatly in the past decade as no fewer than ten Pentecostal Christian colleges have claimed university status. The Christian college phase of Pentecostal higher education seems to be giving way to the university phase, with increasing emphasis being placed on graduate and professional studies. This trend may be related to the pragmatic orientation of Pentecostalism and its lack of a liberal arts tradition.

Pentecostal educators interviewed for this chapter identified a number of encouraging signs, such as the growing numbers of outstanding students, greater commitment to education within the Pentecostal movement, opportunities related to the globalization and diversification of Pentecostalism, a broadened understanding of Christian calling, expanding scholarly excellence, growth in institutional capacity, and better integration of dynamic spirituality with academic and professional excellence. As one President stated: "While we will always have an uneasiness about over-reliance on education, there is a growing number of people who do not accept an either-or view of education, but see dynamic spirituality and thorough education as not mutually exclusive. I see there to be a willingness to remove ourselves from the historic bifurcations and to chart our course as 'both-and' people."

Visions for the Future and Significant Challenges

In Spring 2004 I sent emails to personnel at each of the endorsed AG institutions, requesting interviews. The number of requests corresponded to the enrollment of the institution, from two requests at the smallest institutions to seven requests at the largest. I also made contact with personnel at ORU, Lee University, Regent University, and Vanguard College in Canada (a Type 2 institution) for the sake of comparison. Based on the responses I received, I carried out 39 interviews, some via email, some via phone, and some in person. The profile of the interviewees skewed in the direction of the institutions with the largest enrollments. Further details regarding the sample can be found in the endnotes.

When asked about their visions for their IHEs and for Pentecostal higher education in general, interviewees referred to the continuation of many of the encouraging developments listed above. More elaborate vision statements are available on the websites of a number of these institutions, but the reflections below capture their essence. The following themes wove through responses to the question: "What would you like your Pentecostal IHE and Pentecostal higher education in general to look like twenty-five or fifty years from now?"

Spiritual Vitality

One junior faculty member commented: "I would like [my IHE] to be a vibrant, spirit-filled community of worship and study which prepares students to have a significant impact on the world for Christ." A veteran administrator responded: "Faith, hope, and love. . . Paul's comments keep coming back to me. This is what it means to be authentically Christian." A President expressed this vision for his campus: "I want this to be a place where the presence of God is sensed from the moment someone arrives on campus." Another administrator observed: "Spiritual formation must lead students toward Pentecostal experience, including regular prayer for the sick and the regular exercise of the gifts of the Spirit." Another President emphasized key elements of the Pentecostal identity to undergird visions of spiritual formation: "Effective personal and programmatic evangelism and effective discipleship programs that produce biblical holiness in the lives of believers, effective ways of helping people find their unique spiritual gifts and callings, along with programs that allow them to exercise those gifts. All of this is attended by the manifestation of the supernatural in signs and wonders. In addition, Pentecostals have a unique orientation to the supernatural, an openness similar to what we see in non-Western cultures."

Growth of Enrollments, Programs, and Institutional Capacity

Virtually all interviewees envision continuing growth in enrollments and facilities for their institutions. A Vice President for Institutional Advancement said: "I would like to see our institution be double or more our current size with a broader range of academic offerings reflecting the broad range of ministry, both vocational and marketplace, that our constituents embrace." Regent University envisions a distance education enrollment in the hundreds of thousands over the next twenty-five years, which would make it the largest university in the world. Given that the Pentecostal movement is, arguably, the fastest growing religious movement in the world, and certainly the fastest growing movement in Christianity, this vision of growth in higher education is not surprising. Many Pentecostal IHEs are now offering master's degrees and a few have begun to offer doctoral degrees. In the coming generation, many more will become comprehensive universities. One administrator commented: "Pentecostal higher education has a tremendous mission, to provide leadership to this extraordinary worldwide Pentecostal movement."

Academic Quality

An AG university President stated: "I would like to see Pentecostal higher education continue to take its place as a legitimate member of the academic community, with well-trained minds and high-quality research, continuing to draw well-qualified students, with an open and not exclusive admissions policy. I would hope that that would be done without compromising our commitment to spiritual priorities." Another administrator commented: "I would like for [our Pentecostal IHE] to be fully engaged in the academy. I hope we admit serious Christian students even if they aren't AG, and I hope we recruit serious Christian scholars as faculty even if they aren't AG. I hope we will begin to write textbooks and become the leaders in professional organizations. I would like for us to offer master's and doctor's degrees in a variety of disciplines. I hope we are leaders in non-traditional education delivery systems, and I hope our study abroad programs are fully developed and offer our students a plethora of options for experiencing the world." Another President commented on the distinctive Pentecostal concern for students who have not had prep school or other privileged preparation. "We come from a slice of American culture that was not privileged. . . As institutions, we should have a stronger commitment to second-chance kids." The desire for increasing academic quality and enhancing research efforts is strong. More than one interviewee mentioned the desire to be to Pentecostalism what Notre Dame is to Catholicism or what Wheaton is to evangelicalism.

More Collaborative Relationships among Pentecostal IHEs

A number of interviewees expressed a desire for greater collaboration among institutions, often across denominational lines. One faculty member commented, regarding faculty seminars sponsored by the AG, "It was enjoyable to meet colleagues from other AG institutions and share ideas and concerns." An administrator at a Type 1 Bible institute talked about the possibilities of linking with a Pentecostal university, becoming a college within the university to offer distinctive programs. Another administrator wrote: "I would hope that our colleges would work more closely together. As a team of schools we could provide a powerful and supportive educational resource for each other. Many of the professional program goals I hope we might accomplish some day might be more realistic if we collaborated with our resources, faculty, facilities, and finances." An AG university administrator commented: "We need to look at relationships with other Pentecostal IHEs, like Lee University, growing and building with resources beyond what we have in the AG. How do we link together? How do we have creative dialogue?" This desire for collaboration also envisioned continuing partnerships with evangelical CCCU institutions as well as stronger relationships with other IHEs in their regions.

While encouraging signs abound and visions for the future are strong, Pentecostal higher education faces significant challenges in the coming generation. Some of the most commonly identified follow.

Finances

Virtually every interviewee mentioned the challenges of securing adequate financial resources to support the mission and programs of their institution. These challenges are hardly unique to Pentecostalism,[11] but Pentecostals started late in the higher education game and started from a socio-economic deficit. One administrator put it succinctly as follows: "Finances, finances, finances. Giving, tuition, cost of education, location, faculty salaries, research funds. . . These issues will either help an IHE grow or sink the ship." For faculty, limited resources translate into heavy teaching loads. One faculty member observed: "We are expected to teach four or more classes a semester, to really be involved in the students' lives and to continue to be active in our fields. As we move to university status, I think we will need to open the doors for faculty to do more research and grow in their disciplines. However, the heavy class loads and the lack of financial support make this difficult." Financial challenges are also related to competition within the higher education arena. AG students, for example, do not feel constrained by denominational loyalty to attend the closest AG IHE.[12] Many AG students attend evangelical colleges and universities, like Wheaton, Biola, and Gordon. Many others attend state universities. Highly qualified AG students are even attending elite private institutions like Stanford and Harvard. At the seminary and graduate levels, AG students frequently attend evangelical seminaries or other prestigious graduate schools. Moreover, the modest growth in AG churches over the past decade or more in the United States means that the pool of potential AG students has not increased substantially. Consequently, AG IHEs must recruit not only AG students, but also other Pentecostal and evangelical students. Graduate programs are casting an ever wider recruiting net, sometimes attracting students from non-evangelical and even non-Christian backgrounds. This cultural shift within Pentecostal higher education impacts the identities, the markets, and the finances of Pentecostal IHEs.

Within the AG, most IHEs are affiliated with local districts, and not with the General Council (the central headquarters of the denomination). While districts are supportive partners, their financial resources are limited. While the General Council has, in recent years, invested more in higher education, especially with the faculty seminar initiatives, it has few resources to share with the IHEs it endorses, even the General Council schools that are located in Springfield, Missouri. Consequently, AG IHEs are left to drum up support for themselves in a sort of "survival of the fittest" scenario that favors the entrepreneurial schools who are able to effectively respond to demand in their regional markets.

That market sensitivity can be an asset to an institution in terms of vitality and service, a kind of "indigenization," but can also make it vulnerable to blurring its sense of Christian mission.

Hiring Outstanding Pentecostal Faculty

One President noted: "The biggest challenge is finding good faculty and administrators and building the team. You've got to find outstanding faculty if you want to be a significant institution. At the salaries we pay. . . and considering our lifestyle covenants and who is intellectually and doctrinally complementary with Pentecostalism. . . As you keep adding these criteria, you lop off the number of potential candidates." Another administrator stated: "Because the AG has not championed non-religious higher education, there is not a pool of Pentecostal scholars in the non-religion disciplines." Often, there is no qualified Pentecostal applicant for a particular position in a particular discipline in a particular region. Consequently, Pentecostal IHEs have, in recent years, hired many outstanding evangelical faculty members who have diversified and brought many gifts to Pentecostal campuses. However, that change in the profile of some Pentecostal IHE faculties has, in some cases, created tensions between the IHEs and their denominations and brought about changes in the ethos of the IHEs. This issue will be discussed in greater detail below.

Pentecostal Identity

A number of interviewees mentioned the challenge of defining Pentecostal identity in the twenty-first century. That issue is being discussed elsewhere in this book, but it has tremendous relevance for the question of the future of Pentecostal higher education. On one hand, we are witnessing a "Pentecostalization" of evangelicalism and Christianity, especially in the two-thirds world, but also in the United States. A number of interviewees noted that in recent years non-Pentecostal IHEs and churches have adopted many of the practices and beliefs of Pentecostalism. While some are concerned about students who take pastorates or become faculty members outside Pentecostal churches or communities, the effect of this is, in many cases, to share the experience of the Holy Spirit with the broader church. One President remarked: "We have an ability to penetrate at a lot of different cultural levels. We have a kind of Pentecostal diaspora, blessing so many levels of the social order. Instead of looking at it as a sense of loss, we look at it as a scattering as in the Book of Acts, the 'peppering' of different denominations, the flavoring of other churches. On the other hand, you could hoard it, protect it, and try to keep the kids close. . . The challenge is to carry the Holy Spirit with you, keep your fervor and not lose that even if you go to another kind of church." One President observed, concerning the CCCU institutions: "At first, it was just kind of a tolerance on the part of the group who had strong academic programs, but were steeped in a strong Calvinist position. As time has gone on, they have come to respect our institutions. Within their own ranks, many of their students have come with exposure to Charismatic activity. It has invaded their schools."

On the other hand, Pentecostal higher educators are struggling to define just what makes their institutions "Pentecostal." Given the Pentecostalization of evangelicalism, is there yet a need for a distinctively Pentecostal higher education? Many think so.

The issue of the relationship between Pentecostal and evangelical identity came up often during the interviews. One veteran professor commented: "I hope to find a Pentecostal theology that is more fully-orbed. . . What theology we have is essentially Evangelical theology, with a sector replaced by our distinctive Pneumatology. I would push the discussion in a different direction: What should a Pentecostal Christology look like? What does a Pentecostal hermeneutic look like? What distinctive perspectives does a Pentecostal bring to the Social Sciences? The Arts? Literary Theory?" An AG IHE administrator stressed the distinctions between Pentecostalism and fundamentalism or evangelicalism. "I wish that Pentecostal higher education would find its own voice. Too much mirrors evangelical and fundamentalist models." One administrator outside the AG wrote: "We insist that we are NOT evangelicals, but 'Spirit-filled.' Students are somewhat shocked at first, but soon come to the realization that to live a truly Spirit-filled life one cannot tag on a little bit of the Spirit in their personal or communal Christian expression." The President at another institution commented: "We're Pentecostal in that we lead our students in an exploration of Pentecostal doctrine and practice in our worship. We seek to model worship that includes the Pentecostal emphasis on the gifts of the Spirit. We lead our students in exploring what it means to be Pentecostal. We think a university is a place where you explore those questions and do not just pass down the answers. That sets us apart as a Pentecostal institution. It may not mean that your French teacher is Pentecostal. It does not necessarily mean that the student in the next seat is Pentecostal. A Pentecostal IHE is one that embodies in a contemporary fashion the principles of Pentecostalism."

Even the term "Pentecostal" is not universally embraced at the Pentecostal IHEs. Especially outside the AG, some use "Spirit-filled," others use "Charismatic," and others prefer the term "Renewal." Within the AG, some prefer to use the descriptor "Assemblies of God" more prominently than Pentecostal, in that Pentecostal may mean different things to different people. Some expressed a desire to see AG IHEs perpetuate the AG identity and not simply a Pentecostal identity. Some of this identity issue can be explained by differences in emphasis.

Consider the following identity descriptors:

- *Religious*
- *Faith-based*
- *Christian*
- *Protestant*
- *Evangelical*
- *Pentecostal*
- *Assemblies of God*

Virtually all whom I interviewed would identify with the first six identity descriptors above. Since the majority of my interviewees were from AG IHEs, most would also identify with the seventh identity descriptor as well. However, Pentecostals would differ in the degree to which they would wish to identify their IHEs with each of the descriptors. Some would like the most prominent identity to be that of the denomination. Others would like to put the strongest identity emphasis on a combination of Pentecostal and Christian identifiers. Some would combine Evangelical, Pentecostal, and AG descriptors. One way of assessing the use of these descriptors is to look at the mission statements of the IHEs to see which descriptors are given pride of place. Generally speaking, denominational leaders seem more inclined to give a central place to denominational identity. IHEs (like local churches) vary in their desire to identify denominational affiliation prominently. Among other considerations, some see little market advantage to highlighting denominational affiliation in a post-denominational era. While the denomination and the IHEs share a great deal in terms of their vision to provide outstanding Christian higher education, shaped by a Pentecostal ethos, that will equip people to impact the world for Christ, the difference in emphasis between the denomination and at least some of the IHEs presents significant challenges.

Analysis: Pentecostal Higher Education— the Ring, the Shire, or the Redemption of Middle Earth?

In the past twenty years dramatic changes have occurred in Pentecostal higher education, especially in the development and growth of regionally accredited liberal arts colleges and comprehensive universities. What is one to make of these many changes? Where is Pentecostal higher education likely to go in the next generation? Will it follow the well-worn path of secularization, falling to the seductions of the Ring? Will it recoil from the challenges and seek to return to the comfort and familiarity of the Shire? Or will Pentecostal higher education find ways to become a redemptive force in the complex world of academia and in the larger society? This section seeks to analyze these possibilities by placing the responses summarized above in the larger context of discussions about secularization, particularly as it relates to higher education.

Many books in recent years have examined the historic patterns by which Christian institutions of higher education gradually abandon their Christian mission and become "secularized." The most prominent of these books are George Marsden's *The Soul of the American University* and James Burtchaell's *The Dying of the Light.*

It is important, first, to note what these authors do *not* mean by secularization. Liberal arts education does not inevitably lead to secularization. The creation of graduate and professional studies programs does not assure secularization. An expanded sense of mission, from a singular emphasis on church-related vocations to a curriculum preparing students for an array of vocations serving in many domains, can be very compatible with Christian commitments. The recruitment of a greater variety of students from many different denominational backgrounds does not necessarily lead to secularization. The hiring of a more diverse Christian faculty, representing various Christian streams, does not lead inevitably to secularization. Taking advantage of new market opportunities and new delivery systems (e.g., online, hybrid, and distance education) is not necessarily acquiescence to secularization. So what *is* secularization?

Marsden writes:

> The American university system was built on a foundation of evangelical Protestant colleges. Most of the major universities evolved directly from such nineteenth-century colleges. As late as 1870 the vast majority of these were remarkably evangelical. Most of them had clergymen-presidents who taught courses defending biblicist Christianity and who encouraged periodic campus revivals. Yet within half a century the universities that emerged from these evangelical colleges, while arguably carrying forward the spirit of their evangelical forebears, had become conspicuously inhospitable to the letter of such evangelicalism.[13]

In one sense, the "disestablishment" of Protestant higher education was brought on by the fact that Protestants had, in a sense, controlled American higher education and closed off avenues for expression to Catholics, Jews, and others. According to Marsden, disestablishment was, in many ways, justified. A "secular" public arena, in which people of diverse faiths, or of no faith, are welcomed to participate, seems appropriate for a pluralistic democracy, and Christians, according to Marsden, should be eager and ready to participate.

What is troubling, though, for Marsden, is that this disestablishment, and the opening up of a more pluralistic American higher education system that should have allowed for a greater diversity of distinctive institutions, was accompanied by an aggressive form of secularization that in many cases closed higher education off from religious perspectives and brought about a new naturalistic dogma. Religious views became fenced off in the world of emotion, values, and personal preferences, rather than included in the world of ideas and facts, the domain of the university and the sciences.

Secularization occurred over time in response to forces of American pluralism, modern scientific ideas, and free market capitalism. Rarely did an IHE or
its leader decide, "We are no longer going to be Christian." Instead, this secularization resulted from thousands of daily decisions whose incremental effect
was to distance the institution from its Christian commitments and its Christian
mission. Over time, the worldview of an institution ceased to be rooted in a Biblical understanding of reality and was replaced by a naturalistic understanding
that no longer required the "God thesis." Gradually, distinctively Christian
themes were moderated so as not to offend prospective donors or prospective
students. The desire to serve broader publics and broader markets led to an emphasis on more universally acceptable values and mission statements. Marsden
writes:

> No matter what the denominational identity and the theological issues
> in its background, each Protestant college had to deal with more or
> less the same American market. In such a free enterprise system a
> strong emphasis on theological distinctions could limit a college's
> constituency and be a competitive disadvantage. Hence each college
> was more likely to emphasize the socially unifying aspects of its
> Christian tradition, especially its moral benefits, rather than theologi-
> cal peculiarities.[14]

While there is no inherent dichotomy between mission and market, and
Pentecostals in particular have always been ready to take the mission to the
market and use the tools of the market to share the message of Christ, the power
of the market is such that economic priorities can eclipse all others. This concern
is not unique to Christian higher educators. A vigorous discussion is taking
place even among secular educators about the "marketization" of higher education and the loss of core values and academic quality in American higher education.[15]

Much of Marsden's argument has now become familiar and is discussed in
great detail elsewhere. One final quote provides an application of the lessons of
secularization for Pentecostal (and other Christian) IHEs at the beginning of the
twenty-first century.

> Throughout the era since the rise of American universities, pressure
> has come from many directions for institutions to conform to the ho-
> mogenized national ideal. Many small colleges that long retained a
> more distinctive heritage eventually conformed and lost their identity.
> Today, in addition to confronting an intellectual climate that penal-
> izes anything but pure naturalism, they face practical pressures aris-
> ing from concerns for pluralism, academic freedom, and church-state
> issues that parallel those just considered regarding universities. . . .
> Accrediting agencies sometimes attempt to penalize institutions for
> having a distinctive religious heritage. While the general rule for ac-
> crediting agencies has been that institutions should be allowed to de-

fine their own goals and then be accredited on that basis, accreditors sometimes exert pressure against distinctive religious and cultural traditions.[16]

It is important, also, to note that secularization is not just a matter of abstract worldview. Secularization is the process whereby distinctly Christian ways of living and understanding are supplanted by non-Christian ways of living and understanding. For example, when Christians in or out of higher education begin to value rank and prestige associated with degree, status, title, or wealth above Christian value of the individual as beloved by God whatever their social rank, de facto secularization is underway, regardless of what the mission statement of the institution may say.

Pentecostals view their institutions of higher education as places where students can deepen their Christian understanding of the world. They also affirm that such a worldview will have a very short shelf-life where a living, vibrant experience with Jesus Christ, empowered by the Holy Spirit, is not nurtured in the life of every student, faculty member, administrator, staff member, alum, and trustee.

A difference in emphasis between Marsden and Burtchaell is captured by the latter's sub-title: "The Disengagement of Colleges and Universities from their Christian Churches." Burtchaell, according to his own description, "discerns the dynamics and rationales at various times whereby the link of mutual patronage between college and church was severed in this century."[17] Writing from a Roman Catholic perspective, Burtchaell gives primacy to fidelity to the church and is wary of what he refers to as "Pietism," or revivalist movements (he mentions Wesleyanism and the American churches that arose from the Great Awakening).

> The Pietists propounded the primacy of spirit over letter, commitment over institution, affect over intellect, laity over clergy, invisible church over visible, and they looked to the earliest Christian communities for their models. By holding up the simpler beginnings of the Christian faith as their model, they were able to isolate the original meaning and authentic dynamism of many elements of Christian life that had subsequently been adapted and amended beyond recognition, and seemed spent.[18]

This would be an apt description of Pentecostalism. But Pietism, according to Burtchaell, begets thin ecclesiology, idiosyncratic theology, and unstable movements (failing to embrace the authority and tradition of the church). Consequently, when they launch institutions of higher education, these tend to drift rather quickly toward secular modes given their lack of historical, ecclesial, and theological anchor.

> The pietist view eventually shared by these various denomina-
> tions and churches was that religious endeavors on campus
> should be focused upon the individual life of faith, as distinct
> from the shared labor of learning. Religion's move to the aca-
> demic periphery was not so much the work of godless intellectu-
> als as of pious educators who, since the onset of pietism, had
> seen religion as embodied so uniquely in the personal profession
> of faith that it could not be seen to have a stake in social learn-
> ing. The radical disjunction between divine knowledge and hu-
> man knowledge had been central to classical Reformation think-
> ing, and its unintended outcome was to sequester religious piety
> from secular learning.[19]

While his observation serves as an important caution to Pentecostals, part of Burtchaell's argument is based on this faulty premise: if an institution of higher education remains faithful to its founding church, it will remain faithful to the Gospel of Jesus Christ. The problem with this argument is that churches, like colleges, have their own trajectories in relationship to vibrant Christian faith. Like colleges, denominations are subject to pressures from time, market, and culture. Many denominations and their churches have, over time, blunted their commitment to Christian faith and practice and accommodated culture to the point of losing their spiritual vitality, their prophetic witness, their evangelistic fervor, their social impact, and, ultimately, their membership. Wycliffe, Hus, and Luther are examples of academics who called a wayward church back to faithfulness to Christ.

An institution of higher education that remains faithful to a church that does not remain faithful to Biblical, historic Christian faith will not likely keep its light shining. In his study of the social sources of denominationalism, Niebuhr noted the tendency of revival movements over time to lose revolutionary fervor, due to factors such as "the influence of economic success and gradual assimilation into mainstream society."[20]

There is much to appreciate in Burtchaell's analysis, but secularization is not, primarily, a matter of a college or university cutting its ties to its sponsoring church. Secularization, in fact, impacts both IHE and church, a fact which Burtchaell ultimately acknowledges. Avoiding secularization means that IHE and church must be in dynamic relationship to one another and to God, to "spur one another on."

Partnership between college and sponsoring church is important and can be enriching for both. However, denominational strategies that prioritize denominational loyalty and the perpetuation of the denomination are not likely to strengthen, over the long term, either the denomination or the IHEs for the purposes of Christian mission. As AG General Superintendent Thomas Trask stated in his introduction to the *Vision for Transformation* initiative, "First and foremost, we must commit ourselves to seeing lives transformed and the kingdom of God built. I'm convinced that if we will focus our attention on building the kingdom of God, God will take care of the Assemblies of God."[21] A lively discussion is presently taking place in the United States. AG regarding criteria IHEs must meet in order to achieve or retain the endorsement of the denomination. The Task Force for Transforming Assemblies of God Higher Education has made a number of important recommendations to strengthen the partnership between the General Council and the IHEs. Reflection on the temptations of secularization as well as entrenchment (the Ring or the Shire) are important to this discussion.

Are Pentecostal IHEs immune to the forces that have reshaped the missions of other Christian IHEs over the past century? Are concerns about secularization, or "the dying of the light (of the Gospel)," ill-founded? Clearly, those concerns *are* legitimate. Pentecostal IHE administrators and faculty face daily decisions that will determine the long-term directions of their institutions. Drawn from responses to interview questions and from Marsden's analysis of historical patterns, the following are some of the kinds of questions which Pentecostal higher educators face, especially those engaged in the development of, or laying the groundwork for, universities:

- *Mission:* How do the mission statements of the university and its academic programs make clear the Christian mission and frame of reference? How does the IHE engage with partner churches to focus continuously on its Christian mission?
- *Personnel:* How does the IHE assure that each faculty member hired is committed to Jesus Christ, and to the spiritual and intellectual mentoring of students consistent with Pentecostal, evangelical, and historic Christian commitments? Administrators? Staff members?
- *Professional Development:* How does the IHE equip faculty to integrate faith, learning, and life so that they are able to bring Christian perspectives to bear on their curriculum, research, and instruction?
- *Curriculum:* How do courses reflect strong Christian integration, across all disciplines? What opportunities do students have to reflect on implications of Pentecostal experience for the understanding of the world in its various domains?
- *Graduate and Professional Studies:* How does the IHE address the issue of the relationship of Christian faith to the graduate, professional, or specialized technical programs emerging in the IHE?
- *Spiritual Formation and Ministry:* How does the IHE engage students, staff, and faculty in Christian spiritual formation and Pentecostal worship and ministry?
- *Community:* How does the IHE ensure that the relationships among administrators, faculty, staff, and students are reflec-

tive of Biblical principles of community and supportive of
Christian lifestyles?
- *Scholarship:* What opportunities does the IHE provide faculty
  and students to engage in scholarly inquiry grounded in rich
  understandings of the relationship between scholarship and
  Christian faith? How does the IHE assure the quality of its
  academic programs?
- *Marketing:* How do the efforts at "branding" or marketing the
  institution (through advertising, publications, community engagement, etc.) make clear its Christian commitment and mission?

For each of the questions above, I could recount stories told by interviewees
or colleagues in other institutions, both Pentecostal and non-Pentecostal, where
failure to adequately consider the issue has had unfortunate repercussions. These
questions should not suggest a list of commandments, but rather a call to intentionality.

Recommendations: Toward a Pentecostal
Renaissance in Higher Education

Not one of the Pentecostal higher educators with whom I spoke desired a
future characterized by secularization, or the Ring. Nor did any feel we could
retreat to the Shire and abandon the effort to bring Christian and Pentecostal
understanding and experience to bear in a redemptive way in the realm of higher
education. But how are we to proceed? One way of describing what is needed
might be "Pentecostal Renaissance."

The term Renaissance means "re-birth." It subsumes the ideas of revival
and renewal. If the Pentecostal movement in the United States does not experience a rebirth it is highly unlikely that its IHEs will remain Pentecostal in any
meaningful way. But this Renaissance cannot simply be a replay of earlier Pentecostal revivals. The term Renaissance also evokes an openness that goes beyond a strict "Christ against culture" stance. Renaissance is a rebirth also of the
arts and sciences, of music, of ideas, of architecture, of systems, of professions,
of culture. A Pentecostal Renaissance in higher education would take students
and faculty deeper into relationship with God and into engagement with culture.
Such a Pentecostal Renaissance would affirm:

Intimacy with God. Pentecostal Christians are called to draw their moment-
by-moment lives, their continuous vitality, from the personal, intimate, loving,
communal, bountiful Spirit of God who speaks the Lordship of Christ and the
love of the Father. This desire for intimacy with God and the practice of His
presence should be at the center of the life of each Pentecostal higher education
community.

Spirit Inspiration. As institutions, Pentecostal IHEs must plan and function in a real world of markets and budgets, but more essentially each IHE is a gathering of people of the Spirit called to seek God's guidance and to serve the world in Christ's love. Pentecostal IHEs must be "supernaturally natural," drawing on the power of the Holy Spirit to engage in the pragmatic work of higher education.

Global Mission. The message of Pentecost is not Pentecost. The message is Jesus Christ as Savior and Lord. Pentecostal IHEs encourage the globalization of this Gospel of Christ. Empowerment for mission, which includes evangelism and service, has been at the heart of the Pentecostal movement and must continue to be our focus if we are to be faithful to Christ's calling. This global character also should be evident in the demographics of our campuses, a gathering of all peoples, from all cultural backgrounds, for community and mission.

Intellectual Exploration. Pentecostal IHEs offer opportunities for students and faculty to pursue inquiry, develop worldviews, and generate scholarship, rooted in personal relationship with God, inspired by the Holy Sprit, guided by the authority of Scripture, and open to exploration, seeking out truth, beauty, and goodness wherever they are found. All of Christian history is resource and all of human history offers lessons for critical examination.

Artistic Expression. Pentecostal IHEs should also give special attention to the imagination, as a Pentecostal epistemology is necessarily open to modes of knowing that include the rich variety of ways in which God the Spirit leads us into all truth. New generations of Pentecostal Christians are especially interested in the inspiration of the Spirit in the arts and Pentecostal IHEs are uniquely equipped to nurture and channel this interest.

Cultural Engagement. The cultures of the world are proper domains of Pentecostal engagement and witness. No culture owns the Gospel and all cultures are broken and subject to the Fall. Every culture contains the "dynamic equivalents" that allow for expression and understanding of the Gospel. Pentecostal IHEs uniquely equip Pentecostals and other Christians to engage every cultural domain both prophetically and creatively. Vocational service in any cultural domain can be an act of worship and ministry for those who see no dichotomy between the secular and sacred aspects of their lives.

Collaborative Service. Pentecostal IHEs have unique opportunities to collaborate with and bless all those who believe in Christ and to serve and bear witness to those who do not. Pentecostal IHEs cannot wall themselves off, nor would they survive if they did. Our calling is to bless the world through service to all those in need of healing, hope, and redemption. This service gives special attention, as Pentecostal mission always has, to those who are poor, abused, neglected, imprisoned, addicted, following the lead of Jesus Christ who said: "I was poor, and you fed me. . ."

Conclusion

Over the past century, American Pentecostals have birthed scores of vibrant institutions of higher education initially focused exclusively on the training of ministers, but more recently expanding into liberal arts, professional, and graduate education. Drawing on the power of the Holy Spirit and the lessons of history, Pentecostals have the potential to develop their IHEs over the next twenty-five years into creative and transformative centers of learning if they are able to avoid the traps of secularization and entrenchment while continuing to grow in Christ-centeredness, Spirit-empowerment, educational effectiveness, and institutional capacity, indigenizing themselves within their academic, economic, cultural, and geographic contexts, and experiencing a Pentecostal renaissance.

In this endeavor, Pentecostals have much to learn from the history of Christian higher education in the United States. Burtchaell frames the challenge as follows:

> If Christian scholars have the insight and the nerve to believe that the gospel and its church are gifted, that together they offer a privileged insight, a 'determinative perspective,' then they will be grateful to grapple some more, using the very insights of the gospel to judge critically both the church and the academy and the culture. But if they lose their nerve and are intimidated by their academic colleagues. . . they, too, will end up judging the church by the academy and the gospel by the culture. In time, they will probably lose the capacity to tell them apart.[22]

To return to the metaphor of the Lord of the Rings, the hobbits rejected the lure of the Ring, ventured beyond the boundaries of the Shire, and chose to engage in the redemption of Middle Earth. Pentecostal higher educators have also chosen a redemptive mission. Their quest has only begun.

Notes

1. George Marsden suggests this metaphor: "Suppose we scholars thought of our understanding of things as equivalent to that of the Hobbits in Tolkien's world. The most important thing to take into account is that we are involved in a great spiritual struggle between forces of darkness and light." Marsden, *The Outrageous Idea of Christian Scholarship,* (Oxford: Oxford University Press, 1997), 95. Douglas and Rhonda Hustedt Jacobsen object to the metaphor: "While aware of the existence of good and evil and of the subtle forms those realities can take, scholars, like most other people, usually do their work in a world colored by shades of gray—a world of people and situations that are partly good and partly not so good." Hustedt and Hustedt, *Scholarship and Christian Faith* (Oxford: Oxford University Press, 2004), 24. While accepting the Jacobsen's caveat against simplistic arrogance, this Pentecostal scholar finds the Hobbit metaphor still pertinent, especially within a Pentecostal context, in which the struggle between spiritual forces of good and evil is a central concern.

2. These 39 interviews were carried out via email, or telephone, or in person. The profile of the interviewees skewed in the direction of the institutions with the largest enrollments. Consequently, findings related to these interviews will have greatest relevance for universities and, to a lesser degree, seminaries and regionally-accredited Christian colleges. Personnel at a total of sixteen U.S. Pentecostal institutions were interviewed, thirteen of these being AG institutions and the others being Lee, Regent, and Oral Roberts Universities. I also interviewed one Pentecostal educator at an evangelical seminary, another at a Canadian Pentecostal IHE, and another at an Australian Pentecostal IHE. I requested interviews at nine other institutions, without receiving a response. Interviewees were primarily leaders and faculty who had many years of experience on their campus, though ten had been at their current IHEs for five years or less. The mean number of years spent as faculty member or administrator at their current campus was fifteen. By position, the interviewees had the following profile: Presidents (11), Faculty Members (12, including one emeritus), Other Administrators (15). One denominational administrator (with experience at a Pentecostal IHE) was also interviewed. It should be noted that a number of these IHE administrators also have teaching responsibilities and a number of the faculty members have some sort of administrative responsibility (e.g., department chairmanships).

3. See Douglas Sloan, *Faith and Knowledge: Mainline Protestantism and American Higher Education,* (Louisville, KY: Westminster John Know Press, 1994) for a thorough examination of this process.

4. Joel 2:28–32: "And afterward, I will pour out my Spirit on all people. Your sons and daughters will prophesy, your old men will dream dreams, your young men will see visions. Even on my servants, both men and women, I will pour out my Spirit in those days. I will show wonders in the heavens and on the earth, blood and fire and billows of smoke. The sun will be turned to darkness and the moon to blood before the coming of the great and dreadful day of the Lord. And everyone who calls on the name of the Lord will be saved." New International Version.

5. Beulah Heights Bible College (International Pentecostal Church of Christ); Central Bible College (AG); Eugene Bible College (Open Bible Churches); Heritage Bible College (Pentecostal Free Will Baptist); King's College and Seminary (Foursquare); International Bible College (Church of God, Cleveland, TN); Messenger College (Pentecostal Church of God); Zion Bible Institute (AG); Several Canadian IHEs are also affili-

ated with ABHE, including Central Pentecostal College, Master's College and Seminary, and Vanguard College, all associated with the Pentecostal Assemblies of Canada.

6. Middle States Association of Colleges and Schools, Northwest Association of Schools and Colleges, North Central Association of Colleges and Schools, New England Association of Schools and Colleges, Southern Association of Colleges and Schools, and Western Association of Schools and Colleges.

7. American Indian College (AG); Emmanuel College (Pentecostal Holiness Church); Life Pacific College (Foursquare); Trinity Bible College (AG); Valley Forge Christian College (AG).

8. Charles H. Mason Theological Seminary is affiliated with the Interdenominational Theological Center in Atlanta, Georgia.

9. Bethany University (AG); Evangel University (AG); Lee University (Church of God, Cleveland, Tennessee); North Central University (AG); Northwest University (AG); Oral Roberts University (Independent); Patten University (Church of God, Cleveland); Regent University (Independent); Southeastern University (AG); Southwest Assemblies of God University (AG); Southwestern Christian University (International Pentecostal Holiness Church); Vanguard University (AG).

10. Enrollment data for AG institutions is provided by the Council on Christian Higher Education (COCHE). For additional information about these institutional types see Jeff Hittenberger, "Education" entry, in *The Encyclopedia of Pentecostal and Charismatic Christianity* (Berkshire Publishing: Great Barrington, MA, 2006).

11. See for example, George Keller's *Academic Strategy: The Management Revolution in American Higher Education.* (Baltimore and London: Johns Hopkins University Press, 1983), 5, where he writes: "American colleges and universities occupy a special, hazardous zone in society, between the competitive profit-making business sector and the government owned and run state agencies. They are dependent yet free; market-oriented yet outside cultural and intellectual fashions. The faculty are inventors, entrepreneurs, and retailers of knowledge, aesthetics, and sensibility yet professionals like the clergy or physicians. The institutions pay no taxes but are crucial to economic development. They conduct their business much as their European counterparts did in the Renaissance, still proud and pedantic as Rabelais saw those forerunners; yet modern corporations pay them to sniff out the future. They constitute one of the largest industries in the nation but are among the least businesslike and well-managed of all organizations. Whatever, like large animals in a bleak landscape, they are perpetually in search of vital financial nourishment."

12. In 1989, Blumhofer estimated the percentage of AG college-aged students who attend AG colleges at less than 4%. See Edith Blumhofer, *The Assemblies of God, Volume 2-Since 1941.* (Springfield, MO: Gospel Publishing House, 1989), 110. AG General Secretary George Wood estimated the current rate to be 3% in his presentation to the AG Faculty Seminar, July 21, 2004.

13. George M. Marsden, *The Soul of the American University* (New York: Oxford Press, 1994), 4.

14. Marsden, 80.

15. See, for example Henri Giroux and Susan Searls Giroux, *Taking Back Higher Education: Race, Youth, and the Crisis of Democracy in the Post-Civil Rights Era* (New York: Palgrave MacMillan, 2004) and David L. Kirp, *Shakespeare, Einstein, and the Bottom Line: The Marketing of Higher Education* (Cambridge: Harvard University Press, 2003).

16. Marsden, 436.

17. James T. Burtchaell, *The Dying of the Light* (Grand Rapids, MI: Eerdmans, 1998), ix.

18. Burtchaell, 840.

19. Burtchaell, 842.

20. H. Richard Niebuhr, *The Social Sources of Denominationalism.* (New York: Meridian, 1957), 54.

21. Thomas Trask, "The Vision for Transformation," http://ag.org/top/about/biennial _reports/br_01_visiontrans.cfm (accessed June 28, 2004).

22. Burtchaell, 851.

Chapter 7

The Symbolic Dilemma and the Future of Pentecostalism: Mysticism, Ritual, and Revival

Margaret M. Poloma

Thomas O'Dea's well-known "five institutional dilemmas" point to the inherent tension found to some degree in all religious organizations. Each dilemma reflects the "basic antimony" or "fundamental tension" that exists between charisma (that is, the immediacy of direct religious experience) and institutional forces. The ongoing tension between spontaneity and stability that permeates all five dilemmas can be described as "transforming the religious experience to render it continuously available to the mass of men (sic) and to provide for it a stable institutional context."[1] Once free-flowing, non-normative and seemingly chaotic, charisma must (at least to some extent) be transformed into something that is stable, normal, and ordered. Although an important catalyst in the development of all world religions, charisma is usually quenched in favor of the patterned and predictable institutional features of social life. Each of the five dilemmas—*mixed motivation, symbolic, delimitation, power,* and *administrative order*—provides a unique vantage point to explore the essence and future of Pentecostalism.

Of these five institutional dilemmas that face religious organizations perhaps none is more critical for maintaining the charismatic spirit than the symbolic dilemma described below by Thomas F. O'Dea.

> The object of the apprehension of the "sacred" or the experience of the "holy" as well as the kinds of attitude involved in the response of the adherents must be given some form of objectified expression if they are to survive the moments of such experiences themselves, especially generation to generation. . . . But this process of the socialization of the religious experience and its concomitant attitudes can proceed so far that it loses any close meaningful connection with the interior dispositions and attitudes of the participants. It can become for them a sheer formalization carried out merely because of duty or a general reverence for what somehow embodies sacredness or because of a diffuse respect for tradition.[2]

Symbols are central to any religious system, especially symbols that are dramatized in religious rituals. As I have discussed at length elsewhere it is the Pentecostal worldview—a spiritual perspective that regards the supranatural as normal phenomena—that distinguishes Pentecostalism from a myriad of non-
Pentecostal evangelical churches.[3] Persons are variously encouraged to seek the
baptism of the Holy Spirit and the experience of *glossolalia*, to be attuned to
ways God leads and speaks to individuals, to pray for and expect to receive
miracles and healings, and to regard as "normal" experiences that non-
Pentecostals may deem paranormal or even abnormal. Yet religious experiences
are fragile, and the social reality that depends upon them is often tenuous. The
situation is made even more delicate because the forces of institutionalization
and accommodation militate against the experience of the Pentecostal charismata.

The data used in this article to assess the state of contemporary American
Pentecostal ritual comes from my involvement in the larger Organizing Religious Work project conducted by the Hartford Institute for Religious Research
in the late 1990s.[4] A random sample of pastors from one of America's largest
Pentecostal denominations, the Assemblies of God (AG), was selected for a
general survey about the denomination that yielded a total of 447 usable responses.[5] The survey included items pertinent to the ritual dimension, including
pastoral experience and use of the charismata in his personal life, the life of the
congregation, ritual practices, and experience with the 1990s revivals. The quantitative survey data were supplemented by my participant observation of the
1990s global revival in the larger Spirit-filled movement. One of the epicenters
of the revival in North America was Brownsville Assembly of God in Pensacola, Florida, with a revival that attracted hundreds of thousands to its meetings
during its seven years of revival.[6] The fresh revival fires that swept across the
Pentecostal/Charismatic world were catalytic for revitalizing some sectors of
American Pentecostalism.[7]

The Symbolic Dilemma:
Assessing the Prevalence of Pentecostal Experience

The distinct worldview of the early Pentecostals not only accorded ideological legitimacy to the paranormal experiences reported in biblical times but restored them to a normative position in contemporary Christianity. Albrecht has
succinctly summarized the essence of Pentecostal spirituality that ideally finds
expression in corporate ritual:

> Pentecostalism is predicated on the rejection of the theory that the
> charismata have ceased to operate, which has held sway in the West-
> ern Church since Augustine. Essentially, Pentecostals believe in, ex-
> perience, and "stress the power and presence of the Holy Spirit and

the gifts of the Spirit directed toward the proclamation that Jesus
Christ is Lord to the glory of God.[8]

Albrecht takes issue with those who have reduced Pentecostalism to being a
"tongues movement," noting that this "reductionist assessment mistakes a dis-
tinguishing characteristic for the central feature." The danger of assuming this
reductionist position is not limited to scholars who fail to capture the complexity
of Pentecostal thought but also to some leaders in the Assemblies of God who
have placed undue emphasis on tongues.

Part of the confusion about *glossolalia* comes from the pivotal role of this
practice in the doctrine of Pentecostal denominations and sects. Undoubtedly
accounts of divine healing, prophetic words, miraculous myths, and demonic
exorcisms were always important parts of the Pentecostal package. But so were
the controversial strange physical manifestations that generated the pejorative
label "holy rollers" that was ascribed by outsiders to early Pentecostal believers
who sometimes fell in a faint to the floor, jumped pews, violently jerked and
shook, laughed, barked, or rolled in the aisles under the alleged influence of the
Spirit. Despite the denials of many contemporary cultural Pentecostals about
their prevalence in early Pentecostalism, these same controversial manifestations
erupted again during the New Order of the Latter Rain movement, others could
be found in the "second wave" as Pentecost came to mainline denominations,
and the unusual physical manifestations intensified during the contemporary
"third wave" revivals.

A dilemma facing Pentecostal believers from the earliest days of Azusa
Street was how to allow the Spirit free movement while controlling excesses
judged to be fanatic. This challenge was met by sorting out the more controversial physical responses (often difficult to justify from biblical texts) from less
controversial experiences (more readily defined as "biblical") that frequently has
accompanied the perceived presence of the Holy Spirit. In the AG *glossolalia*
and healing became doctrines while many other alleged expressions of the
Spirit's presence were relegated to the realms of fanaticism and heresy.

Despite the solid ideological support for revival expressed in pastoral responses to questions on Pentecostal identity, much ambiguity continues around
the incarnation of this ideology. What is perceived to be "extreme" and "fanatical" has fluctuated in AG history, thus contributing to a mixed message about
the current streams of revival. This ambivalence about once commonly experienced revival phenomena can be gleaned in reviewing survey the data collected
from AG pastors through the lenses of the symbolic dilemma. Rather than seek
to get at the meaning of the manifestations (and their effects on the lives of believers) it is often easier to suppress them. The same has held for so-called
"word gifts" of prophecy, revelation, and knowledge. Although accepting the
validity of prophecy in principal, prophetic words are often discouraged as being
detrimental to the orderly flow of more formalized services.

At the heart of the symbolic dilemma is ritual: "the cultic re-presentation of the religious experience [that] is central to the life of the religious group."[9] In Pentecostalism, however, the goal was never to simply remember the past but rather to provide a forum for on-going religious experiences. As described at some length in *The Assemblies of God at the Crossroads*, the report card on this dilemma is mixed, as noted in this concluding paragraph of the chapter titled "Maintaining a Pentecostal Worldview through Ritual:"

> The symbolic dilemma is deemed one of the most important in maintaining charisma, yet it is, paradoxically perhaps the most difficult to keep alive. In an attempt to minimize the dangers of both disorder and inauthenticity, some pastors are placing less emphasis on experiences in their services. Opting for set programs, well-times services, and a high level of professionalism, these pastors are often openly critical of "emotionalism" in services. The dilemma is further jeopardized by the fact that some very successful Assemblies of God congregations have exchanged charisma for institutional techniques to promote church growth.[10]

Findings from the new data set confirm results from the 1980s study. In short, the dilemma is still viable in many cases with a healthy tension between experience and organized ritual that is integral to Pentecostal identity. Many pastors and their congregations, perhaps in an effort to reduce the tension between the supernatural and the practical, appear to be choosing the path of formalized ritual over a service that that allows the Spirit to freely move. To further explore this observation in light of the survey results we will first consider the core ritual experiences in the AG and then discuss the ambiguity that exists around the professed Pentecostal beliefs, practices, and experiences.

Core Ritual Expressions within the Assemblies of God

The debates within the AG about choirs and choir robes, printed bulletins, and ritualized services have over the years been increasingly resolved in favor of order and predictability. Pragmatic decisions to accommodate multiple services, to make services more inviting for non-Pentecostals, and to deal with time-conscious Americans have produced a ritual in many churches that is indistinguishable from non-Pentecostal evangelical services. Mechanisms used to maintain order, however, are the same ones that stifle the free flow of Pentecostal experiences. Earlier years of distinctive Pentecostal ritual (when congregants commonly "tarried," waiting for the Holy Spirit to move in the gathering sometimes with unpredictable results) have largely been relegated to AG history.[11] Some recall this history with fondness and longing; others are more cautious about feared abuses found in unregulated meetings. The result is for the Pentecostal spirit to be unevenly distributed as can be seen from statistics on the personal religious experiences of pastors as well as from pastoral reports about congregational services.

As reported in Table 1, the most frequently practiced Pentecostal expression reported by pastors is speaking in tongues or *glossolalia*. All ministers must sign a document annually when their credentials are renewed certifying to the fact they accept the doctrine of tongues as the "initial physical evidence" of Spirit baptism. Although the doctrine repeatedly has been challenged by those outside the denomination as well as some within, it appears to have strong support among pastors. 85 percent of the pastors agreed with the statement: "A person who has never spoken in tongues cannot claim to be Spirit baptized." However, there appears to be an increase in the number of pastors who do not agree with the AG position on tongues as initial evidence of Spirit baptism. 16 percent of the pastors indicated that they disagreed with this AG doctrinal position in the late 1990s, up from the 2 percent figure in the survey I conducted in the 1980s.[12] Although increasing numbers of AG congregants do not speak in tongues and a significant percent of pastors disagree with the doctrinal statement, the experience of *glossolalia* and professing the creed of "initial evidence" remains a prerequisite for receiving and retaining AG ordination papers.[13]

The overwhelming majority of pastors in this survey (82 percent) did report praying in tongues weekly or more, with no pastor reporting not having prayed in tongues this past year. Tongues (at least on occasion) is a nearly universal part of the prayer lives of AG pastors. Pastors are somewhat less likely, however, to use this gift in church ritual. Eighteen percent reported that they had not given an utterance in tongues or an interpretation of a glossolalic word during the past year, with another 36 percent indicating that they did so only a few times. 47 percent gave expression to *glossolalia* in a congregational setting more regularly, reportedly giving an "utterance" or an "interpretation" once a month or more. The fact that pastors *pray* in tongues in private ritual but are less likely to use the *gift of tongues* in a corporate setting suggests a dissonance that exists in this expression of Pentecostal identity. Despite a more vocal yet clear minority who has reservations about the *doctrine* of tongues, it appears that the *use* of *glossolalia* is nearly universal for pastors in private prayer. Its corporate form of expression as "tongues and interpretation," however, is practiced regularly by less than half the pastors surveyed.

Glossolalia is central to AG doctrinal identity, as reflected in its inclusion as one of the sixteen items found in the AG Statement of Fundamental Truths. It is, however, only one of many paranormal expressions found in early Pentecostalism or in the larger Spirit Movement within Christianity. Experiences of other gifts and manifestations common at Azusa Street, during the early history of the AG and during subsequent renewals and revivals, are now seemingly few and far between. This narrowing range of Pentecostal experiences was true for the pastors' accounts of their personal experiences (see Table 1) as well as for their reports of corporate experiences within their congregational services (Table 2).

Only a minority of pastors regularly experienced prophecy, healing, deliverance or other phenomena believed by many to be signs of the activity and presence of the Holy Spirit. For example, 34 percent claimed to have given a prophecy once a month or more. 46 percent reported being a prayer facilitator for a physical healing and 41 percent for a mental and emotional healing. Only 13 percent, however, claimed regular involvement in deliverance from demonic oppression as a result of prayer. Put another way, 66 percent responded that they never or rarely gave a prophecy, 55 percent never or rarely witnessed a physical healing through their prayer, 60 percent were never or rarely a witness to emotional or mental healing, and 88 percent never witnessed deliverance (see Table 1).

Other physical manifestations common to contemporary revival meetings outside the AG were similarly less likely to be part of experiences reported by pastors: 94 percent were never or rarely slain in the spirit; 83 percent had never or rarely experienced holy laughter; and 76 percent had never or rarely experienced the bodily manifestation of shaking or jerking, all of which were commonly experienced during the recent revivals.

A similar pattern was found for corporate ritual experiences (Table 2). Tongues and interpretations was reported as a regular experience for only 43 percent of the congregations. While only 2 percent of the pastors reported that tongues and interpretation (as dictated by Pentecostal protocol) was never a part of their public ritual, for the remaining majority it was an infrequent occurrence. Only 33 percent reported regular experiences of prophecy, a gift that serves a function similar to that of tongues and interpretations. Both are regarded as inspired words or messages from God delivered to the congregation, with prophecy being a simple message without the glossolalic prelude.

Although prayer for healing was a regular feature of 90 percent of congregational services, less than half of the congregations (41 percent) provided regular opportunity for sharing healing testimonies. It appears that healing prayer has become a nearly universal ritual in AG churches but that fewer churches include opportunities for testimonials commonly used to encourage and build faith for miraculous healing.[14] The fact that testimonies about healings received were far less likely to be reported than regular prayer for healing may point to underlying ambiguity about healing ritual as well as *glossolalia*. The frequencies found in Tables 1 and 2 reporting the major findings on pastoral involvement in the expression of charisma during worship services and the pastoral reports of congregational use of the spiritual gifts during worship demonstrate how ongoing charismatic practices vary widely within the AG.

Ambiguity and the Ritual Dilemma

The history of AG is one of a revitalization movement that emphasizes an experiential baptism distinct from baptism with water. In the words of David du Plessis, a central Pentecostal actor in the Charismatic Movement of the 1960s and 1970s, "God has no grandchildren." Because the identity of Pentecostals is rooted in paranormal religious experiences, their children cannot rely on their parents' experiences to claim Spirit baptism. Many adherents, however, appear to be lapsing into a cultural Pentecostalism that increasingly assumes an Evangelical identity at the expense of Pentecostal experience. This may be demonstrated by the changes in Pentecostal ritual over the decades, particularly the decrease in revival meetings and Sunday night services where signs and wonders once drew both the faithful and potential converts to be refreshed by Pentecostal experiences. In a discussion of the history of Pentecostalism, Everett Wilson emphasized the important role revival plays in the spread of this global movement:

> Whatever success the historian has in identifying the succession of Pentecostal outpourings in the early century, the issue is not 'who begat whom,' but who or what brought to life and enthusiasm those many different specimens of Pentecostalism in diverse settings and sequences. A pedigree can show the relationship of each ascending generation to its predecessor, but each new generation still has to be born in reproductive passion. Revivals last not because the movement had an impressive beginning, but rather because periodic renewal keeps the enthusiasm vibrant despite energy-sapping generational, organizational and circumstantial changes.[15]

Revivals, once common in the AG, have gradually taken a back seat to "seeker-sensitive" churches and well-promoted programs, in many sectors of the denomination. They were first banished from Sunday morning time-slots and relegated to Sunday evening church gatherings and summer camps. They increasingly have been replaced by other more formal and predictable rituals in many AG churches, lingering only as rumors from a seemingly distant historical past, as fewer pastors and their congregants experience the range of the charismata found in early Pentecostalism. When new outpourings of charisma come along that revive the larger Spirit movement, the AG has been reluctant to accept them as authentic moves of God. That isolationist and protectionist mentality has cost them opportunity to participate in charismatic outpourings in other sectors of Christianity.

Blumhofer's observations about the consonant notes found in the New Order (Latter Rain) revival of the 1940s and early Pentecostalism provide some insight for understanding the ambivalence of the AG toward the fresh outpouring of charisma:

Some first-generation Pentecostals had begun within a decade to bemoan their movement's waning power and had pointed to a future, more copious showers of the latter rain. Consequently, there was even precedent for the eschatological innovation by the New Order advocates. Daniel Kerr, for example, noting a declining focus on healing as early as 1914, had heralded a coming dispensation in which healing would have the prominence accorded to tongues at the turn of the century. As Pentecostal groups had organized and charismatic fervor had waned in some places—or was largely confined to revival campaigns and camp meetings—voices had been raised asserting that the turn-of-the-century Apostolic Faith Movement had seen only the beginning of a revival whose more copious latter rains were yet to come.[16]

While Blumhofer goes on to describe the AG rationale for rejecting the Later Rain or New Order Movement (particularly its rejection of religious organizations and its indictment of "old Pentecost"), the fact remains that the AG has been at times ambivalent and at times hostile to Pentecostal experiences in other streams of the larger Spirit-filled movement. The Latter Rain, the subsequent healing revival of the 1950s, and the Charismatic movement of the 1960s and 1970s, for the most part, occurred outside the AG. It had a positive effect on AG growth during this period largely through pastors who risked the criticism of their peers and sometimes censure from leadership for their support of the newer movement

Most pastors in this survey did seem to be aware that the Pentecostal worldview is in continual need of revitalization. A vast majority (84 percent) either agreed or strongly agreed with the statement "The AG must actively seek to revitalize its early Pentecostal roots." Very few (5 percent) agreed that in order to reach the unchurched "the AG must downplay the public use of the gifts of the Spirit" which are believed to accompany baptism with the Holy Spirit. The overwhelming majority of pastors verbally support AG identity as a Pentecostal denomination in which paranormal gifts are openly displayed, even if these manifestations should cause some discomfort for first-time visitors. Moreover, 85 percent of the respondents reported that their congregations are of "one mind" regarding "expressive worship practices" which have at times caused divisions and disagreements in the past.

Despite the verbal acquiescence, there appears to be an unresolved paradox between the widely acclaimed support for revival with openness to the paranormal gifts and the absence or near-absence of Pentecostal vitality in at least half of the AG churches. With the possible exception of tongues and interpretations (experienced regularly in 43 percent of the congregations included in this study), other gifts and manifestations commonly witnessed in the larger Spirit movement do not appear to be a regular part of AG ritual. The discrepancy between sentiments and behavior—between what people say and what they do—has been long observed by social psychologists and can be once again seen in the responses to questions about the Brownsville Outpouring and other renewal tributaries.

The revival/renewal of the 1990s in North America can be traced to a revival began with the Assemblies of God in Argentina—a revival that continued into the twenty-first century (although with less intensity).[17] The revival in North America first found an epicenter in Ontario Canada at the then Toronto Airport Vineyard (a Third-Wave congregation) where it caught the attention of both the secular and religious media because of the unusual physical manifestations said to be caused by the Holy Spirit.[18] It spread quickly to the United Kingdom (largely in independent "new" or "restoration churches" and Anglican charismatic churches). In 1995 similar revival phenomena found a home in a traditional AG congregation, Brownsville Assembly of God, in Pensacola (Florida) that had been praying for revival.[19]

Brownsville Assembly of God (BAOG) quickly became a pilgrimage site for Spirit-thirsty Pentecostals and Charismatics alike. Its leaders soon offered a traveling version of the revival as Awake America Crusades began monthly treks to local communities. In June 1997, the *Pentecostal Evangel* (the official magazine of the AG) devoted a special issue to the question "Is America on the verge of spiritual awakening?"—presenting revival updates on 24 AG congregations located throughout the United States. Full-length articles appeared on the "Golden State" (AG churches in Sacramento, Modesto, and Bakersfield, CA); First Assemblies of God in Fort Wayne, Indiana; The Tabernacle in Orchard Park, New York; Bethel Temple in Hampton, Virginia; and Bettendorf, Iowa Assembly of God. Editor Hal Donaldson acknowledged that this issue is "by no means a comprehensive report. . . [but the churches] featured here are merely representative of congregations across America—large and small, urban and rural—that are recognizing fresh spiritual life." The tone of the issue was affirming of renewal sprinkled with only a bit of caution. As Hal Donaldson opined in his editorial comment, "Historians will judge whether the burgeoning revival in America deserves to be dubbed the next great awakening. But signs suggest this is more than a spiritual tremor. . ."[20]

The Response Paper adopted by the General Presbytery in August, 2000, "Endtime Revival—Spirit-Led and Spirit Controlled," appeared to be more cautionary than affirming in its concern about the excesses of renewal. While stating that the "last thing any sincere Pentecostal believer wants to do is to quench or grieve the Holy Spirit," much of the paper was devoted to cautioning against "revival extremes." These two publications—the special issue of the *Pentecostal Evangel* and the "Response Paper to Resolution 16" dealing with "Endtime Revival"—demonstrate the ambiguity that readily can be found in the AG about revival/renewal.

The survey data collected from AG pastors about the 1990s revivals reflects this same dissonance. As reported earlier, 86 percent of pastors identify with Pentecostal *renewal* or *revival* (R/R), reporting that being involved in R/R is extremely important or very important to them. Nearly all (98 percent) were aware of the R/R movement found at BAOG and other congregations in North America through reading articles in AG literature (100 percent) or in other Christian magazines (86 percent) and by talking with AG leaders/pastors (72 percent), with church members (70 percent), or with other persons who have visited popular R/R sites (86 percent). The overwhelming majority of the pastors appear to be aware of the current Pentecostal revival and seem to have a single mind about the importance of reviving authentic Pentecostal spirituality. This does not necessarily mean, however, that AG pastors are of one mind about BAOG and the revival of the 1990s. Pastors were evenly divided on the issue as to whether "America is in the midst of a revival similar to the one that gave birth to Pentecostalism." Despite the fact that the national leaders of the AG have given cautious approval and support to the revival at BAOG, the average pastor appears to be reluctant to embrace it.[21]

Nearly all the pastors surveyed support revival in principle and nearly all had heard about BAOG and the R/R movement, but far fewer had experienced this latest outpouring of charisma for themselves. It is noteworthy that despite the verbal assent to the importance of revival, approximately 2/3 *have not* personally checked out the nightly meetings at the BAOG in Pensacola or any of the other AG and non-AG renewal sites which dot the nation. The vast majority have not invited R/R speakers to their churches (67 percent) nor have they attended an Awake America Crusade sponsored by BAOG in various cities throughout the United States (80 percent). Given this lack of first-hand contact, it is not surprising that only thirty percent of the pastors report their churches "to be actively engaged in the Renewal/Revival."

In sum, it is clear that most pastors perceive a decline in Pentecostal practices within the denomination. It is noteworthy that 70 percent either strongly agree or agree "the gifts of the Holy Spirit are losing their prominence in AG churches as a whole." They report concern about the loss of Pentecostal power, an embracing of a renewal/revival identity, are informed about the various renewal sites, but surprisingly most have made little effort to check out the rumors of revival for themselves.[22] Being of one-mind around the core value of revival has apparently not translated into an acceptance revival in contemporary dress. It appears that many present-day AG pastors, much like their predecessors, have been reluctant to accept charisma as it has taken flesh in periodic revivals of the latter half of the twentieth century. At least among some pastors, revitalization in Pentecostalism is being relegated to doctrine rather than personal experience. Revivals are often acknowledged to be "messy"—even by their supporters. Established Pentecostal denominations like the AG may well prefer the safety of doctrine to the unpredictability of religious experience.

The Future of Pentecostal Ritual: Summary and Conclusions

The findings reported here in this article provide a mixed report card for the future of distinct Pentecostal ritual in AG congregations. Although the data come from one particular Pentecostal denomination, there is little reason to assume that other white American Pentecostal denominations (e.g. Church of God, Cleveland, TN; International Church of the Foursquare Gospel) would present a different profile. Pentecostal ritual is difficult to maintain in historic Pentecostal denominations—at least white denominations—in North America. Uniquely Pentecostal rituals have been revived, however, through the different waves of the Pentecostal spirit that have refreshed believers and brought in new believers throughout the past century. These waves of revival tend to spawn new denominations and new networks that quickly experience a routinization of ritual similar to that against which the AG continues to struggle.

Hope for the future of a unique Pentecostal identity as reflected in ritual is not bright for the white American sector of the movement. It is in danger of becoming another indistinguishable voice within the larger Evangelical movement. Where distinctiveness can be found is among ethnic congregations that are quietly growing in number both within the AG and among other groups in the Pentecostal/Charismatic movement. These groups mirror the assessment Philip Jenkins made about the state of global Christianity in which nations south of the equator demonstrate "a breathtaking ability to transform weakness into strength."[23] This description may hold true not only for the growth of Pentecostal Christianity south of the equator but also within North America as well.

Appendix

As part of the larger Organizing Religious Work Project, in 1997 a questionnaire focusing on doctrine, identity and revival was sent to a random sample of Assemblies of God pastors, yielding 447 responses. The survey was part research conducted through the Hartford Institute for Religion Research. A full report of the larger study can be found in David A Roozen and Scott Thumma's forthcoming edited volume titled *Church, Identity, and Change: Theology and Denominational Structures in Unsettled Times* (Eerdmans, 2005). Tables 1–3 report findings for Assemblies of God pastors referenced above. The full questionnaire is available from the author.

Table 1: Pastors' Charismatic Experiences (within past year)

	Never	Few times	Monthly	2X Month	Weekly +
Tongues & Interpretations	18% (76)	36% (154)	12% (52)	19% (83)	16% (69)
Prophecy to Congregation	18% (78)	48% (209)	16% (69)	14% (61)	4% (15)
Used in prayer: physical healing	3% (12)	52% (222)	21% (88)	18% (76)	7% (32)
Used in prayer: mental healing	7% (28)	53% (225)	17% (71)	17% (72)	7% (28)
Used to pray for Deliverance	29% (118)	59% (245)	7% (27)	4% (17)	2% (6)
Prayer in tongues	-------	7% (29)	4% (17)	7% (30)	82% (361)
Sing in the spirit	19% (83)	34% (185)	12% (50)	17% (72)	18% (78)
Slain in the spirit	44% (186)	50% (212)	3% (14)	2% (8)	1% (5)
Physical Manifestations	43% (113)	33% (86)	12% (30)	9% (23)	4% (10)
Holy Laughter	46% (172)	37% (137)	8% (29)	5% (17)	5% (10)
Dancing in the Spirit	42% (183)	35% (152)	8% (35)	7% (28)	8% (36)

Source: Organizing Religious Work Project (1997). N=447, parentheses indicate actual responses.

Table 2: Congregational Experiences & Ritual Practices (within past year)

	Never	Rarely	Sometimes	Regularly
Tongues and interpretation	2% (8)	13% (57)	42 % (183)	43% (188)
Prayer for Spirit baptism	1% (3)	9 % (41)	43% (187)	47% (206)
Prayer for healing	-------	-------	10% (42)	90% (394)
Prophecy	4% (16)	19% (81)	45% (195)	33% (142)
Prayer for deliverance	3% (11)	19% (82)	44% (191)	35% (151)
Altar call for salvation	--- (2)	2% (8)	6% (26)	92% (402)
Healing testimonies	--- (1)	7% (30)	52% (229)	41% (177)
Salvation testimonies	1% (5)	9% (41)	54% (235)	36% (156)
Dancing in the spirit	20% (86)	39% (176)	32% (139)	10% (43)
Singing in the spirit	10% (43)	31% (134)	33% (143)	26% (115)
Slain in the spirit	10% (43)	30% (129)	47% (205)	14% (60)
Physical manifestations	27% (117)	40% (173)	24% (104)	9% (37)

Source: Organizing Religious Work Project (1997). N=447, parentheses indicate actual responses.

Table 3: Revival Attitudes and Behavior

Attitudes	Strong Disagree	Disagree	Agree	Strong Agree
America is in midst of revival	6% (27)	44% (188)	44% (188)	5% (26)
Must downplay public use of Spirit gifts	61% (265)	34% (150)	3% (14)	2% (8)
Loss of gifts of Holy Spirit in AG	3% (14)	26% (109)	55% (233)	15% (70)
AG must seek revitalization of early roots	2% (10)	13% (55)	45% (192)	39% (174)
AG experiencing loss of Pentecostal ID	6% (25)	34% (140)	48% (202)	12% (51)
Importance of personal ID w/revival	4% (18)	10% (44)	32% (139)	54% (234)
Importance of congreg. ID w/revival	6% (25)	18% (80)	35% (151)	41% (178)
Involvement	Yes			
Aware of present renewal movement	98% (431)			
Read AG articles on revival	100% (422)			
Read other Christian articles on R/R	86% (382)			
Discussed R/R with AG leaders/pastors	72% (319)			
Talked with members who visited	70% (312)			
Talked with others who visited	86% (382)			
Surfed R/R websites	24% (105)			
Visited Toronto revival site	7% (32)			
Attended Awake America Crusades	20% (90)			
Visited Brownsville Assembly of God	34% (158)			
Visited other BAOG-like sites	34% (151)			
Other R/R contacts	11% (48)			
Church actively involved in renewal	30% (135)			
Use renewal music	65% (290)			
Invited renewal speaker	33% (147)			

Source: Organizing Religious Work Project (1997). N=447, parentheses indicate actual responses.

Notes

1. Thomas F. O'Dea and J. Milton Yinger. "Five Dilemmas in the Institutionaliza-tion of Religion," Journal for the Scientific Study of Religion 1, no. 1 (October 1961): 38
2. O'Dea and Yinger, 78–79.
3. Margaret Poloma, The *Assemblies of God at the Crossroads: Charisma and Insti-tutional Dilemmas* (Knoxville: University of Tennessee Press, 1989); Poloma, *Main Street Mystics: The Toronto Blessing and Reviving Pentecostalism* (Walnut Creek, CA: AltaMira Press, 2003).
4. Details of the survey are available in the appendix.
5. I would like to acknowledge the assistance and helpful feedback from others in-volved in the Organizing Religious Work project at the Hartford Institute for Religious research, especially David Roozen and Scott Thumma.
6. Margaret Poloma, "The Spirit Bade Me Go: Pentecostalism and Global Religion." Paper Prepared for Presentation at the Association for the Sociology of Religion Annual Meetings, August 11-13, 2000, Washington, D.C.
7. See Poloma 2003.
8. Albrecht 1999, 29.
9. O'Dea and Yinger, 58.
10. Poloma 1989, 206.
11. See Grant Wacker, *Heaven Below: Early Pentecostals and American Culture* (Cambridge, MA: Harvard University Press, 2001).
12. Poloma 1989.
13. Data from the CCSP (Cooperative Congregational Studies Project) found that "40% of churches estimated that half or less of their members has been baptized in the Holy Spirit with evidence of speaking in other tongues" (Doty and Espinoza, 2000.)
14. In reviewing these statistics, I was reminded of a comment made by an AG graduate student in one of my courses during which I was discussing my research on divine healing. The young man commented. "I have heard stories like you are reporting all of my life, but I have never seen one case of such healing in my church. Healing is professed but I have seen little evidence of its being practiced or experienced."
15. Everett Wilson, *Strategy of the Spirit* (London: Paternoster Press, 1997), 92.
16. Edith Blumhofer, *Assemblies of God: A Chapter in the Story of American Pente-costalism* (Springfield, MO: Gospel Publishing House, 1989), 58.
17. For a scholarly discussion of Pentecostalism in Argentina see Daniel Miguez's *Spiritual Bonfire in Argentina: Contrasting Current Theories with an Ethnographic Ac-count of Pentecostal Growth in a Buenos Aires Suburb*, Latin America Studies Series, no. 81 (Buenos Aires: CEDLA, 1998).
18. See Poloma 2003.
19. For accounts of Brownsville see Steve Robey's *Revival in Brownsville: Pensacola, Pentecostalism, and the Power of American Revivalism* (Nashville, TN: Thomas Nelson, 1998); Renee Deloriea Portal's *Pensacola: The Real Thing Hits Brownsville* (New York: Destiny Image Publications, 1997).
20. Hal Donaldson, *Pentecostal Evangel* 54, no. 2 (June 1997), 4.
21. It was interesting to review the selection of readings found in the 85th Anniver-sary Edition 1913–1998 of the *Pentecostal Evangel*, the weekly publication of the AG. An article on Pentecostal revival was reprinted from the July 12, 1924 issue that lamented how "many folks are blind" to the Pentecostal revival that was still in process. The anni-

versary issue, although published three years after the revival began at BAOG, failed to mention the Pensacola Outpouring (as it is often called) as one of the significant events of AG history.

22. Ambiguity and ambivalence appear to be heightened by the fact that only 6 percent of the respondents did not believe that the denomination is responsible for promoting revival. Sixty percent of the pastors surveyed believed it was the task of the National Office and another 34 percent reported it was the task of the District Offices to promote revival.

23. Phillip Jenkins, *The Next Christendom: The Coming of Global Christianity* (Oxford: Oxford University Press, 2002), 220.

Chapter 8

The Future of Oneness Pentecostalism

David K. Bernard

This chapter focuses on the future of Oneness Pentecostalism, also known as the Jesus Name or Apostolic Pentecostal movement.[1] To project where the Oneness Pentecostals of North America will be in twenty-five to fifty years, the essay begins with the movement's historic and present distinctives. Next it will identify the major processes of change at work, examine the impact they have already had, and discuss counterbalancing influences. Finally, the chapter offers conclusions and projections for the future.[2]

Oneness Pentecostal Distinctives

First and foremost, the Oneness Pentecostal movement is characterized by a distinctive teaching about God commonly known as the Oneness doctrine or the almighty God in Jesus Christ. It has also been somewhat pejoratively called "Jesus Only," although most Oneness Pentecostals reject this label as inaccurate and misleading.

The Oneness doctrine can be stated succinctly in two propositions: 1) there is one indivisible God with no distinction of persons in God's eternal essence, and 2) Jesus Christ is the manifestation, human personification, or incarnation of the one God. All the fullness of God dwells bodily in Jesus Christ, and all names and titles of deity properly apply to him.[3]

God has revealed himself as Father (in parental relationship to humanity), in the Son (in human flesh), and as the Holy Spirit (in spiritual action). These manifestations describe God's work in salvation history, but they do not represent different centers of consciousness or personalities. The scriptural distinction between Father and Son does not describe two divine persons but the transcendent, eternal Deity and his manifestation in flesh as the man Christ Jesus. Closely related to this teaching is the practice of baptizing in water by invoking the name of Jesus Christ only. Oneness Pentecostals believe that a scriptural baptismal formula should feature the name of Jesus, after the examples in the

Book of Acts, rather than the "Father, Son, and Holy Ghost" formula. They regard Jesus as the only saving name and the one name that encompasses God's
redemptive work as Father, Son, and Spirit.[4]

Oneness Pentecostals teach that God's standard of full salvation for the New
Testament church is repentance, water baptism in the name of Jesus Christ, and
the baptism of the Holy Spirit with the initial sign of speaking in tongues. They
affirm both that salvation is by grace through faith and that these three steps
constitute the application of grace and the expression of faith.[5] Along with receiving the Holy Spirit, they encourage demonstrative, spontaneous, joyful worship as well as signs, wonders, and miraculous gifts of the Spirit.

Most Oneness Pentecostals acknowledge the importance of a separated lifestyle. They believe that holiness should characterize believers both inwardly and
outwardly. To a great extent, they still affirm practical guidelines of righteousness in lifestyle, amusements, and dress that predominated in the Holiness-
Pentecostal movement until the latter part of the twentieth century.[6]

While many Pentecostals baptized in the name of Jesus during Pentecostalism's first decade, including Charles Parham and some in Los Angeles during
the Azusa Street revival, Oneness Pentecostalism began as a distinct movement
when Frank Ewart (a close associate of William Durham) and Glenn Cook (a
close associate of William Seymour) rebaptized each other in the name of Jesus
Christ on April 15, 1914. Soon after this event, many early leaders of the Pentecostal movement were baptized in Jesus' name, and for a time it seemed that this
message might prevail throughout Finished Work Pentecostalism. In 1916, however, the Assemblies of God rejected the Oneness doctrine, and Oneness Pentecostals became relatively isolated from other Pentecostals.[7]

The major Oneness Pentecostal organizations in the United States and Canada are:

- United Pentecostal Church International (UPCI)
- Pentecostal Assemblies of the World (PAW)
- Church of Our Lord Jesus Christ of the Apostolic Faith (COOLJC)
- Bible Way Churches of Our Lord Jesus Christ Worldwide (BWC)
- Apostolic Assembly of the Faith in Christ Jesus (AAFCJ)
- Assemblies of the Lord Jesus Christ (ALJC)
- Apostolic Church of Pentecost of Canada (ACPC)

Total constituency in the United States and Canada is approximately 2.5 million, not counting the many Charismatics who have been baptized in Jesus'
name. Worldwide constituency is estimated at 24 million or more.[8]

Factors Influencing Change

Several major factors have influenced change in the Pentecostal movement
over the past century.[9] We discuss them because they are likely to exert contin-

ued influence in the decades ahead and have the potential to affect Oneness Pentecostals.

First, there is *the generational effect*. In the early stages of a revival movement, growth is fueled by the high commitment of converts who radically change their beliefs and lifestyle, defend their new-found beliefs against great opposition and at great cost, and experience first-hand the benefits of their commitment. Subsequent generations tend to have less appreciation for this conversion and the sacrifice it entailed. Consequently, they typically have less zeal and commitment, unless there is ongoing renewal coupled with a continued influx of converts.

A second influence is *upward social mobility* with a corresponding increase in the desire for social acceptance. Like most revival movements and like Christianity in the beginning, Pentecostalism appealed first and foremost to the common people, especially to the socially disadvantaged, the dispossessed, and the oppressed. Such people had the least to lose and the most to gain by taking the step of faith.

As Pentecostals began to move upward in society, they had the means to enjoy greater participation in society. As their churches grew, they drew the attention of the establishment and were able to influence the establishment to some extent. At this point, they acquired a greater stake in society and thus a greater concern for how society viewed them. As part of the price of participating in and influencing the larger religious and secular communities, however, they encountered greater pressure to conform to the expectations of those communities.

A third source of change has been the influence of conservative Protestantism—*Fundamentalism and later evangelicalism*. Pentecostals have tended to borrow theology from other conservative Christians on matters that did not involve their unique beliefs. Thus, on subjects from the Atonement to the inspiration of Scripture to eschatology to political positions, they often received direction from Fundamentalists and evangelicals.

Fourth, the Latter Rain movement in the 1950s and especially the *Charismatic movement* in the 1960s and beyond have had a significant impact on Pentecostalism. Initially, Pentecostals had great reservations about close fellowship with the Charismatic movement because of its diverse theology and praxis. Today, however, there is widespread acceptance, interaction, mutual influence, and transfer of ministers, churches, and members between Trinitarian Pentecostals and Charismatics. Indeed, in 1994, major Trinitarian Pentecostal and Charismatic organizations joined together in the Pentecostal/Charismatic Churches of North America, which replaced the Pentecostal Fellowship of North America. Charismatic beliefs and practices have significantly affected Pentecostal views on holiness, fellowship, worship, end-time prophecy, spiritual warfare, and the initial evidence doctrine.

Fifth, *technological revolution and accompanying globalization* are forcing movements to adapt or become irrelevant. The pragmatism of Pentecostals causes them to be open to new technology, such as television and the Internet,

but the challenge is to harness it without allowing it to compromise basic identity. As the experience of televangelism has shown, this is not always easy.

Sixth, North American culture has been heavily influenced by *postmodernism*, which is characterized by relativism and epistemological pessimism. Consequently, there can easily develop a gap between official teaching based on
moral absolutes and the everyday decisions of believers, which may conform to
the situation ethics of society.

Serving to accentuate the foregoing factors is a desire for growth. As a new
group becomes established, there is an inherent temptation to diminish the level
of intensity, uniqueness, and strictness in order to appeal to more people, especially if its growth has slowed. Pentecostals have an especially strong desire to
see church growth, as the missionary impulse is integral to their existence. As a
result they are quite pragmatic and adaptable on secondary matters.[10] There is
even a tendency to reclassify some distinctives as secondary. The influence of
the Charismatic movement is significant here, for in many ways it represents a
merger of Pentecostal experience with mainline Protestant and Catholic doctrines and mainstream American lifestyle.

All of these factors have motivated change in both Trinitarian and Oneness
Pentecostalism in North America. The theological isolation and cultural sepa-
rateness of Oneness Pentecostalism has served to lessen their impact, however.
Consequently, Oneness Pentecostals have preserved more of the doctrinal approach, experience, worship, lifestyle, and intensity of the early Pentecostals
than Trinitarian Pentecostals have.

Impact upon Oneness Pentecostals

What impact will these factors have upon Oneness Pentecostals in the next
fifty years? We can answer this question in part by considering the impact they
have already had, identifying any countervailing influences, and then extrapolat-
ing. While it would be difficult to evaluate the impact of each factor separately,
we can observe their cumulative effects.

Oneness Pentecostals have been influenced by the generational effect as well
as upward social mobility. To a great extent, they have entered the middle class
and have embraced middle-class values. Consequently, much like Trinitarians,
they have moderated some of the earlier Pentecostal positions. For example,
many early Oneness believers refused to consult doctors or take medicine, instead trusting in God alone for healing. Today, Oneness Pentecostals still emphasize divine healing and the need to trust God, but they endorse the use of
doctors and medicine. Likewise, many early Oneness Pentecostals were suspicious of higher education as well as professional occupations. Today, however,
there is general acceptance of both. The predominantly black organizations have
been at the forefront in this regard.

As another example, the early Oneness organizations opposed the taking
human life in warfare, and the UPCI still retains such a statement in its Articles
of Faith. In recent years, however, UPCI publications have featured the contri-

bution of its members in the military, and pacifism may now be a minority position.

The influence of evangelicalism has been much less pronounced on Oneness Pentecostalism than on Trinitarian Pentecostalism. The doctrinal division in 1916 was a defining moment in the experience of Oneness Pentecostals. It has guided their trajectory over the past ninety years and will continue to do so in the foreseeable future. Oneness people considered that they were choosing apostolic precedent over ecclesiastical tradition and thereby faithfully following and applying the primitivist, restorationist ideas that had produced Pentecostalism in the first place. As Edith Blumhofer noted, not necessarily with approval, "The doctrinal departure aside, if one admits the strong restorationist component at the heart of the definition of Pentecostalism, Oneness proponents were more zealously restorationist, more doggedly congregational, and more Christocentrically spiritual—in short, in some important ways more essentially Pentecostal than the mainstream."[11]

Oneness Pentecostals saw Trinitarians as choosing tradition and ecumenical unity over scriptural and experiential truth. It was a painful split among Spirit-filled believers who had received the Holy Spirit together, faced denominational opposition together, and labored together to spread the Pentecostal message. Nevertheless, Trinitarian Pentecostals began to identify instead with Fundamentalists, who did not receive the Spirit and who generally denounced the move of the Spirit as carnal or demonic. Early Assemblies of God leaders such as Stanley Frodsham and J. R. Flower spoke of themselves as Pentecostal Fundamentalists—Fundamentalists whose only important difference from the others was that they spoke in tongues.[12] Trinitarian Pentecostals were invited to help form the National Association of Evangelicals in 1943, and from the 1940s onward the influence of evangelicals upon them became even stronger. When the Pentecostal Fellowship of North America was formed in 1947, it simply adopted the statement of faith of the National Association of Evangelicals and added a Pentecostal paragraph.

This Trinitarian Pentecostal self-identification with evangelicalism has resulted in significant changes of theology and praxis. Theologically, there is less emphasis on the baptism of the Holy Spirit and more emphasis on Evangelical-style conversion. By contrast, while the earliest Pentecostal leaders such as Charles Parham, William Seymour, and William Durham spoke of being justified before receiving the Holy Ghost, they stressed the importance of receiving the Holy Ghost. They taught that believers need to receive the Spirit in order to have full salvation, to enter the New Testament church, and to go in the Rapture.[13] Similarly, while the initial evidence doctrine is still affirmed officially, support for it has diminished considerably. Experientially, only 5 to 35 percent of members now speak in tongues.[14] There has also been a departure from practical expressions of holiness in lifestyle and dress that formerly distinguished Pentecostals from the secular world and even from most evangelicals.

By contrast, Oneness Pentecostals have continued to proclaim that the baptism of the Holy Spirit is part of Christian initiation and the experience of full salvation in the New Testament church. In doing so, they considered that they were remaining more true to Scripture and also more true to the initial impulse of the Pentecostal movement. Because of this emphasis, it is the norm for Oneness Pentecostals to receive the Holy Spirit with tongues, and it is generally a requirement for church membership. In a typical UPCI congregation, 90 percent of the regular attendees, aged ten and above, have spoken in tongues.[15]

Regarding the doctrines of God and Christ, Oneness Pentecostals realized that they could not follow traditional formulations. As a result, they developed the nuances of their message with little regard to historic or contemporary beliefs in Christianity. Over the years, some explored and debated the major Christological positions of ancient Christendom (such as Apollinarianism, Nestorianism, and Monophysitism), although the participants usually were not aware of the theological antecedents. This process has led to many doctrinal innovations, but it has also helped to refine beliefs. While Oneness Pentecostalism will continue to encompass theological diversity, there is a strong affirmation of the essential elements of the Oneness position and greater consensus on Christological matters.

An example of both the doctrinal diversity and the trend toward consensus on key elements is the Pentecostal Churches of the Apostolic Faith Association, which split from the PAW in 1957. Its founder advocated a form of adoptionist Christology, but in recent years the organization has abandoned this position in favor of classic Oneness theology. Similarly, the Apostolic Church of Ethiopia, founded by UPCI missionaries, drew from its Monophysite cultural heritage to develop the view that Christ had "heavenly flesh" and was genetically unrelated to Mary. In 2003 the UPCI rejected this teaching, and in 2004 its General Board readily adopted a comprehensive statement on Christology.

On secondary doctrinal issues, Oneness Pentecostals, like Trinitarians, have been more susceptible to Fundamentalist and Evangelical influences. For instance, most of them uncritically adopted the full system of dispensationalism and related eschatological schemes from the Fundamentalists. In recent years, some have called for a critical appraisal of such areas with the goal of formulating a more consistent and comprehensive Oneness theology.

Historically, Oneness Pentecostals have developed and allowed great diversity on secondary matters, while some Trinitarians sought more definitive formulations in line with Fundamentalism. For example, the Assemblies of God officially teaches the pretribulation Rapture and opposes the doctrine of annihilation. The UPCI has no official position on the timing of the Rapture and has generally treated annihilation as a part of eschatology and therefore open to different interpretations. In the 1980s, however, the UPCI passed a rule against licensing new ministers who teach annihilation, while still allowing ministers to hold the view.

The subject of women in ministry is an interesting study of the interplay of various influences. In the early Oneness movement, women composed almost two-thirds of the constituency and one-third of the ministerial roll, although organizational leadership was male. Over the years, the proportion of women ministers and pastors has diminished greatly. We can discern several reasons, including the increasing number of men who entered the movement and the ministry, the influence of Fundamentalism and evangelicalism, and a backlash against the women's liberation movement of the 1960s and 1970s. Pentecostal women did not want to be seen as rebellious or radical, and many came to prefer a role of joint ministry with their husbands. Sometimes, a woman maintained the primary role of preaching while her husband sought ministerial license as well. In many cases, women who felt a call to ministry married ministers and worked alongside their husbands without seeking credentials of their own.

More recently, many have sought to return to the roots of the movement by affirming and encouraging women in ministry. In part, this new awareness may stem from changing attitudes in the larger culture as well as the prominent role of women in Charismatic circles. (There does not seem to be a strong desire, however, to emulate the common Charismatic pattern of labeling husband and wife as co-pastors of a local congregation.) In the UPCI, which has always allowed the ordination of women, there have been calls for greater affirmation of women in ministry, but the top positions of district and national leadership are reserved for men. The PAW has gone even farther by appointing women as district elders and national executives.

Turning to the influence of the Charismatic movement, it has become an attractive option for those who felt that the doctrinal positions of Oneness Pentecostalism were too restrictive. Over the years, a number of talented singers and speakers have left the fellowship of Oneness Pentecostal organizations to minister in the larger Pentecostal/Charismatic world. Typically, they have maintained their beliefs in the Oneness of God and baptism in the name of Jesus Christ but have adopted an Evangelical soteriology and a Charismatic identity, lifestyle, and ministry.

In many cases, their expressed goal is to appeal to a larger audience or to experience greater church growth, and some have been quite successful in this regard. Others have found, however, that a change of identity does not always result in church growth. A church that makes this transition typically loses much of its committed core and faces the immediate challenge of attracting a new base of support without the former advantage of a distinct identity. To grow, it must become viable and competitive in the larger Pentecostal/Charismatic world.

In view of the size and influence of the Evangelical and Pentecostal/Charismatic communities, Oneness Pentecostals will continue to face pressures for doctrinal change, and there will always be some who call for a fundamental shift of direction. There is already much diversity within and among Oneness organizations as well as among independent Oneness churches. Therefore, many who desire to make changes can do so within the context of Oneness Pentecostalism. Nevertheless, for the foreseeable future it appears that Oneness Pentecostalism as a whole will maintain its distinctive doctrinal core, and those who want fundamental change will seek a place outside the movement.

For example, in 1992 the UPCI General Conference passed a resolution calling for a reaffirmation of its doctrinal distinctives. A total of 50 pastors—1.3

percent—chose to withdraw at that time, and they were gradually joined by a few others later. While significant, this withdrawal fell far short of the split predicted by both *Christianity Today* and *Charisma*. Instead, the organization has continued to grow without noticeable effect.

Technology, globalization, and postmodernism are all influencing Oneness Pentecostalism, yet so far they do not seem to be causing a change of identity. Rather, it appears that the movement is finding in them new opportunities for evangelism without compromise of identity. For example, the UPCI has used the Internet effectively while trying to limit the negative influence of televangelism. Technology and globalization are providing the opportunity for believers in other countries to influence and assist the North American church.

While postmodernism does not advance the truth claims of Christianity, it has caused people to examine preconceptions and unstated assumptions more critically and thus to become more open to voices that have been marginalized. Oneness Pentecostals seem to be competing well in this pluralistic, individualistic environment by appealing to personal testimonies and divine miracles that confirm the gospel.

Counterbalancing Factors

Countering the generational effect and the effect of upward social mobility has been the continued growth of the Oneness movement with a *steady influx of converts from all walks of life, including ethnic minorities*. While growth has slowed, it has not reached a plateau. In the 1990s, for instance, the UPCI grew by 9 percent in number of churches and 27 percent in church attendance in the U.S. and Canada. (In the rest of the world, its growth was 118 percent and 154 percent respectively.) A home missions campaign in 2002–2003 resulted in commitments to plant 1,000 new churches, which should translate into an increased growth rate. Already in the past five years (summer 1999 to summer 2004), the UPCI has grown by 8 percent in the number of churches.[16]

It is also significant that half of the Oneness Pentecostal movement in the U.S. and Canada consists of African-Americans, Hispanics, and Asian-Americans. The PAW, COOLJC, and BWC are overwhelmingly African-American, while the AAFCJ is Hispanic with primary ministry in Spanish. Three large Oneness bodies overseas—the True Jesus Church (one of the largest Christian groups in China and Taiwan), the Spirit of Jesus Church (the largest Christian group in Japan), and the United Pentecostal Church of Colombia (the largest Protestant group in Colombia)—have sizeable constituencies in North America.

The UPCI, which is the largest Oneness body, has grown rapidly among ethnic minorities. Approximately 20 percent of its constituents in the United States and Canada are African-American, Hispanic, Asian-American, or Native American.[17] By the electoral process, there is minority representation on the General Board, on the boards or regional directorates of the six general divisions that have such a structure, and in the leadership of one-third of the districts.

There is also significant growth among immigrants. UPCI churches in North America minister in sixty-seven languages. Moreover, the UPCI is active in 172 nations around the world, and many of the national churches have connections with immigrants in America.

The UPCI has fostered growth by forming new districts in areas of increasing opportunity and need. For example, the South Texas District was formed in the fall of 2002. In its first two years, it grew from 164 churches and daughter works to 209, for an increase of 26 percent. Some of this growth was due to greater recognition of existing efforts as well as strong emphasis and strategic planning in the formative months. Much of the growth, however, represents the ongoing dynamics in an area where the population is 90 percent urban and 55 percent ethnic minorities. Ministerial constituency has grown from 333 to 376 for an increase of 13 percent, which seems to be indicative of overall growth. Again, much of the growth has been among minorities, with congregations that are predominantly Hispanic, African-American, and Asian-American now comprising 38 percent of the total.

Thus, there is strong growth among first-generation converts, minorities, immigrants, urban residents, and lower economic classes. If this trend continues and accelerates, it will do much to keep Oneness Pentecostalism close to its roots and counterbalance the effects of social change. The resulting diversity of the movement will help it to remain relevant in an era of technological advancement, globalization, and postmodernism.

Several other important factors appear to be working to maintain Oneness identity, including conferences and camp meetings, strong pastoral leadership, publications, and educational institutions.

Camp meetings and conferences for ministers, youth, men, and women are thriving in the Oneness movement. The annual camp meeting of the Louisiana District UPC is the largest of any group in North America, attracting 10,000 participants annually. Because of the Times, a ministerial conference in Alexandria, Louisiana, draws over 3,000 ministers and spouses each year. The biennial North American Youth Congress (UPCI) had 17,000 in attendance in 2003.

Meetings such as these promote Pentecostal worship and renewal. Observers have noted that they exhibit the fervency of worship, physical demonstrations, and racial integration of audiences that were characteristic of the early Pentecostal movement but have diminished over time in Trinitarian ranks.

On the local level, almost all Oneness Pentecostal churches have *strong pastoral leadership*. The senior pastor is the primary shepherd, teacher, manager, and vision caster. While the pastor is accountable to the congregation and to fellow ministers, more than anyone else he or she is the one who determines the character of the church. The foremost reason for stability or change is not the denomination but the local pastor. This means that fundamental change does not come from a decision by an organization but from the grass roots over time.

Publications have always been important for the dissemination and inculcation of Oneness beliefs, but in the early movement they were mostly periodicals, tracts, and booklets. In the past twenty-five years, however, the UPCI has published about 150 books on biblical, theological, and ministerial subjects. The UPCI operates the only Oneness denominational publishing house (Pentecostal Publishing House) and publishes the only Oneness Sunday school curriculum (Word Aflame Publications).

The Oneness movement has lagged behind Trinitarians in the development of *educational institutions*, but that is beginning to change. The UPCI has seven endorsed Bible colleges in the United States and Canada and 170 overseas. Other organizations also operate Bible colleges, including the PAW, COOLJC, ALJC, and AAFCJ. A group of Oneness ministers is currently in the process of establishing the first liberal arts college. Oneness students increasingly seek higher education, both secular and theological.

In 1986, the UPCI began sponsoring biennial symposiums on Oneness theology. In 1989 representatives from the UPCI began participating in the annual meetings of the Society for Pentecostal Studies.

In 2001, the UPCI founded Urshan Graduate School of Theology, the only seminary in the movement and the only educational institution formally in the process of accreditation. As of 2004, it had obtained letters of equivalency from Pentecostal, Charismatic, and mainline Protestant seminaries; associate membership in the Association of Theological Schools; and participation in the U.S. Army chaplain candidate program. Its student body was about one-fourth female and one-fourth ethnic minorities. The graduate school has begun the sponsorship of annual symposiums and is preparing a study Bible.

These developments have fostered an increase in the number of Oneness teachers, writers, and scholars, as well as increased interaction among them. There is a growing awareness that Oneness scholars need to work together to articulate distinctive, coherent Oneness perspectives in hermeneutics, theology, praxis, and ministry. It appears that the emerging Oneness academy does not seek radical change but rather ways to express the Oneness message and lifestyle with credibility, practicality, relevance, and self-consistency in the twenty-first century.

Over the years there has been fellowship among the Oneness organizations but not close cooperation. There are signs of a desire for greater interaction, especially with regard to matters of common interest and concern, such as promotion of the Oneness message itself. In the past, tentative initiatives by the UPCI did not translate into definite action, and a proposed union of the COOLJC and BWC ended abruptly.

In recent years there has been greater interaction because of the factors we have mentioned rather than because of organizational initiatives. Many members of various Oneness organizations and independent churches attend conferences, symposiums, and Bible colleges together. One-half the customers of the Pentecostal Publishing House are from outside the UPCI. While most students of Urshan Graduate School are from the UPCI, it also has students from the PAW, AAFCJ, and ALJC. It is too soon to project the degree of interaction that may result from these efforts, but there is a developing influence for maintaining cohesiveness in the Oneness movement.

Conclusions and Projections

The editors of this book asked the contributors a number of questions regarding classical Pentecostal denominations, which this section answers with regards to Oneness Pentecostalism. First, what will become of the Oneness Pentecostal movement in the United States and Canada over the next fifty years? It will continue to grow, in large part due to its success among immigrants and ethnic minorities. Hispanics, African-Americans, and Asian-Americans will assume greater roles and have even greater influence. Churches in urban areas will become more influential. The movement will continue to be diverse ecclesiastically, but the major organizations will continue to set the direction and pace.

There will be an increasing emphasis on education and scholarship, but the constituency will not allow these to become a substitute for spirituality or apostolic ministry. There will be continued separation from the Trinitarian mainstream, but less isolation and more interaction. As the movement continues to grow and gain visibility, it will seek opportunities for social influence and social action without abandoning its primary emphasis on evangelism.

Second, what will be the "distinctives" of Oneness Pentecostalism? Oneness Pentecostals will continue to proclaim the oneness of God and the full deity of Jesus Christ; the full salvation message of repentance, water baptism in the name of Jesus Christ, and the baptism of the Holy Spirit with the sign of speaking in tongues; a lifestyle of holiness; exuberant, spiritual worship; and miracles and gifts of the Spirit.

Some will modify or abandon one or more of these tenets, but in doing so they will align themselves with the broader Charismatic and independent Pentecostal movements. The core Oneness Pentecostal constituency will remain unique in doctrine and praxis.

Third, how can the movement sustain its original impulses? If it is to maintain its unique character, it must promote zealous preaching, doctrinal teaching, fervent prayer, joyful worship, the miraculous work of the Holy Spirit, a separated and dedicated lifestyle, aggressive missionary outreach, faithful pastoral leadership, expectancy of the Second Coming, and above all, an intense personal devotion to Jesus Christ. In view of the pressure from the larger secular and religious communities, the movement will only sustain its original impulses by growing significantly through the integration of first-generation converts; by reaching out effectively to all classes and races of people; by pursuing personal and corporate renewal through the Spirit; and by formulating its unique message in credible, consistent theological expressions.

Fourth, what will Oneness Pentecostalism contribute to the larger American culture? Oneness Pentecostals will continue to bear witness to the Bible as the inspired Word of God, to Jesus as Lord and Savior, and to the supernatural work of the Holy Spirit to liberate and transform lives. In a pluralistic society, their emphasis on personal holiness of attitudes, activities, and dress will cause them to be visibly distinct and so to bear witness of an alternative life that does not conform to the values of the world. Their experience of the supernatural power of God will give them a hearing amid the many voices of religion, philosophy, materialism, and postmodernism.

Oneness Pentecostalism is one of the most racially diverse movements in history. From 1918 to 1924 and again from 1931 to 1938, the largest Oneness organization was completely interracial in a time when American society was strictly segregated. Unfortunately, intense social pressures and lack of vision and fortitude, especially among whites, led to reorganization along racial and regional lines. Nevertheless, the increasingly interracial character of the UPCI along with greater interaction among all the organizations will enable Oneness people to bear effective witness in North American culture. The movement will continue to make significant contributions to society by fostering racial harmony, assimilating immigrants, strengthening marriages and family relationships, offering assistance to the socially disadvantaged, and providing deliverance and new life to the spiritually bound.

As an early example, during the 1960s the city of Indianapolis escaped much of the racial turmoil and rioting that characterized most urban areas of the day. Civic leaders attributed this in large part to the legacy of G. T. Haywood, a Oneness pioneer and organizational leader. An African-American who was greatly respected by both blacks and whites across North America, he served as pastor of a large interracial church in the city until his untimely death in 1931.

The predominantly black churches have long contributed much to their communities, especially the large churches in urban areas. Smallwood Williams, founding bishop of the BWC, became quite active in the Civil Rights movement of the 1960s, serving as president of the Southern Christian Leadership Council in Washington, D.C. He worked closely with Martin Luther King Jr. and met with various federal officials, including President Lyndon Johnson. In other areas where Oneness Pentecostals are numerous, such as Louisiana, Mississippi, and Texas, they have exerted social and political influence on moral issues, sponsored community projects, and assisted with social services.

Fifth, will Oneness Pentecostalism be subsumed by the larger Evangelical ethos? Will it have proven itself to be just a revival movement following the earlier Great Awakenings? No. The Oneness Pentecostal movement is now ninety years old; it has already outlasted the life span of a revival movement. Moreover, it has maintained the doctrinal uniqueness that caused it to separate from Trinitarian Pentecostalism in 1916, and it will continue to do so over the next fifty years. This is indicated by the relative stability of Oneness Pentecostal beliefs and practices over the past ninety years; the ongoing separation from the larger Trinitarian Pentecostal, Evangelical, and secular worlds; the relatively limited effect of the factors for change that we have identified; and the counterbalancing factors that are working for stability.

Finally, will Oneness Pentecostalism have a prophetic voice within the larger range of Christendom? Yes. In the face of postmodernism subjectivism and theological liberalism, Oneness Pentecostals will continue to insist upon the authority of Scripture, a grammatical-historical interpretation of Scripture, and fidelity to the teachings of Scripture. They will advocate an apostolic hermeneutic that emphasizes the teaching, experience, and practice of the first-century church. Their emphasis on the oneness of God will enhance the appeal of the Christian message to Jews and Muslims, as is already occurring overseas. They will remind Christendom not to subordinate the message of Scripture to philosophical, cultural, or traditional modes of thinking, expression, and application.

Although other conservative Christian groups object strongly to certain Oneness tenets, they may find that the growing Oneness movement is a welcome ally in important areas. They can depend on Oneness Pentecostals to be strong in defense of marriage, family, sexual morality, and modesty and strong in opposition to homosexual conduct, abortion, euthanasia, and moral relativism. evangelicals can appreciate their strong advocacy of the deity of Jesus Christ in contrast to mainline liberals and new religious movements. Trinitarian Pentecostals will welcome their support of the baptism of the Holy Spirit as a definite experience for all believers; speaking in tongues as the initial evidence; and a balanced, biblical approach to spiritual warfare, divine healing, and spiritual gifts. Both Trinitarian Pentecostals and Charismatics will benefit from the fervent prayer, preaching, teaching, singing, worship, and manifestations of the Spirit that characterize Oneness Pentecostals.

Along with the larger Trinitarian/Charismatic world, Oneness Pentecostals will proclaim the urgent need of the miraculous work of the Holy Spirit for salvation, healing, deliverance, victorious Christian living, and world evangelization. In addition, Oneness Pentecostals will issue a unique prophetic call to exalt the name of Jesus in everything and to manifest God's holiness in all aspects of life.

Notes

1. The major organizations include the words "Pentecostal," "Apostolic," or "Jesus" in their official names.

2. I wish to acknowledge the helpful comments of Ken Gurley, Rodney Shaw, and Johnny Celey.

3. See David K. Bernard, *The Oneness of God*, rev. ed. (Hazelwood, MO.: Word Aflame Press, 2000); David K. Bernard, *The Oneness View of Jesus Christ* (Hazelwood, MO.: Word Aflame Press, 1994). For the scriptural basis, see Deuteronomy 6:4; Isaiah 44:6–8, 24; 45:21–23; Mark 12:28–31; John 10:30; 14:9–11; 20:28; Colossians 2:8–10; 1 Timothy 3:16.

4. See David K. Bernard, *In the Name of Jesus* (Hazelwood, MO.: Word Aflame Press, 1992). For the scriptural basis, see Acts 2:38; 4:12; 8:16; 10:48; 19:5; 22:16; 1 Corinthians 1:13; Romans 6:3–4; Galatians 3:27.

5. Most regard this threefold experience as constituting "the new birth," but some identify the new birth with repentance only. All acknowledge that people begin a genuine relationship of faith in God at repentance but should continue to walk in obedience as God leads them. For the belief that these steps constitute the new birth, see David K.

Bernard, *The New Birth* (Hazelwood, MO: Word Aflame Press, 1984). For the scriptural basis, see John 3:5; 7:37–39; Acts 2:1–4, 37–39; 10:42–48; 11:13–18; 19:1–6; Romans 6:1–5; 1 Corinthians 6:11; 12:13; Titus 3:5.

6. The principle is generally affirmed, but on practical applications there is considerable variation among churches and even within churches. For standard UPCI teaching on the subject, see Loretta Bernard and David K. Bernard, *In Search of Holiness* (Hazelwood, MO: Word Aflame Press, 1981); David K. Bernard, *Practical Holiness: A Second Look* (Hazelwood, MO: Word Aflame Press, 1985). For the scriptural basis, see Romans 12:1–2; 1 Corinthians 11:13–16; 2 Corinthians 6:14–7:1; Galatians 5:13–26; 1 Timothy 2:8–10; Hebrews 12:14–15; 1 Peter 1:15–16; 2:9; 3:1–5.

7. See Fred Foster, *Their Story: 20th Century Pentecostals*, rev. ed. (Hazelwood, MO: Word Aflame Press, 1981).

8. In 1999, there were about 2.2 million in the U.S. and 20 million worldwide. Talmadge L. French, *Our God Is One: The Story of the Oneness Pentecostals* (Indianapolis: Voice & Vision, 1999), 86, 253–283.

9. For further discussion of the first four factors, see David K. Bernard, *A History of Christian Doctrine, Vol. 3: The Twentieth Century* (Hazelwood, MO: Word Aflame Press, 1999), 158–63. See also the similar discussion of how "sects" become "churches" in Rodney Stark, *For the Glory of God: How Monotheism Led to Reformations, Science, Witch-Hunts, and the End of Slavery* (Princeton, N.J: Princeton University Press, 2003), 23–24.

10. See Grant Wacker, *Heaven Below: Early Pentecostals and American Culture* (Cambridge, MA: Harvard University Press, 2001).

11. Edith Blumhofer, *The Assemblies of God: A Chapter in the Story of American Pentecostalism* (Springfield, MO: Gospel Publishing House, 1989), 1:238.

12. Robert Mapes Anderson, *Vision of the Disinherited: The Making of American Pentecostalism* (New York: Oxford University Press, 1979), 149; Walter J. Hollenweger, *Pentecostalism: Origins and Development Worldwide* (Peabody, MA: Hendrickson, 1997), 192–93.

13. Bernard, *History* vol. 3, 17–18, 28–31, 48–52, based on Charles Parham, *A Voice Crying in the Wilderness* (1902; rev. ed. Baxter Springs, KS: Apostolic Faith Bible College, 1910); William Seymour, ed., *Apostolic Faith* (Los Angeles, 1906-8), repr. in *The Azusa Street Papers* (Foley, AL: Together in the Harvest Publications, 1997); William Durham, *Pentecostal Testimony*, Jan. and Aug. 1912.

14. David Barrett, "Global Statistics," in Stanley Burgess and Eduard van der Maas, eds., *The New International Dictionary of Pentecostal and Charismatic Movements*, rev. and exp. ed. (Grand Rapids: Zondervan, 2002), 291. Assemblies of God officials say the number for their group is 50% (*Charisma*, October 1993), but some scholars say informally that the figure could be as low as 30%.

15. No general survey has been taken. This statistic was valid for New Life United Pentecostal Church of Austin, Texas, in September 2004, when it had almost 500 people ages ten or older in regular attendance. The 10% who had not spoken in tongues were mostly newcomers or people who did not seek the Spirit. Conversations with pastors around the country indicated that this statistic corresponded closely to their situation also.

16. On September 7, 2004, the UPCI reported 4,209 churches, including daughter works, compared to 3,892 in 1999.

17. Bernard, *History* 3:98–103.

Chapter 9

The "Almost Pentecostal:"
The Future of the Church of God in the United States

Kimberly Ervin Alexander

On July 25, 1741 John Wesley preached a sermon at St. Mary's, Oxford University titled "The Almost Christian." His text, Acts 26:28, assumed that one could be almost persuaded to be a Christian. In his introduction he commented on this state,

> But seeing it avails nothing before God to go *only thus far*,
> it highly imports us to consider.
> First. What is implied in being *almost*,
> Secondly. What in being *altogether, a Christian.*[1]

Wesley described the "almost Christian" as having a form of godliness or the outward appearance of a Christian. This Christian may abstain from what is evil and may do good. But while practicing the outward form of Christianity, he or she lacks, according to Wesley, sincerity or "a real, inward principle of religion, from whence these outward actions flow."[2] However, Wesley allows that one can be "altogether a Christian." Rather than being motivated by a fear of punishment this Christian is motivated by the love of God and neighbor and by real faith.[3] As a result, this Christian has assurance and faith working by love.

As an heir to Wesley's experiential theology, twenty-first century Pentecostalism must ask itself a similar question: are we altogether Pentecostal? Do we have a form of godliness but not the power of godliness? To put the question in more recent terminology, do we have style but no substance? In order to assess the state of Pentecostalism we must initially ask what is the substance of Pentecostal theology?

Many attempts at defining the Pentecostal substance have focused on phenomena associated with its revival ethos, most famous among these is speaking in tongues (*glossolalia*). But recent discussions have concluded that the movement cannot simply be defined in terms of *glossolalia*. The most helpful of the recent suggestions is that of Steven J. Land who defines Pentecostalism under the rubric of "the fivefold gospel": Jesus is Savior, Sanctifier, Spirit-Baptizer, Divine Healer, and Soon Coming King. Land identifies five theological motifs which are at the heart of the movement's theology:

1. Justification by faith in Christ.
2. Sanctification by faith as a second definite work of grace.
3. Healing of the body as provided for all in the atonement.
4. The pre-millennial return of Christ.
5. The baptism in the Holy Spirit evidenced by speaking in tongues.[4]

Pentecostals understand themselves to be "in the way" or "in the light." Each of the crisis experiences provided by grace are steps along the way. Therefore, Pentecostalism constitutes a way of life or a way of being. Land explains,

> The journey toward God was a journey with God in God. It was walking toward the Father with Jesus in the Spirit. But this journey was also fundamentally a journey into God: a kind of mystical, ascetical journey which was ingredient in knowing God and going further, deeper and higher. To know God was to be directed by God's will, motivated by God's love and strengthened by God's power.[5]

As Land's work goes on to illustrate, the substance or power of Pentecostalism's theo-spirituality comes from a transformation of the affections. With the experiences of initial salvation, sanctification, and Spirit Baptism come the accompanying affections of gratitude, compassion, and courage.[6] This transformational/relational understanding of salvation is at the heart of Pentecostal theology. And it is against this transformational/relational dynamic, not a reductionistic approach in light of *glossolalia*, that the future of Pentecostalism should be assessed.

The following quote from A. J. Tomlinson, first General Overseer of the Church of God, illustrates how these early Pentecostals saw their calling as one which transformed them into warriors:

> Satan is mustering his forces and drafting every man and woman into his service that is possible for him to procure. The smoke of an awful battle is already rising from the battle field where the skirmishers are engaged. But it is now high time for the regulars, to advance with the full equipment of Pentecost, and to pour into the ranks of the enemy the shot and shell, grape and canister of gospel truth and power until the roar of the cannons can be heard all over the world as they belch forth with tremendous fury their deadly discharges.[7]

The Church of God was understood to be a holy army of God and every member was charged with the mission to preach the gospel to every creature. To *be* anything less, to *do* anything less was to fail.

This chapter will focus on the future of the Church of God (Cleveland, Tennessee) in the context of its birthplace, the United States. The COG, like other classical Pentecostal churches, is experiencing the majority of its growth outside of North America and like other classical Pentecostal churches, the denomination is feeling the effects of its "coming of age." After one hundred years of organization,[8] the Church of God is facing the very real challenge of maintaining the movement's vitality amid institutional stagnancy. How does a denomination that was born in the mountains of North Carolina and Tennessee, one that has emerged as one of the fastest growing Pentecostal denominations in the world with over six million members worldwide, cope with the accompanying growth pains?

To examine this struggle, three areas of concern will be addressed: doctrine, mission, and polity. If there is integrity in the Church of God, there should be congruity between doctrine, mission, and practice. Because the Church of God is still considered to be a Wesleyan-Pentecostal denomination, the doctrine of sanctification and the accompanying doctrine of holiness as a standard of living will be discussed. Specifically, will the Church of God *remain* a Wesleyan-Pentecostal church in the next century? In addition, the church's understanding of its mission in the twenty-first century will be explored. Will this Pentecostal denomination remain zealously evangelistic? Finally, the issue of the women's roles in the church, according to Church of God polity, will be examined. Will the Church of God, informed by the conservative complementarians within the Evangelical movement, finally silence its daughters and thereby violate its historic communal ethos?

Spirit and Doctrine

Context

The Church of God stands in the Holiness-Pentecostal trajectory of North American Pentecostalism. Though its roots go back to an organizational meeting in 1886, called by Baptist preacher R. G. Spurling, a revival in 1896 imprinted the church with the Holiness Movement's expectation of sanctification as a subsequent experience to the New Birth. Many reportedly spoke in tongues at that same meeting and in the ensuing years. The church intersected with the Azusa Streeet Revival in 1908 when its persuasive leader, Ambrose Jessup Tomlinson was baptized in the Holy Spirit following a sermon by G. B. Cashwell.

The Church of God was relatively untouched by the other doctrinal divisions which rocked the rest of the early Pentecostal world. The 1910 division over the Finished Work doctrine of sanctification had little or no effect.[9] It is possible to attribute the survival of the southern Pentecostal groups (Church of God, Church of God in Christ, Pentecostal Holiness Church) to William Durham's early death; he simply never got to these groups. However, each of these groups was strongly centralized, with formidable leadership (Tomlinson, Charles H. Mason and J. H. King, respectively), and a governmental approach congruent with their Wesleyan stance. It is doubtful that Durham's message could have penetrated these strongholds. As a result the early Church of God was also untouched by the New Issue of Oneness theology, a trajectory of the Finished Work view.

However, the Church of God did face a theological test in the 1940s that was a challenge to its Wesleyan-Holiness commitment. During the 1930s, there had been an influx of Finished Work adherents into the movement. For example, Finis J. Dake had an influence as a popular Bible teacher. Parallel to this, the Church of God and other Pentecostals were participating in the National Association of Evangelicals, a group with a decidedly non-Wesleyan (and non-Pentecostal) statement of faith. Meanwhile, at the denomination's Bible Training School, D. C. Barnes contributed to the Finished Work controversy by teaching a different view of sanctification from the Wesleyan-Holiness understanding. After several years of deliberation, the Church of God General Assembly finally adopted a Declaration of Faith which emphasized *subsequence*.[10] Though this tenet was clearly Wesleyan in principal, it did not define sanctification as either a crisis or a process. This confusion over *how* one is sanctified after the new birth was still a matter of debate. As more and more Church of God ministers found a new "home" within Evangelicalism, a place where they had previously been unwelcome, and as many were trained in Reformed theology, there was a corresponding decline of the Wesleyan emphasis on the crisis experience of entire sanctification. As the Charismatic movement of the 1960s and 1970s began to bring other voices into the church, whether through media or direct personal involvement, there was a further chiseling away at the doctrine of subsequence.

The alliance with Evangelicalism in the 1940s, seen by many as the "coming of age" of Pentecostalism, in retrospect, has been viewed by others as the beginning of the blurring of the distinctiveness of Pentecostalism.[11] The sons and daughters of first generation Pentecostals, including those in the Church of God, wanted to throw off the shame of being "peculiar" and the church from "the other side of the tracks."

As early as 1958 the effects of the ambiguity over the sanctification doctrine were apparently being felt. At the 1958 General Assembly a particularly heated debate ensued over the wearing of wedding bands. The debate centered on the issue of holiness as a standard. A reassessment of what it meant to be a "holiness church" was needed. The General Assembly of 1960 responded by issuing the "Resolution on Holiness" which warned, "We must, therefore, beware lest we become conformed to the world or lest a love for the world take root in our hearts and manifest itself as lust of the flesh, lust of the eye, or the pride of life."[12]

A move which has had unforeseen repercussions was made in 1974. In that Assembly, the teachings of the church were divided into two categories: doctrinal and practical. Though the clear intention was merely to clarify what kinds of things fell into the doctrinal and practical categories, the move had the effect of moving the Practical Commitments to a place of subordination. Gradually, the Practical Commitments were treated as nonessentials or as optional.

Having fallen into the trap of too easily identifying or reducing holiness to external appearances, the Church of God, after several revisions, in 1988 arrived at a statement of Practical Commitments which delineates general categories of spiritual and moral commitment with more specific subcategories. Though this document did not change the letter of the law—it expanded the understanding of a holiness standard in many ways—its adoption for some people became a "license" to see few real absolutes.

Challenge

With the afore noted history in mind, the doctrinal question confronting the Church of God is will it continue in the Wesleyan-Pentecostal trajectory? After surviving the Finished Work controversy which divided Pentecostalism in 1910, will the Church of God in the United States stay true to its heritage, even while it adapts to an ever-changing context?

Like the Evangelical churches, the focus on righteousness in most contemporary Pentecostal preaching has moved from a focus on individual responsibility to those issues most often identified with the Religious Right. Church of God ministers and members, like their sisters and brothers in other United States classical Pentecostal denominations, by and large, seem to be enjoying their newfound affluence and freedom of conscience with regard to dress and lifestyle. So it follows that issues of modesty and simplicity are rarely addressed. When and if holy living is discussed it *may* include discussions about prayer and devotion. Contrastingly, issues such as the sanctity of life and marriage have tended to dominate preaching on righteousness.

While there has been a much needed new emphasis on caring for the poor in the Church of God, with the result that the Division of Care Ministries has been restructured to include benevolence ministries, there has *not* been a corresponding de-emphasis on materialism and consumerism. In fact, the influence of televangelism, the Charismatic movement and/or Word of Faith movement has led many into identifying gain as godliness.[13] The holiness message of *victory*, traditionally understood as a message of victory over sin, is now preached by some as victory over bad health and poverty. This over-realized eschatology forgets the classical Pentecostal worldview of the *already-not yet*. Ayodeji Adewuya's recent treatment of Romans 6-8 is a classical Wesleyan-Pentecostal understanding of this worldview:

> Although Paul's primary concern is not to answer the question of why the righteous suffer, he, nevertheless, shows that sanctification does not provide immunity from trials and sufferings. . . . In Romans 8.1-17, it has been shown that holiness or life in the Spirit is characterized by both freedom and responsibility. From this point on, Paul portrays the sanctified life as that of hope in the midst of suffering. . . . Whatever the cause of the believers' suffering, they can endure when they remember the glory of the life to come. Paul is thinking about a finished redemption, of our sharing in the glory of Christ in eternity. What steadying assurance this should give to those who suffer from the ravages of disease such as AIDS, to those who are victims of injustice and wickedness, to persecuted saints in many places, and to all Christians who have felt the hard blows of inescapable tragedy and cruel circumstances and crushing affliction.[14]

Since 9/11 the contexts of both the United States and the world have changed, and will likely continue to change. Just one result is that the twenty-first century context is now characterized by suffering. Those Pentecostals who have embraced a theology which does not actively propagate a life of victory over sin, a theology which depends upon the continuing prosperity and upward mobility of the church, may be left having nothing to offer a suffering world. What is encouraging is that there has been an observable emphasis on holy lifestyle from a younger generation of Church of God ministers. Influenced by recent revivals, many in this generation are finding ways to make "holiness preaching" relevant in a postmodern context.

Recently pastor Loran Livingston, at Central Church of God in Charlotte, North Carolina (with more than 6,000 in attendance), made news by adopting a "cover and conceal" code of dress for its worship services. The policy states:

> As we strive to be holy in all we do, please be mindful of your attire when dressing for church services. Shorts are inappropriate for everyone. Gentlemen, no tank tops, please. Ladies, please be modest in determining appropriate hem lengths (no short skirts!), refrain from tight or revealing clothing, and conceal all undergarments. Make a special note: spaghetti-trapped tops are not acceptable attire for church. Thank you for honoring the Lord and His house![15]

Two years later, at the General Assembly, Livingston assumed the leadership of the General Executive Council by virtue of his being the first elected to the eighteen member council. This election may be indicative of the fact that Livingston's stand on standards of dress has not negatively affected his status in the denomination or it may indicate that Livingston's stand is respected by those who are aware of it.

While this accent on holy living as it relates to lifestyle and even dress is needful, what may be lacking in these approaches is a theological grounding of holy living as a fruit of a transforming experience of sanctification. Without an experience which produces the fruit of holy living, communities which embrace holiness as a lifestyle or standard *tend* toward legalism. The addictions and bondages of the twenty-first century can only be broken through the transforming power of sanctifying grace, not just legislated righteousness. The experience of inward holiness is required. Adewuya said, "We can gain a victory over sin, not because of the law forbidding it, but through the power of grace by which we have been saved. The compulsions of grace are those of inner spiritual power and spiritual gratitude. There is inner aversion to sin, moral energy to resist sin, and constraining motivation to please the holy God."[16]

It is incumbent, then, upon the Church of God to continue to articulate Wesleyan-Pentecostal doctrine in a twenty-first century context. Elsewhere it has been shown that removing one doctrine from the integrated "fivefold gospel" has far-reaching implications.[17] Though *on paper* the Church of God has not removed the doctrinal commitment, it has been *practically* removed through negligence on the part of many.[18]

A positive and hopeful sign in this regard may be seen in the selection of Steven J. Land as President of the denomination's seminary. Noted for his scholarship in the area of Wesleyan-Pentecostal studies, Land's identification of the Fivefold Gospel as the heart of Pentecostal spirituality has greatly informed the direction of the Seminary for several years. The Church of God Theological Seminary, having been called a "guardian of the faith" whose mission statement identifies it as a Wesleyan-Pentecostal institution, is intentional in its approach to passing on the "faith once delivered." The curriculum offerings include required courses in pneumatology, the doctrine of holiness, and Pentecostal spirituality. Faculty research efforts also revolve around this Wesleyan-Pentecostal commitment. For instance, recent publications have focused on Pentecostal hermeneutics,[19] healing and deliverance,[20] communal holiness,[21] Wesleyan-Pentecostal readings of scripture,[22] and Pentecostal practice.[23] The effects of these teaching, research and publishing efforts are already being seen and heard, and may well steer the denomination back toward its Wesleyan moorings.[24]

Another positive sign, which has the potential of affecting the polity of the Church, is the launching of the Center for Pentecostal Leadership and the "Walking in the Spirit" project funded jointly by the Church of God Theological Seminary, the denomination and the Lilly Sustaining Pastoral Excellence fund. "Walking in the Spirit" revives the polity of the denomination by encouraging accountability, holy friendships, and covenant relationships among pastors at the district level.

Spirit and Mission

Context

At the first General Assembly, 1906, the group of twenty-one men and women agreed to do their best "to press into every open door this year and work with greater zeal and energy for the spread of the glorious Gospel of the Son of God than ever before."[25] The earliest missionary efforts of Church of God ministers carried the Pentecostal message into the Caribbean (Bahamas, Cuba and the Virgin Islands), China, and Latin America.[26] Missionary efforts in Egypt were also supported by early Church of God members.[27] At the same time the denomination was expanding throughout the Southeastern United States.

There is nothing which so characterized the early period of the church and its ethos than A. J. Tomlinson's *The Last Great Conflict*. In his *magnum opus* Tomlinson set out his worldview for the church of which he was Overseer. Therein he said that the Church of God is an army engaged in conflict with the forces of Satan. He exhorted,

> 'Press the battle' as a slogan or war-cry should be taken up by every lover of truth and echoed and re-echoed over every plain and hilltop until those who have had a tendency to compromise healing, tongues, the gifts of the Spirit, etc., will become ashamed, ask forgiveness of their Captain, raise the red flag of war and rush into the battle with a holy zeal such as no people of past history have ever manifested.[28]

Through the years, the Church of God became a fierce evangelistic movement noted for its "fire": loud and "spirited singing," anointed preaching, missionary zeal, and physical manifestations of the Spirit.[29] The Church of God grew as a result of revivals that were often held in small towns where prayer meetings or Sunday Schools had already been established. According to John C. Jernigan, "The preacher stayed in a private home and fasted, prayed and preached 'until the power fell.'"[30]

Throughout the twentieth century these evangelistic and missionary efforts were organized into major departments of the denomination. Within the Department of Evangelism and Home Missions specific efforts were directed toward various ethnicities making up the ever-changing American fabric: Native Americans, Hispanic Americans, and African Americans.

Challenge

Denominations have the *tendency* to turn inward, to support the mechanisms necessary to maintain the structure. Pentecostalism, as a dynamic Spirit movement, perhaps more than other religious group, has felt the tension of the dialectic between structure and Spirit. As the movement has come of age in many areas of the American expression, there has been what Land has called a "rush to respectability" with all the trappings of such a status: upward mobility, materialism, consumerism, and a numbing narcissism.[31] The Church of God, originally a movement that saw itself as a "mighty army," has often relegated the work of evangelism to the designated evangelism department within the structure. A monthly monetary contribution is merely sent to those who are delegated to the work of evangelism.

The agenda for the General Council of the 70th International General Assembly in 2004 called for a "special order of the day" to consider the mission and vision of the Church of God. This order was preceded by two years of study which had included input from over 140 persons from both inside and outside the United States. This study called for an insertion of commitment statements into the mission statement of the Church of God. These commitments included a commitment to prayer, Pentecostal worship, world evangelization, church planting, leadership development, leadership care, and leadership interdependence. The commitment to world evangelization would be demonstrated by calling every local church to adopt an intentional goal of interceding for and reaching unreached people groups.[32] A "Resolution on Home Missions" was also adopted. This resolution recognized that the United States has "the third largest pre-Christian population in the world" and that the United States is itself a mission field.[33]

These two measures have the *potential* to renew the Church of God by refocusing its priorities. If the Church of God community begins to think and, more importantly, pray for those outside of its structure, it may again find its original ethos, its "holy zeal." There is nothing more spiritually troubling, nothing that shakes up the status quo more, than the realization that the harvest is truly great and as yet unreached. Intentionally praying for the world harvest may have the effect of turning the Church of God away from its introversion and away from its identity with the "American dream." Pentecostalism, by definition, is a celebration of the first fruits of the harvest, implying that the rest of the harvest will be gathered. Pentecostalism at its heart has "a passion for the Kingdom."[34] At the point Pentecostalism moves away from this *passion,* it has a diseased heart, and possibly has ceased to be truly Pentecostal.

Viewing unconverted America as a mission field should cause the American Pentecostal church to look beyond the four walls of its structure.[35] Outstanding among the unconverted are those immigrants who have come to make America their home and who have brought with them their own religious practices. Pluralism should not be viewed as a threat to the "American way of life" but rather as an opportunity for advancing the Kingdom of God.

Another challenge, one not readily recognized, is the subtle devolution which has occurred in the Pentecostal understanding of the salvation experience. Most are aware of the monumental paradigm shift which occurred in 1910 when most of American Pentecostalism was swept into the Finished Work soteriology introduced by William Durham. What has rarely been explored, or admitted, are the implications of this shift for evangelism and discipleship. Elsewhere it has been shown that by removing the doctrine of sanctification as a second work of grace, and by recasting initial conversion in a more Reformed way, the salvation experience was seen in more positional terms, where all experiences in God are "claimed" as "already accomplished." This shift had the effect of nullifying, or making unnecessary, any further works of grace in the life of the believer. One result is that the experience of Spirit Baptism has been divorced from the *via salutis* and understood merely as empowerment for Christian service. The result is that the experience of Spirit Baptism has become optional and not a part of the *via salutis* for all believers. Thus, Spirit Baptism has become necessary only for those called to minister and serve. A second development of the Reformed perspective on positional salvation is that some Pentecostals believe that an "already accomplished" salvation also includes divine health.[36]

Moreover, this reconfiguring of Pentecostal soteriology results in a nearly uncritical acceptance of a view of salvation which reduces salvation to a "decision for Christ." This reduction too easily leads to a doctrine wherein there is nothing else beyond that simple first step of mental assent. Once unsatisfied with a neighbor's mere "profession of faith" or "decision for Christ," which was not evidenced by the fruits of repentance (true conversion), the evangelistic zeal of the average American Pentecostal, including that of the Church of God adherent, has been subsumed by an emphasis upon "privatized religion." More significantly, Pentecostals have too easily bought into the Evangelical Movement's definition of Christian experience. This definition, with its tendency toward an overemphasis on juridical understandings, has led to a salvation in which there is no real conversion. Wesleyan-Pentecostals must ask, as Wesley did in his day "are we almost Christian, almost Pentecostal?"[37]

Kenneth C. Collins has recently demonstrated that the decline of both British and American Methodism may be traced to its shift in priorities. According to Collins the church has lost its mission and therefore its identity. Collins cites William J. Abraham, who bemoans the Methodist Church's move away from its central focus on God, "As a consequence 'pastoral care is reduced to therapy, mission to sociopolitical action, evangelism to church growth, academic theology to amateur philosophical inquiry and church administration to total quality management.'"[38] Collins has also re-conceptualized Wesley's ministry to the poor in terms of a soteriological orientation. Collins warns, "without holy love as its impetus, without a concern for 'souls' as its highest ministry, the church runs the risk of self-righteousness, a partisan spirit, an incipient materialism, and much worse, a fostering of perhaps all those unholy tempers which Wesley so often warned against."[39]

If Wesleyan-Pentecostalism, as typified by the Church of God, is to survive and thrive in the twenty-first century, it must revive its missionary zeal and its concern for lost souls. It will not be enough to develop new programs or even to train ministers and members in evangelistic methods. Instead, it is necessary that Pentecostals recover their passion for the Kingdom. As Land has shown, this passion only comes as the result of a rebirth of the affections. The transformation of the affections is the fruit of the sanctification experience. Mission, then, is vitally linked to holiness.

Spirit and Polity

Context

A movement whose methodology and/or polity does not flow from its ideology has no integrity. For instance, Methodism and the Wesleyan movement carefully explicated a system of accountability and a propagation of the message which had integrity with its doctrine. Wesley variously believed that salvation was available to all, was a "full" salvation, and could be perceived by all who experienced it. He carefully crafted a system of bands and class meetings that incorporated the accountability necessary for maintaining one's experience of salvation. His lay preachers, both men and women, carried the movement's message and lay class leaders provided pastoral care for those within their cell group. The bands and classes maintained strict rules of discipline, all with a goal of personal and corporate holiness. Church polity, then, should reflect the theology of the denomination. A Wesleyan-Pentecostal denomination would be expected to operate with a polity which held the tension of accountability and empowerment in dialectic.[40]

Concerning leadership and inclusiveness, the Church of God now will be examined regarding its ideological-polity integrity. Specifically, do the criteria for the credentialing of ministers or eligibility for leadership reflect a Holiness-Pentecostal doctrinal commitment? Has this full salvation truly reversed the curse?[41] Because it has roots in the Southeastern United States, the leadership of the Church of God has traditionally consisted of white Southern men. In spite of the fact that the majority of membership is now to be found outside the United States, there has been a noticeable absence of ethnic diversity among the elected officials of the church. This is in part owing to the fact that the biennial International General Assembly is held within the continental United States. Parallel to the tremendous expansion of the Church of God into the rest of the world was the alliance with Evangelicalism. The sometimes competing forces of internationalization and Evangelicalism have pressed upon the polity and traditions of the Church of God in the last decades of the twentieth century.

Remarkably, as early as 1921, there had been appointments of persons of color to "The Other Seventy," a group of seventy ministers who led the church alongside the General Overseer and the Council of Twelve.[42] Tomlinson had granted license to African Caribbeans, Mexican Americans, Native Americans and African Americans from 1909 forward. In a 1919 address to the General Assembly Tomlinson exhorted, "Our dark skinned brothers and sisters have received the Holy Ghost as well as we, and we have long ago learned that God is no respecter of persons." This address came as an explanation for giving a formal place on the program to African Americans.[43] Sadly, this progressive vision of inclusiveness did not prevail in the Church of God as it did in the Church of God of Prophecy.

Nevertheless, a growing awareness of the diversity of the Body of Christ, as a result of internationalization, and a somewhat forced recognition of diversity based on civil rights legislation, has led the ministers of the Church of God to recognize the inequities which exist. Most promising in this regard was the election of Wallace J. Sibley, an African American, to the position of Assistant Director of Evangelism and Home Missions in 2004 and to Director in 2006. The 2004 election made history: Sibley was the first person of color ever elected to an office in the International Church, excluding the Executive Council.[44] The election was understood by all present to be a move toward reconciliation. One resolution that came from the floor of the General Council (Ordained Bishops present), and which was passed by the General Assembly (all members present) in 2004, calls for further study with regard to inclusion of persons of color in positions of leadership in the Church of God. Less hopeful are the signs surrounding the inclusion of women in all areas of the ministry of the Church of God. Nowhere is the fallout of the influence of Evangelicalism felt more than in the ambiguity with regard to participation of women.[45]

Early in the history of the Church of God, as in other early expressions of Pentecostalism, women were full participants; they addressed the earliest General Assemblies on issues such as prayer and Sunday School and they preached in worship services at the Assemblies. Rebecca Barr and Nora Chambers were licensed by the Church of God in 1909 and 1910, respectively. Lula Jones, Sallie O. Lee and Clyde Cotton evangelized the Southeastern states and planted churches. It is estimated that as many as 12.2 percent of the licensed ministers in the Church of God in 1912 were women.[46] However, as early as 1914 a different form of license, the Evangelist's License, was prescribed for women. This license held certain restrictions for women: they were not allowed to administer the ordinances of water baptism, footwashing, or the Lord's Supper.

While these women were recognized as capable preachers, evangelists, and church planters, their role in governing the church was easily dismissed, at least for A. J. Tomlinson. The view that has held sway in the Church of God is that women are not to be involved in the governing of the church. In what may be a unique interpretation, Tomlinson presented his view of church government. He declared, "Church then means government—Christ's government; His Church."

He continued, as if responding to a question, "Here then is where women are to keep silence: that is, they are to have no active part in the governmental affairs." Citing 1 Corinthians 14, Tomlinson continued by discussing the regulation of tongues. He concluded, "There were no women speaking in the council at Jerusalem: no one talking in tongues. They were a judicial body, searching for and applying the laws to a particular case." The implication is that the Holy Spirit does speak through women in prophetic ways, such as with messages in tongues. But because the business of the Council is governmental and specifically judicial, then those kinds of spiritual manifestation are not needed, and therefore women's input is non-existent.[47]

David Roebuck and Karen Mundy have shown that following World War 2 the percentage of licensed ministers who were female reached a peak at 18.2 percent. Following the war, there was a trend in American society for men to take their rightful places in the work force and in the home.[48] While the idyllic "Leave It To Beaver" image was being projected by Hollywood, and ironically by the Evangelical Church, in reality the majority of Pentecostal women were employed outside the home out of economic necessity.

Accompanying the alliance with the National Association of Evangelicals in 1948 was a change in the nomenclature for ministerial ranks that eliminated the role of Evangelist for men and instituted the rank of Licensed Minister. The rank of Evangelist remained in tact for women, however.[49] Apparently women were still recognized as being gifted by the Spirit for Evangelism but were not to be recognized professionally as clergy. More changes in nomenclature and status were to follow. By1958 the term "Female Minister" appeared in the General Assembly Minutes and in 1964 the title "Lady Minister" appeared in lists of qualifications for ministry (alongside three ranks for male ministers: Exhorter, Licensed Minister, Ordained Minister). In 1972 the credential of "Lady Evangelist" was issued for the first time.[50] Sacerdotal rites were granted in 1990 when the offices of Exhorter and Licensed Minister were made gender inclusive.[51]

A real challenge to the Tomlinsonian interpretation occurred in 1994 when the constituency of the General Assembly, the highest governing body, was changed to include both male and female members who were present and of the age of 16 or higher. In 2000, the title of the second rank of licensure for Church of God ministers was changed to "Ordained Minister," in effect granting ordination to women. However, women were still excluded from the highest rank, "Ordained Bishop," and thereby from the positions of leadership.

By a small margin in 2002 the General Council of the Church of God voted not to place on the agenda of the General Assembly a measure that would allow women to serve on local church councils. The opposition to the motion cited Paul's admonitions for women to be silent and not to usurp authority over men. Though Tomlinson's name was not invoked, his interpretation prevailed. More radical opposers saw this possibility of women serving in governance of the local church as concession to liberalism. Two years later, the measure was again defeated. A motion from the floor to remove references to gender with regard to the highest rank of ministry, Ordained Bishop, was tabled for further study. Sadly, after study by the Doctrine and Polity Committee, papers presenting both views were circulated to Ordained Ministers, but the discussion was not placed on the 2006 General Council agenda.

Challenge

It is easy to see the inconsistencies of the Church of God polity at the beginning of the second century of Pentecostalism. Women variously may answer the call to preach, evangelize, plant churches and may even be appointed to serve as pastor, but they may not serve on the Church and Pastors' Council. Therefore, in one ironic scenario it is conceivable that a woman may serve as a pastor of a church with the oversight of an all-male Council![52] Women serve in local congregations in nearly every role (treasurer, teachers, pastors of youth and children, worship leaders) but may not serve in the position most closely associated with that of deacon. Incongruous with the Church of God's understanding that women are not to be a part of the administration of the church, women are, as members of the General Assembly, a part of the highest governing body in the Church of God. Nevertheless, they cannot be elected or appointed to positions of leadership in the state or general church. Though restricted from authoritative positions as preachers, or as bearers of prophecies or messages in tongues or interpretation of tongues, women are given the ultimate authority over their hearers as they assume the role of speaking the voice of God.[53]

Not surprisingly, the percentage of credentialed ministers in the Church of God who are women has reached a low of 4 percent. The message to Pentecostal daughters rings loud and clear and is an echo of the position voiced by many in Evangelicalism.[54] By buying into the Evangelical hermeneutic, the church has betrayed herself. Traditionally, Pentecostalism exhibited a dynamic and pneumatic interpretation of Scripture, in which the Word, the community, and the Spirit were each engaged.[55] This hermeneutic was far from the literalistic reading of Fundamentalists. In true Wesleyan form, the Church of God and other Wesleyan-Pentecostals, like those at Azusa Street, were able to integrate their experience and tradition into their reading of the text.[56] This concession to Evangelicalism has robbed the Church of God and other classical Pentecostals of a vital part of its identity: "a church where everybody's a preacher."[57]

The restriction of any ministerial or church office to one gender is a violation of the Holiness-Pentecostal understanding that full salvation is *for* all. If the seed of the woman has bruised the head of the serpent, then those who are saved are no longer cursed. The victorious work of Christ through his life and death has restored humanity to the *imago dei* and the Holy Spirit continues that work in the church. As the gifts are given to the church, the life of God infuses it.[58] If there is a place where one would not expect to see the remnants of the curse of oppression and prejudice it is in the Wesleyan-Pentecostal movement. Where this sin remains, there is a question of the integrity of the movement. Communal holiness—full salvation—requires that the church be a place where everyone is liberated from the curse of the law.

Conclusion: "And are we yet alive?"

In the past, the Methodist Conference often began with the singing of the Wesleyan hymn which began with the question "And are we yet alive?" The lyrics go as follows,

And are we yet alive,
And see each other's face?
Glory and praise to Jesus give
For his redeeming grace!
Preserved by power divine
To full salvation here,
Again in Jesu's praise we join,
And in his sight appear.

What troubles have we seen,
What conflicts have we past,
Fightings without, and fears within,
Since we assembled last!
But out of all the Lord
Hath brought us by his love;
And still he doth his help afford,
And hides our life above.

Then let us make our boast
Of his redeeming power,
Which saves us to the uttermost,
Till we can sin no more;
Let us take up the cross,
Till we the crown obtain;
And gladly reckon all things loss,
So we may Jesus gain. [59]

Like the Methodists, the Pentecostals in the early Church of God believed that they had been kept and preserved by the power of God, and brought into a full salvation. They were saved, sanctified, filled with the Holy Ghost, and a member of the "Great Church of God." No matter what troubles they experienced from without, and no matter what fears lie within, they were united by a strong sense of identity and a unified purpose, a passion for the Kingdom. They were saved to the uttermost, looking forward for salvation from the very presence of sin. To be in the army of the Church of God was to be charged with taking up the cross until such day as the crown was obtained. The testimony of Euterpie Saunders of the Bahamas bears this out:

> Cooper's Town, Bahamas [sic]
>
> Dear Brother Tomlinson and Saints,
>
> Greetings in Jesus' Name: I praise God for saving and sanctifying me. John 17:17, and later on He baptized me with the Holy Ghost and fire and I spoke in other tongues as the Spirit gave utterance. It is so sweet to trust in Jesus, He is so good to me. He is my Healer, bless His name. I can join in with the Psalmist David in saying, "Bless the Lord, oh, my soul and all that is within me, bless His holy name." Oh, how I long to get closer to the Lord and to be a soul-winner for Him.
>
> The Devil is hard against the children of God but I am determined to go through. Just one glimpse of Him in glory, will the toil of life repay. I am a member of the great Church of God. Pray for me.
>
> Your sister under the blood,
> Euterpie Saunders[60]

At the dawning of the second hundred years of Pentecostalism, the Church of God must assess whether or not it has *both* the form *and* power of godliness. The question is not either/or. Wesleyan-Pentecostals understand both that fruit flows from true repentance and cannot precede it, and that outward demonstrations flow from holy love. To remain vibrant the Church of God must measure its works against its heart. It is not enough to profess to be a Pentecostal. One must *be* a Pentecostal. To be a Pentecostal is to have a holy love, one that is exhibited by a holy zeal for lost souls. To be a Pentecostal is to live in holy covenant community with God and each other. If the Church of God is going to be *altogether Pentecostal*, like Sister Euterpie Saunders, it must recover a commitment to holiness as a real experience so that it can be renewed in its mission and practice.

Notes

1. John Wesley, "The Almost Christian," http://gbhm-umc.org/UMhistory/Wesley/sermons/serm-002.stm (accessed January 17, 2006).

2. Wesley, 2–3.

3. Wesley, 4–5.

4. Steven J. Land, *Pentecostal Spirituality: A Passion for the Kingdom*, JPTS 1 (Sheffield: Sheffield Academic Press, 1993), 18.

5. Land, 76.

6. Land, 139.

7. A. J. Tomlinson, *The Last Great Conflict* (Cleveland, TN: The Press of Walter Rodgers, 1913), 21.

8. The beginnings of the Church of God can be traced to an organizational meeting in 1886, a holiness revival in 1896 and a reorganizational meeting in 1901. See David G. Roebuck, "Restorationism and a Vision for World Harvest: A Brief History of the Church of God (Cleveland, Tennessee)" at http://web2010.com/pctii/cyber/roebuck.html (accessed May 24, 2006).

9. See Vinson Synan, *The Holiness-Pentecostal Tradition: Charismatic Movements in the Twentieth Century* (Grand Rapids, MI: Wm. B. Eerdmans Publishing Co., 1997), 149–152 for a discussion of this first doctrinal division.

10. David G. Roebuck "Declaration Prevents Church Division," *Church of God History and Heritage* (Summer 1998), 1–2, 5–6.

11. See Margaret Poloma, *The Assemblies of God at the Crossroads: Charisma and Institutional Dilemmas* (Knoxville, TN: The University of Tennessee Press, 1989).

12. "Resolution Relative to Principles of Holiness of Church of God," *Church of God 69th General Assembly Minutes 2002* (Cleveland, TN: Church of God Publishing House, 2002), 93.

13. See James P. Bowers, *You Can Have What You Say: A Pastoral Response to the Prosperity Gospel*, Pentecostal Leadership Series (Cleveland, TN: Center for Pentecostal Leadership and Care, 2004).

14. J. Ayodeji Adewuya, *Transformed by Grace: Paul's View of Holiness in Romans 6–8* (Eugene, Oregon: Cascade Books, 2004), 74.

15. Central Church of God bulletin, August 29-September 12, 2004, available at www.centralchurchofgod.org. See also Ken Garfield, "Casting off casual Sundays: Central Church of God tells flock to honor God with appropriate dress," *The Charlotte Observer* www.charlotte.com/mld/observer/living/religion/4072287.htm?template=content Modules/printstory.jsp (posted on September 14, 2002).

16. Adewuya, 30.

17. For studies of the trajectory of early Pentecostalism as a result of the collapsing of sanctification into initial conversion with the introduction of Durham's "Finished Work" theology see Kimberly Ervin Alexander, *Pentecostal Healing: Models of Theology and Practice* (Blandford Forum, Dorset, UK: Deo, 2006); and William David Faupel, *The Everlasting Gospel*, JPTS 10 (Sheffield: Sheffield Academic Press, 1996).

18. It is noteworthy that the denomination's website utilizes an introductory graphic which identifies the Church of God as Christian, Protestant, and Evangelical but not Wesleyan or Holiness.

19. Kenneth C. Archer, *A Pentecostal Hermeneutic for the 21st Century: Spirit, Scripture and Community*, JPTS 28 (London: T & T Clark International, 2004).

20. Alexander, *Pentecostal Healing: Models of Theology and Practice* and John Christopher Thomas, *The Devil Disease and Deliverance: Origins of Illness in New Testament Thought*, JPTS 13 (Sheffield: Sheffield Academic Press, 1998).

21. J. Ayodeji Adewuya, *Holiness and Community in 2 Corinthians 6:14–7:1: Paul's View of Communal Holiness in the Corinthian Correspondence* (NY: Lang, 2001).

22. Rickie D. Moore, *God Saves: Lessons from the Elisha Stories* (Sheffield: JSOT Press, 1990) and John Christopher Thomas, *The Pentecostal Commentary on 1 John, 2 John, and 3 John* (London: T & T Clark International, 2004).

23. Cheryl Bridges Johns, *Pentecostal Formation: A Pedagogy Among the Oppressed*, JPTS 2 (Sheffield: Sheffield Academic Press, 1993).

24. An outgrowth of the Seminary's intentionality in promoting constructive Pentecostal theology is its housing of the *Journal of Pentecostal Theology*, and the corollary Supplement Series, edited by three Seminary faculty members.

25. Minutes of the First General Assembly (1906).

26. Church of God ministers Rebecca and Edmond Barr, R. M. Evans, Sam C. Perry, Jenny and Brinson Rushin and F. L. Ryder were responsible for these first missionary efforts.

27. Lillian Trasher and Sarah A. Smith founded mission stations in Assiout and Nikhela, Egypt, respectively.

28. A. J. Tomlinson, *The Last Great Conflict*, 20.

29. See Ray H. Hughes, *Church of God Distinctives* (Cleveland, TN: Pathway Press, 1968).

30. Jernigan quoted in Roebuck, 23.

31. Land, "The Nature and Evidence of Spiritual Fullness" in *Endued With Power: The Holy Spirit in the Church*, Robert White, ed. (Nashville: Thomas Nelson, 1995), 61.

32. "2004 International General Assembly Agenda, Part 1" (unpublished), 6.

33. "2004 International General Assembly Agenda, Part 1" (unpublished), 7.

34. Land, *A Passion for the Kingdom*.

35. Ironically, there has been a recent move to re-structure the financial system of the denomination by decreasing the amount of money sent from each congregation to denominational headquarters. A counter-move has proposed reducing the amount each church contributes to the World Missions department as well as consolidating all incoming funds to be dispersed by the Executive Committee of the denomination.

36. See Alexander, *Models*.

37. Kenneth C. Collins, *A Real Christian: The Life of John Wesley* (Nashville, Tennessee: Abingdon, 1999). In this, and other works, Collins proposes that the heart of Wesley's soteriology is his understanding of the *real*, transforming power of regeneration.

38. Abraham quoted in Collins, "The Ongoing Decline of British and American Methodism: A Modernistic Saga" in *Asbury Theological Journal* 56 no. 2 (Fall 2001–Spring 2002), 68.

39. Kenneth Collins, "The Soteriological Orientation of Wesley's Ministry to the Poor," *Wesleyan Theological Journal*, 36, no. 2 (Fall 2001), 34.

40. It is a fact that the vast majority of these denominations (the Church of God, Pentecostal Holiness, Church of God in Christ) all operate with a strongly centralized government.

41. See Janet Evert Powers, "Reversing the Curse: Women in the New Testament," unpublished paper. Powers maintains that Pentecostals who restrict women from ministry are in violation of a Holiness soteriology which saw the curse of Genesis 3 as being reversed by the work of Christ.

42. Curry was appointed to this position in 1923. Louis F. Morgan, "Bishop J. H. Curry: An Eminent Church Leader," *Church of God History and Heritage* (Winter/Spring 2003), 4.

43. Harold H. Hunter, "A. J. Tomlinson's Journey Toward Racial Reconciliation," *Church of God History and Heritage* (Winter/Spring 2001), 6. See also Doug Hogsten, "A Man of Zeal and Progressive Vision: Ambrose Jessup Tomlinson," unpublished paper.

44. Bishop J. H. Curry was elected to the International Executive Council in 1932. See Morgan, 3–4.

45. Poloma, 107.

46. See David Roebuck, "Perfect Liberty to Preach the Gospel: Women Ministers in the Church of God," *Pneuma* 17, no. 1 (Spring 1995), 30.

47. Tomlinson quoted in R. Hollis Gause and Kimberly Ervin Alexander, *Women in Leadership: A Pentecostal Analysis*, Pentecostal Leadership Series (Cleveland, TN: Center for Pentecostal Leadership and Care, 2006). The irony is that there were often messages in tongues with interpretation at the business sessions of the General Assembly.

48. David G. Roebuck and Karen Carroll Mundy, "Women, Culture, and Post-World War Two Pentecostalism" in *The Spirit and the Mind: Essays in Informed Pentecostalism* (Lanham, MD: University Press of America, 2000), 193. A similar phenomenon is observed by Margaret Poloma in the Assemblies of God. In 1983, the percentage of credentialed women had declined from 18.9% (1918) to 14%. One third of those ordained were retired. The number of women who served as pastors had "eroded" from 13.5% (1915) to 1.3% (1983). Poloma, 109.

49. See Roebuck, "Perfect Liberty," 30.

50. David G. Roebuck, *Limiting Liberty: The Church of God and Women Minister. 1886–1996* (Ph.D. diss., Vanderbilt University, 1997), 161–164. Roebuck points out that the action of granting licenses with the title "Lady Evangelist" was never authorized by the General Assembly.

51. Roebuck, 330–332.

52. In the Church of God, with its Episcopal polity, the Church and Pastor's Council is given the responsibility, "under the direction of the pastor" to "promote the general and state outreach programs of the church," to "assist the pastor, "when called upon, in the institution and direction of the local church programs." In every area of responsibility, according to the *Minutes*, the Council works "under the direction of the pastor." The irony is that a pastor may *direct* the Council, but a female is not seen fit to *serve* on the Council! See *Minutes*, 180–181.

53. See Gause and Alexander for a more detailed analysis of the incongruity of this situation in the Church of God. It should be especially noted that the situation is remarkably different in the majority-world, where Church of God women serve in positions of district, regional, and national leadership.

54. See Stanley Grenz with Denise Muir Kjesbo, *Women in the Church: A Biblical Theology of Women in Ministry* (Downers Grove, Il.: InterVarsity Press, 1995) for a careful comparison of the egalitarian and complementarian views.

55. John Christopher Thomas, "Women, Pentecostals and the Bible: An Experiment in Pentecostal Hermeneutics," *JPT* 5 (1994), 41–56.

56. Albert Outler has identified the "Wesleyan Quadrilateral" as the way in which Wesley determined doctrine. The elements of this quadrilateral are scripture, reason,

tradition and experience. For examples of this type of reading see Alexander, *Models* and John Christopher Thomas and Kimberly Ervin Alexander, "'And the Signs Are Following': Mark 16.9-20—A Journey into Pentecostal Hermeneutics," *Journal of Pentecostal Theology* 11, no. 2 (2003), 147–170.

57. This was a common designation for the Church of God, generally attributed to "outsiders" and observers of worship services where participation of the whole congregation was expected. Anyone, or everyone, might testify or exhort and therefore be described as "preaching." Frank Bartleman described this phenomenon in his eyewitness account of the Azusa Street Revival, "The Lord was liable to burst through any one. We prayed for this continually. Some one would finally get up anointed for the message. All seemed to recognize this and gave way. It might be a child, a woman, or a man." Bartleman, Frank, *Azusa Street* (Plainfield, NJ: Logos International, 1980), 59.

58. Gustav Aulen, *Christus Victor: An Historical Study of the Three Main Types of the Idea of the Atonement* (NY: MacMillan, 1969).

59. http://www.ccel.org/w/wesley/hymn/jwg04/jwg0478.html (accessed November 21, 2005).

60. *Church of God Evangel*, 7, no. 19 (May 6, 1916), 3.

Chapter 10

Heritage and Horizons:
The Derivation and Destiny of Open Bible Churches

David Cole

"Open Bible Standard Churches[1] is a vital organ in the body of Christ." At the national convention of Open Bible Standard Churches (OBSC) in 1997, these words of declaration by denominational president Jeff Farmer became a rallying cry for the ministers and delegates as they were challenged to accept a sense of vision and purpose for the future of the organization. The statement was a reference to a word of prophecy spoken many decades earlier by a church leader, and the search for its meaning and fulfillment symbolizes the denomination's quest for identity and destiny within the larger Pentecostal movement throughout its history.[2]

The following is a consideration of the ongoing struggle of a Pentecostal denomination to come to terms with its ecclesial self-understanding. From its very beginning (and even in its pre-amalgamation years prior to the coming together of Bible Standard Churches and the Open Bible Evangelistic Association in 1935) this church family has postured itself in reaction to one extreme or another in the greater Pentecostal movement while searching for its own clear mandate. Like other Pentecostal denominations, it has been challenged to know when to pursue unity and cooperation in step with other churches, and when to distinguish itself in uniqueness. An understanding of the OBSC movement,[3] as it has emerged in the Pentecostal landscape, is instructive as one considers its possible contributions to the larger Church in its ongoing journey to fulfill its perceived mission.

Heritage: Open Bible Standard Churches

OBSC, whose headquarters are in Des Moines, IA, was formed in 1935 as an amalgamation of two smaller Pentecostal bodies, the Bible Standard Mission of Oregon, and the Open Bible Evangelistic Association, based in Iowa. Both of these organizations were formed in response to difficulties between parties in the parent organizations. In the case of Bible Standard Mission, Fred Hornshuh and several fellow ministers chose to form their organization in 1919 after having left Florence Crawford's Portland-based Apostolic Faith Mission (AFM).[4] A decade later a group of thirty-two ministers in the Midwest, led by Rev. John R. Richey, decided in 1932 to separate from the International Church of the Foursquare Gospel (ICFG) and its leader, Aimee Semple McPherson.[5] Three years later, the Iowa and Oregon churches joined one another to form OBSC.

Once the followers of Hornshuh and Richey had a chance to get to know one another, the decision was made in 1935 to officially come together. There was much that the two groups had in common, including their Pentecostal experience, their dissatisfaction with dominant (and probably coincidentally, female) leadership, and their insistence that local churches should own their own property and maintain some autonomy with regard to the running of their affairs.[6] The arrangement has been workable, in that the unified group has survived for over seventy years, with close to 400 churches in the United States and over 1,000 internationally, in over forty nations.

However, in another sense it can be said that descendants of the two groups have maintained some of their original, and separate, loyalties. Geographically, by far the two largest of OBSC's five regions are the original two, now named the Pacific and Central regions. They are separated by the Rocky Mountains and by occasional differences in their political approaches to church business. During elections for national leadership positions, the location of the convention and support from the home region can play a major role in the success of a candidate for national office. Another example of regional territorialism can be seen in the merger of the denomination's Bible colleges over the years. OBSC now has only one officially recognized Bible college, Eugene Bible College (EBC), located in the Pacific region. Over the years three other schools merged with the college in Eugene after periods of declining enrollment. Most significant by far was the merger of Open Bible College (OBC) in Des Moines with EBC in 1986. OBC trained hundreds of pastors, missionaries and leaders since opening in 1930. OBC was accredited by the Accrediting Association of Bible Colleges (AABC),[7] and when OBSC leadership announced (taking many members quite by surprise) the closure of OBC/merger with EBC, many in the Central region were unhappy with the decision. Many wondered why, if there was to be only one school, it shouldn't be in Des Moines, where the denominational headquarters were, even though EBC was more stable in terms of enrollment and finances.

The merger went through, and since then EBC has attempted to serve the higher education needs of the entire OBSC constituency. However, after two decades statistics show that students from regions outside EBC's "home" Pacific region have not enrolled at their denominational school in the numbers that EBC and OBSC leadership had hoped. Other signs of separation between OBSC regions can be seen in issues related to the OBC/EBC merger. One is that when OBC's campus was sold at the time of the merger, proceeds from the sale were not all used for the development of EBC; some were retained for ministry purposes in the Central region. Thus, it was not a true merger in some senses, and certainly not in the minds of some of the constituents. Second, and possibly related to the first, EBC has never legally become OBSC's national college, in the sense that the property and assets of EBC continue to be under Pacific region trusteeship. Thus, while it is said that EBC is OBSC's national school, leaders know that in some aspects it is still under Pacific region control, although a national board of directors has been organized. On these and similar matters, leaders from the founding regions have at times seen church issues through their territorial lenses.[8]

Cooperation and Lines of Demarcation

OBSC was among the very first Pentecostal denominations to make a strong stand with the National Association of Evangelicals (NAE) once offered the opportunity to do so in the early 1940s. Thus when the Pentecostal Fellowship of North America (PFNA) was organized a few years later, OBSC leaders were in the early pool of the PFNA's executive officers and board of administration for the first two decades of PFNA history. Indeed, OBSC seems to have exerted considerable leadership and influence in cooperative efforts among Pentecostals for a denomination of its size.[9]

While OBSC's participation among the larger Pentecostal bodies was at a very high level during these years, the organization's questions about its identity and distinctiveness continued to be asked in earnest. Quietly, among top levels of leadership, OBSC and the Assemblies of God were discussing the possibility of a merger.[10] Indeed, the prophetic word mentioned in the opening paragraph of this writing was delivered in the context of a leadership meeting where such a merger was being considered. The prophetic word was presented as the Lord's response to the question of a possible merger: OBSC has a role to play (is a vital organ) and thus should continue as an entity. Other OBSC leaders dismissed the relevance of the prophetic word to their conversations/negotiations, although such a merger never materialized. There have even been expressions of public repentance among some OBSC ministers in the past decade for the sin of rejecting the prophetic word of the Lord, as people struggled with OBSC's perceived failure to respond to what God was saying.[11]

Meanwhile, it seems that OBSC's prioritizing of relationships with the NAE and PFNA in general and the Assemblies of God in particular had the corresponding residual effect of its distancing itself from persons and movements who fell out of favor with the prioritized friends. An example of that is the case of the Latter Rain Movement (LRM).

The LRM, rising in the later 1940s out of an independent Bible school in Saskatchewan, Canada and having major impact in the United States through Bethesda Tabernacle in Detroit and elsewhere, has been called "the most dramatic controversy to affect the Pentecostal Movement since World War II."[12] The LRM developed a teaching that "emphasized extreme congregationalism with local authority committed to a restored order of apostles, who through receiving a special dispensation derived from the laying on of hands, could in turn dispense a variety of spiritual gifts."[13] The Detroit work was a successful Assemblies of God church, and many Assemblies leaders were attracted through it to the LRM, including *The Pentecostal Evangel* editor Stanley Frodsham, who ultimately left the Assemblies of God organization. Attacks on existing "apostasized" Pentecostal groups brought open conflict, and Assemblies of God leadership took measures to address what it perceived to be chaos and doctrinal error.[14] The Assemblies' strong corrective action demonstrated sentiments that were shared by the larger PFNA body. After criticism from PFNA leaders, Elim Missionary Fellowship president Ivan Spencer, who had openly embraced the LRM, resigned from the PFNA Board of Administration in 1949.[15]

Keeping in step with the Assemblies and PFNA, OBSC also took a stand with the LRM in 1949–1950. In the *Message of the Open Bible*, the LRM was critiqued by several leaders for grieving the Holy Spirit, minimizing the Pentecostal outpouring and aligning the Pentecostal movement and leadership with "the old apostate Church of England."[16] OBSC general chairman Fulton declared that the LRM had "drawn lines of demarcation in their doctrinal position which are diametrically opposed" to OBSC teaching, with unscriptural teachings that are "either a spiritual delusion or a wresting of Scriptures."[17]

Thus OBSC chose a path of caution, of balance, of moderation. Indeed, "Moderation" became a tenet among the Articles of Faith of the movement, and the historical self-description in the introduction to its *Policies and Principles* includes the statements that OBSC is known for "freedom from fanaticism" and "Pentecostalism without fanaticism."[18] But some in OBSC circles seem to have wrestled with the decision of the leadership to officially distance the movement from Latter Rain ties, or were at least sympathetic with the spiritual emphases of the LRM.[19] In recent years, an openness to prophetic ministry in general has characterized many OBSC national and regional gatherings, and in particular, a relationship with Elim Missionary Fellowship has been developing. OBSC president Jeff Farmer has served as a member of the board of directors of Elim Bible Institute (EBI) in Lima, New York, and EBI president Paul Johannson was a keynote speaker at OBSC's 2003 national convention, delivering a word of prophecy to the OBSC family. OBSC seems to be attempting to overcome a possible overreaction to earlier LRM excesses by choosing to act on its desire for prophetic and apostolic ministry, even accepting it from those once rejected.

Leaders Who Left

A national OBSC leader has recently described a phenomenon within the movement that he called "The Big Fish that Got Away." That phenomenon is the reality that many wonderful leaders in the Body of Christ were once, but are no longer, members of OBSC. Some were strong leaders of some responsibility before moving on to another movement. Others were emerging leaders who were reared in OBSC churches and/or attended an OBSC college before leaving, and sometime after their departure they found fruitful or even notorious success elsewhere. A partial, categorized list can be drawn of those formerly with OBSC:[20]

- Early examples (1920s–1940s)[21]
- OBSC ministers who left to work with Oral Roberts Evangelistic Association[22]
- Ministry figures of recent notoriety[23]
- Academics/scholars[24]
- Former pastors of key churches who are no longer in OBSC ministry[25]
- Former OBSC ministers and students who are now with other movements[26]

Of course, there are many ways to interpret or reflect on this movement of people from one organization to another. One can certainly acknowledge that all denominations (and perhaps especially Pentecostal ones) experience such migration to one extent or another. Other possible responses include the following:

1. OBSC is a resource and a blessing to other ministries and Movements.
2. Other ministries and movements steal good OBSC leaders.
3. there is a lack of loyalty to OBSC among its emerging leaders.
4. OBSC is a stepping stone to greatness elsewhere.
5. OBSC is not a strong enough entity to hold good people.

No matter what the most accurate combination of interpretations might be, it is true that OBSC has at times been distracted by the challenge to develop strong leaders who are willing to stay in the organization. And since the movement is seventy years old, and yet still has only 400 U.S. churches, the loss of these leaders is sometimes mentioned in discussions about why the movement has not grown as large as other Pentecostal groups.[27] Even among the faithful who have not left the fold, vision-casting and building excitement about the future are dependent on overcoming disappointment over both the loss of those who have left and the overall modest size of the movement compared to sister organizations.

Healing Old Wounds

While the post-amalgamation history of the new organization has not recorded ongoing conflict with the previous parent organizations, recently the board of directors of OBSC issued a separate "Statement of Reconciliation" to each of the organizations from which ties had been severed. This was announced by OBSC President Jeff Farmer during the June 1997 national convention. The statements both declare that OBSC acknowledges "in a spirit of repentance and reconciliation" that there were "organizational governance decisions and personnel issues" between "our mutual founding fathers and mothers in the faith."[28] After mentioning the respective dissolutions and their dates, each statement declares that OBSC "eagerly invites the Holy Spirit to examine its past and present, exposing any sin, offense, stronghold of the enemy, or unforgiven and unhealed wound of division that might hinder the flow of God's river."[29] Finally, the statement asks forgiveness of the parent group for its actions:

> When, in the separation of organization and the breaking of fellowship, we said things and did things to sin against, to offend, and to hurt the men and women of. . . and the Body of Christ, which is His Church. Open Bible recognizes the providence of God in many streams flowing out of His river, and multiple branches growing out of His Root. But we reject spirits of competition and sectarianism, and affirm our unity in the Body of Christ. We are one in Christ, and by the grace of God declare our intent to walk in love and mutual support for the advancement of Christ and His Kingdom.[30]

In the case of the ICFG response to the actions of the ministers in the midwest, the Statement to the ICFG recalls that its leadership responded to the departure by saying, "Let us continue with our eyes on the Lord and see if He doesn't heal this breach."[31]

The president of AFM, Rev. Dwight L. Baltzell, was not able to personally attend the convention as had been hoped. He did send a letter of response, read by Farmer.[32] Baltzell's comments on behalf of AFM were generally words of forgiveness and blessing. Neither Farmer nor Baltzell made reference to specific actions or personalities, other than the separation itself. Dr. John R. Holland, then president of ICFG, was present and spoke words of blessing and forgiveness, remarking that God was doing a work of reconciliation in the Body of Christ, of which this is a part. He made reference to wounds from an "attempted abortion" on the ICFG movement as it was being born, not only in this instance, but also via the events of earlier years, including 1901, 1906, and 1927. He asked forgiveness on behalf of ICFG for actions related to that "woundedness." He considered himself a "shirt-tail relative that came to a family reunion" at the convention, and presented a plaque to OBSC on behalf of the ICFG Board,[33] expressing fellowship and common heritage and callings of the two movements.

This series of gestures between OBSC and their immediate Pentecostal ancestry is not even close to a reunion of churches. Nothing was said about credential transferability or pulpit sharing agreements, or any organizational ramifications of these expressions. Certainly one should expect to see greater understanding, fellowship, and cooperation in the aftermath of this, whatever that might look like. But in a distinctly Pentecostal way, these overtures can be seen to reflect a similar spirit as that which motivated the lifting of sixteenth century anathemas between various historic Protestant churches, and between those churches and the Catholic Church, in recent years.

Horizons: What OBSC Will Look Like in 25 Years?

OBSC will, it is hoped, be a vital organ in the Body of Christ. The form that the fulfillment of this prophetic pronouncement will take is contingent upon several factors discussed below, within the context of parameters connected to OBSC's DNA (mission, vision, core beliefs, and values). The following are questions for consideration, both here and beyond the scope of this writing:

- In what way will OBSC be seen to be a Pentecostal organization? What distinctly Pentecostal characteristics will OBSC manifest? Granted that OBSC derived from Apostolic Faith (Crawford) and Foursquare (McPherson) roots, does current OBSC culture reflect those parents, or a reaction to them, or both, or neither?
- Unity within diversity: how much mutual respect, cooperation, and multiculturalism can OBSC accept? Will it remain one denomination or disintegrate into five even smaller ones?
- Is OBSC doing more burying than marrying? Is there an inordinate number of churches closing (or needing to close)?
- Can OBSC develop an integrated approach to training ministers and leaders that affects the whole movement? Many of the movement's Bible colleges have closed, and yet EBC's reception across the organization has often been lukewarm. An alternative training approach, Institute for Theology by Extension (INSTE), has been launched, but it maintains clear ongoing distinction from EBC. The credentialing process within the movement often does not clearly correlate training and preparation of ministers with denominational training options.[34]
- Is OBSC a movement that embraces apostolic and prophetic offices and giftings? In what way? Will the return to relationship with the Elim movement be embraced denomination-wide?
- Is the current denominational debate over a restructuring of the organization (centralization vs. decentralization) simply a desire to re-distribute funds? Or are there other compelling reasons (such as finding more effective ways to fulfill OBSC's mission) to keep pushing until the movement takes on a new structure?[35]
- Does OBSC have respect for top-level leaders, or is there within its DNA a disdain for hierarchical leadership that results in a reactionary overcorrection? Does this indicate that there are issues of trust (forgiveness)? How is this issue related to the call for restructuring?[36]

• Is there a denominational psychological complex over its size? OBSC is relatively small. Like the Avis car rental commercials, do they try harder? Should they? Are they jealous of their bigger/older brothers? Has their history of losing key leaders to other movements, through proselytism or otherwise, colored their sense of identity?

While these and other tough questions must be processed, mention should be made of what are likely to be some the clear, distinctive contributions OBSC will be making to the Body of Christ in the decades to come:

• Leadership: OBSC has begun to influence the development of leaders among Pentecostals and Evangelicals in the United States and around the world on a scale beyond its current denominational size. The non-traditional training program INSTE, developed and led by Drs. Leona and Nick Venditti, is being utilized in over thirty nations, and by over a dozen denominations and church groups outside of OBSC. Paul Leavenworth[37] has been a resource for leadership development, teaching and implementing strategy after the model of his mentor Robert Clinton, in numerous movements and organizations in the United States and elsewhere. This favor with other Christian groups is likely to continue in the coming years.
• Ecumenical Participation: OBSC president Jeff Farmer has emerged as a sought-after resource and executive leader among cooperative groups including Mission America, the Sentinel Group, NAE, PCCNA, and the newly forming Christian Churches Together in the USA. For many years OBSC has been sending official delegates to a variety of ecumenical endeavors, including the international Roman Catholic–Pentecostal dialogue. The organization's openness should allow for continuing influence in such circles.
• Church planting: OBSC has prioritized church planting in the last decade, and has been involved in the transfer of resources from dying churches to new church plants in the United States. This focus on the planting of new churches is somewhat of a return to its revival roots, and should bear fruit for decades to come.
• Soul-winning: under Farmer, the movement's core value of evangelism has returned to greater prominence. The extent of his success in helping OBSC to recapture a passion for soul-winning remains to be seen.
• Missions: OBSC has always had more churches outside of the United States than inside. A recent movement among

OBSC youth has produced a rise in short-term missions endeavors. The National Youth office's Global Outreaches Unlimited program, headed by Rob Leitheiser, has had a significant affect on the culture of the next generation of OBSC leaders.

• Training models: Paul Leavenworth has coordinated an emphasis on multiple and overlapping models of leadership development in OBSC. EBC, INSTE, and church-based training centers (such as Master's Commissions) are working together and assisting one another in a more complimentary way than has been characteristic of the movement in the past. Leavenworth is also building training partnerships with Youth With A Mission (YWAM) and other parachurch groups, enabling OBSC to resource itself and overcome a sense of ingrownness.

• OBSC has intentionally addressed the role of women in denominational leadership, and at its 2003 national convention adopted a position paper strongly endorsing the desire to see women functioning at all levels of leadership. This too is seen as a return to its revival roots, as there were many women playing significant roles as pastors, evangelists, church planters and missionaries in the early decades of the movement, following after the models provided by leadership in prior organizations (e.g., Crawford, McPherson).

• Doctrinal flexibility: although some might see this as a weakness, OBSC has shown that it is willing to adjust the way it emphasizes doctrinal distinctives for the sake of clear communication and reaching new generations for Christ. At the 2003 national convention a revised version of the Articles of Faith was approved. Among the more significant changes in articulation involved the doctrines of the Baptism in the Holy Spirit (classical language updated while affirming the experience) and Eschatology (specific millennial and tribulational views deleted).[38] OBSC may prove to become pacesetters in such matters, able to adapt more quickly than older, larger, more institutionalized organizations.

• Even the restructure issue may eventually be seen as a distinctly Pentecostal return to the grass roots, and bring new life to OBSC and its Pentecostal relatives in coming decades.

Several current Open Bible national leaders were recently asked to consider the future of Pentecostalism from an Open Bible perspective.[39] Paul Leavenworth sees strategic partnerships as key to Open Bible's future, and recently outlined eight different levels of ongoing partnership emerging between OBSC and YWAM.[40] They include, but are not limited to the following:

- cooperative short-term missions ventures involving denomi-
  national children and youth
- exchanges of speakers (OBSC leaders speaking in YWAM
  venues and vice versa)
- OBSC youth attending YWAM Discipleship Training
  Schools (DTSs)
- OBSC developing its own DTSs after YWAM's model
- YWAM alums pastoring or interning in OBSC churches
- Cooperative evangelistic outreaches involving YWAM and
  OBSC in small mid-west cities

Leavenworth's thoughts on OBSC's future have been shaped by the works of Philip Jenkins (*The Next Christendom*) and Donald Miller (*Reinventing American Protestantism*). He accepts Jenkins's assertions that the center of emerging Christianity is outside of the West, and is predominantly evangelical with emphases on the reliability of the Bible, the power of the Holy Spirit, and the social impact of the gospel. He agrees with Miller's picture of the church transitioning toward Bible-centered teaching, contemporary worship styles, active laity, tolerance of personal differences, use of spiritual gifts, and creativity.

Against this backdrop Leavenworth sees OBSC adapting and changing in the next twenty-five years in the following ways:

From	To
Senior Pastor	Equipping Pastor
Board	Team
Building	Community
Programs	Mentoring/Discipleship
Size	Multiplication/Church Planting
Male	Male/Female
Vocational	Bi-vocational
Monocultural	Multicultural
Organization/denomination	Relationship/Network
Formal training	Non/informal training

Leavenworth sees multiple models of healthy churches emerging in OBSC in the next twenty-five years, generally characterized by the above "To" qualities. Current churches unwilling or unable to adapt "From" to "To" will continue to decline, and eventually be replaced by new ministries and church plants guided by an emerging generation of young leaders. He sees apostolic church networks emerging out of OBSC, and while such networks often grow independent of their original denominations, some will remain connected to OBSC and will serve as denominational "orders" after the manner of those that have maintained their relationship to the Roman Catholic Church over the centuries.

Of course, all of this shifting will occur in the context of tension which will cause some to disassociate themselves from OBSC, while others grow to appreciate wider expressions of gifts and offices, including those more apostolic, prophetic, and evangelistic. Such adaptation will enable OBSC to find a way to stay connected to its revival roots, with a (hopefully) large remnant finding a fruitful future. Seeing the considerable change that is needed and coming, Leavenworth would describe himself as "pessimistically optimistic about the future of Open Bible."[41]

OBSC president Jeff Farmer[42] shares a concern that the movement not losing its emphasis on the Baptism and gifts of the Holy Spirit, and would describe that possibility as a challenge and even a threat to the movement. He sees OBSC fulfilling its prophetic mandate to be a vital organ in the body of Christ, including becoming more and more a prophetic voice to the rest of the Church, just as he sees Pentecostals in general taking a stronger leadership role. There is evidence of such in his own life, including his appointments to leadership roles in various interdenominational groups (NAE, PCCNA, CCTUSA, Mission America). Farmer would see parallels between these opportunities for service he has accepted and similar ones that others from Pentecostal-charismatic families have experienced, including Lamar Vest's role as board chairman of the American Bible Society, and the appointment of Bob Burt (OBSC) as Chief of Chaplains for the U.S. Navy.

Farmer sees OBSC as becoming more flexible in structure, maintaining a continuum between old and new wineskins (ministry styles and philosophies). He sees a continuing and increasing diversity among OBSC's churches and ministries, as for the sake of evangelism ministries connect with skateboarders, cowboys, sports bars, and other sub-cultural groups. The denomination's future rests in its ability to serve and resource churches to become healthy and vital.[43]

Paul Canfield sees Pentecostal identity becoming less denominationally oriented and more loose-knit, connected relationally around common goals. [44] That will increasingly affect missions enterprises, as missionaries will receive the bulk of their support from individual churches and small clusters of churches rather than from the denomination as a whole. Training for ministry will become more hands-on and mentoring based. A number of large churches will spring forth from the movement and its churches in general will grow stronger and healthier, but the movement will not attain growth to the level of a large denominational organization. A classically Pentecostal identity will give way to a more general understanding of being "Spirit-filled people" who seek new and fresh expressions of experiences of the Spirit.[45]

Ross Adelmann sees the challenge facing OBSC and other Pentecostal groups who desire to survive the next quarter century (in a significant and effective way) to be related to paradigm changes in the surrounding culture that require change, and OBSC's ability to make successful transitions. [46] Adelmann's short list of necessary transitions includes:

1. Seeing the move and manifestations of the Holy Spirit not as occurring primarily for the "purpose of transforming individuals, but rather for the purpose of forming growing, multiplying communities of people moving in the mission of God." Adelmann critiques Pentecostal theology as being warped by rationalism and individual autonomy, resulting in an exclusionary focus on a) the power of knowledge resulting in conflict over being right; b) salvation and healing on a personal level without adequate regard for community implications; c) exaltation of correct, rational doctrine over lived out results; and, d) too strong a focus on moments in time rather than transformative processes. Vital Pentecostalism in twenty-five years will see each of these primary and secondary foci reversed.

2. A theology of leadership that moves from the focus on an individualized hearing of the voice of God (Moses on the mountaintop) and casting of vision to that of a leader who cultivates vision and leads the community in vision discovery—team leadership will become more prominent as the primary leader becomes a poet of vision empowering the community toward mission involvement, replacing a 20th century model of Pentecostal leadership that has more often than not been focused on a leader-centered church and authoritarian pronouncement.

3. Social transformation as the outcome of mission—this partly involves discerning the work of the Holy Spirit among non-Christians and beginning the discipleship process through relationship that enables non-Christian people to be involved in the mission of being Good News even before they have crossed the threshold of praying the sinner's prayer or being baptized. As was true in the earlier centuries of the Church, baptism will once again become the recognized point of demarcation, as the process of transformation (focusing on the priesthood of all believers and meaningful incorporation into the Body of Christ) becomes prioritized over moments of decision.

Adelmann challenges OBSC to "truly relearn a way of depending on the leading and the power of the Holy Spirit rather than living in our reactions to excess and our attempts to catch up with organizational paradigms of the 1980s and 1990s."[47]

The movement continues to walk through the sometimes painful process of identifying who it is and where it is going. The February 2004 national Strategic Prayer and Planning sessions in Des Moines (a biennial event) brought together over thirty national leaders and a number of pastors to consider issues of direction. A major initiative emerging from those discussions was the recommendation that a special meeting of all five regional boards of directors meet together for the purpose of considering restructuring possibilities for the organization. Later that same month, the OBSC national board approved a motion to create a restructure task force, and to bring the five boards together as was recommended.

In March 2005 the meeting of the five regional boards took place in Orlando, Florida. This event was preceded by a November 2004 session of prayer and fasting carried out by the national officers of OBSC and their spouses. Out of the November event emerged a document entitled *Open Bible Churches Proclamation on Family Unity, Trust, Respect and Authority.*[48] The document seems to have been intended to prepare the way for whatever restructuring journey the movement was embarking on, while challenging constituents to respect the movement's heritage and walk through change in a right spirit.

The March 2005 gathering in Orlando included a session during which the November proclamation was read to the thirty-seven regional leaders present, with an invitation to sign the document as an expression of covenant relationship. Most, but not all, of those present signed the document. The discussions themselves were meant to offer an opportunity to express priorities and values that could be passed along to the restructure task force that had been appointed. The major point of consensus at the gathering was the call for a considerable decentralization of OBSC programs and ministries. It was recommended that leadership and funding for major areas of ministry be moved closer to OBSC's grass-roots (regional, district, and local church levels). Areas specifically identified included Youth, Children's, Men's, Women's, and Development departments, but the general flavor of the recommendation was that anything that can be decentralized should be.

How (and whether) such restructuring will be accomplished remains to be seen. A timeline was established allowing for the restructure task force, national board, regional boards, and national convention to process potential changes. Ultimately, OBSC bylaws were to be rewritten to reflect major changes, and the process was scheduled to culminate in discussion and formal action on the floor of the 2007 national convention in Spokane, WA.

It is also not known how any changes will affect OBSC's ongoing mission. OBSC's stated mission is to make and release disciples, plant churches, and send missionaries. Any organizational restructuring would presumably be for the purpose of more effectively accomplishing that mission. In any event the process seems to indicate two things: that OBSC is dissatisfied with its current level of effectiveness in fulfilling its God-given mandate, and that it is willing to ask difficult questions and take painful steps in order to address that relative lack of effectiveness. In all of this, OBSC wants to posture itself to participate more fully in advancing the Kingdom of God in the years to come.

In a certain sense the movement is showing the same willingness to ask painful questions and consider significant change that characterized the actions of its forebears during the seasons that produced the Bible Standard Mission and Open Bible Evangelistic Association. And it appears that the same values and priorities are being reemphasized: when it is time to more effectively accomplish mission, a move toward decentralization is a part of the corrective process. In 1919 and 1932 the decisions to resist strong central authority resulted in two new movements. It remains to be seen where the current clear call for decentralization will lead. Indeed, a question that was raised, but not answered, at the March 2005 gathering was "Are we five, or are we one?" Decentralization of leadership and resources will likely either result in enough breathing room to add life and health to the movement and thus strengthen it, or it will cause further disengagement from the center to the point that portions of the current denominational roster detach and become entities unto themselves. In any case OBSC appears to be on a course of significant change.

OBSC seems to be finding ways to face its history as it continues to establish its future. As an association formed in 1935, it is a second-generation Pentecostal group whose founders spent up to three decades in other Pentecostal families. Thus it has struggled to find and maintain clarity with regard to identity and mission. From its very beginning it has seen and reacted to conflict and controversy (e.g., Dowie, Crawford, McPherson). In its quest for survival it has formed strategic alliances with those it trusted, and possibly on whose coattails it could ride (e.g., NAE, PFNA, Assemblies of God). Along the way, the movement may at times have sacrificed its own sense of identity while adopting the safer positions of its strategic partners, and correspondingly rejecting causes and groups that were politically/doctrinally incorrect (e.g., ecumenical movement, LRM). That loss of self-assuredness was exacerbated by the choice of some pastors, leaders, and churches to leave the denomination. In more recent years OBSC has attempted to embrace a stronger sense of its unique role in the Body of Christ and the Pentecostal movement, and in so doing it has sought to rebuild some broken bridges from its past (with ICFG, AFM, Elim), while at the same time moving into its future with a growing belief that it could make a vital contribution in God's Kingdom. It continues to struggle as a movement with issues of territorialism (including the debate over the relative centralization of administrative leadership) that is the residue of both the original amalgamation and the congregational polity that was part of the package. To the extent that OBSC continues to face each of these challenges with positive and healthy responses, it will demonstrate maturity as a movement, and more solidly establish and clarify its mission and identity.

Notes

1. Open Bible Standard Churches (OBSC throughout this chapter), headquartered in Des Moines, IA, has officially been doing business as Open Bible Churches since 2001 by national convention action, to the dismay of some ministers from the Pacific region, whose Bible Standard Churches merged with the Open Bible Evangelistic Association in 1935. The reaction of some ministers with Bible Standard roots was that "they just took the 'standard' out of Open Bible."

2. The title of this writing is inspired by the official history of the movement written by R. Bryant Mitchell entitled *Heritage and Horizons: The History of Open Bible Standard Churches* (Des Moines: Open Bible, 1982). For the history of the movement from 1982 to 2007, see the forthcoming *Heart for the Harvest: A 25 Year Biographical History of Open Bible Churches 1982–2007*, ed. Jeffrey E. Farmer and Andrea P. Johnson, to be published by Open Bible Publishers (Des Moines, IA), due out in 2008.

3. Some sections of this writing are adapted from "Open Bible Churches: Forging an Identity Out of Conflict and Cooperation," a paper presented by David Cole at the 33rd Annual Meeting of the Society for Pentecostal Studies at Marquette University on March 13, 2004, along with material found in "Pentecostal Koinonia: An Emerging Ecumenical Ecclesiology Among Pentecostals," unpublished dissertation by David Cole, Fuller Theological Seminary, 1998.

4. Hornshuh and his associates had grown discontent under Crawford's leadership in the following ways: 1) an isolationism, which "resisted and in some cases prohibited fellowship with other full gospel groups;" 2) unkind treatment of those with whom differences arose, often leading to dismissal without hearing; 3) a rigid stand on divorce and remarriage (including requiring remarried persons to renounce the second marriage and return to original mates); 4) centralized authority, which included required attendance of all pastors at a three month summer tent meeting; and though they would not admit it in writing, these men were "chafing under what they thought was feminine domination." See Mitchell, *Heritage and Horizons*, 41–42.

5. Two primary reasons are given for the separation of these ministers from ICFG. First, they were not prepared to surrender their church property titles to the Los Angeles headquarters, which the ICFG leadership then was requiring. Second, they were concerned about the 1931 remarriage of the divorced McPherson. See Mitchell, *Heritage and Horizons*, 145–148. For further information on both groups, see Wayne E. Warner, "Open Bible Standard Churches, Inc.," in the *New International Dictionary of the Pentecostal and Charismatic Movements* (NIDPCM), 945–946. Synan cites John Thomas Nichol (*Pentecostalism* (New York: Harper and Row, 1966), 144–145) in support of his contention that the main reason for the departure of the Iowa ministers was the kidnapping controversy surrounding McPherson ("One permanent outcome of the adverse publicity surrounding the alleged kidnapping was the creation of yet another Pentecostal denomination," and again, Richey led a break "mainly because of the kidnapping incident. . . ." Synan, *The Holiness-Pentecostal Tradition*, 202–203). However, not only does the official history of OBSC (Mitchell) not mention this, but McPherson's most successful campaigns in Iowa took place in 1927 and 1928, after the kidnapping aftermath had largely subsided.

6. Another factor that may have been overlooked has to do with the pre-history of the denomination. Both Hornshuh and Richey have a connection to John Alexander

Dowie's Zion movement. Hornshuh's is more direct, in that he spent two years at Zion College from 1904–06, after having been influenced by the miraculous healings of his brother and sister through the healing prayers of Zion ministers. Hornshuh was said to be "head and heels, heart and soul, mind and body in sympathy with Zion." He was called to ministry at a Zion prayer meeting before joining AFM upon experiencing baptism in the Holy Spirit at one of their camp meetings. He remained with AFM for a decade.

Richey's connection is less direct. The family of his cousin, evangelist Raymond T. Richey (who was later influential in bringing Hornshuh and John Richey together), was intimately involved in Zion's ministry, impacting a generation of Richeys who entered Pentecostal ministry, possibly including John, who was raised in Kentucky and prepared for ministry at LIFE Bible College in Los Angeles. With young Hornshuh still being shaped for ministry while at Zion during its unraveling, and Richey undoubtedly hearing from his family about both the glory days and the demise of Dowie and Zion, the hard lessons learned provide a context for the similar decisions of both at a later date to lead their factions away from strong, charismatic leaders, and for the choice to work together. See Gordon Gardiner, *Out of Zion Into All the World* (Shippensburg, PA: Companion Press, 1990), 101–103.

7. The Accrediting Association of Bible Colleges is now known as the Association for Biblical Higher Education (ABHE).

8. A third, current territorial issue has to do with whether to fund a full-time National Youth Director, or to use OBSC dollars for decentralized youth programs in each of the regions. Issues related to centralized vs. decentralized leadership are ongoing in the movement. For a more detailed treatment of the history of EBC and its merger with OBC, see Chad Davidson's unpublished master's thesis at Oral Roberts University (2005) entitled "Firm Foundations—A Mandate for Generations: the Early History of Eugene Bible College."

9. From 1948 through 1958, OBSC leaders R. Bryant Mitchell, Everett J. Fulton and Frank W. Smith served as either board members or executive officers each year. Smith served as PFNA chairman in the 1960s. See Darrel Klink, "The Pentecostal Fellowship of North America's Ministry of Administration," unpublished master's thesis, Melodyland School of Theology, 1976, 67–72; and Wayne Warner, "Smith, Frank W.," NIDPCM, 1076. That trend of participation and leadership has continued to some extent over the years. Ray Smith provided leadership in the PFNA and NAE for two decades until his retirement in 1995, and Jeff Farmer has been involved and influential in the PCCNA and NAE since then. Under Farmer's leadership, OBSC has moved beyond traditional cooperation in NAE and PCCNA circles. OBSC has either sent Farmer or an official delegate to gatherings such as Mission America, World and National Council of Churches (WCC, NCCC) Faith and Order consultations with Pentecostals, the international Roman Catholic/Pentecostal Dialogue, the recently formed Evangelical/Catholic (U.S. Conference of Catholic Bishops) dialogue, and the newly forming Christian Churches Together in the USA (CCTUSA).

10. At the time, two brothers were in top levels of leadership in the organizations. Frank Smith was pastor of OBSC's flagship church in Des Moines and a national officer, and his brother, R.D.E. Smith, was in executive leadership with the Assemblies of God.

11. There is no written documentation known to the writer for this occurrence. Several former national OBSC leaders have rehearsed the incident with current OBSC pastors and leaders. Three former OBSC leaders and a former Assemblies of God leader are reported to have been present for the private meeting in the 1970s when the prophetic

word was given. Times of repentance among OBSC ministers for rejecting its prophets have occurred at recent regional conferences and national conventions.

12. Menzies, *Anointed to Serve: The Story of the Assemblies of God* (Springfield: Gospel Publishing House, 1971), 321–322.

13. Menzies, *Anointed to Serve*, 322. See also Richard Riss, "The Latter Rain Movement of 1948," in *Pneuma: The Journal of the Society for Pentecostal Studies* (Spring 1982), 32–45.

14. A series of corrective articles appeared in *The Pentecostal Evangel*, and the Assemblies' General Council adopted a resolution in 1949 disapproving of the practices of the LRM, specifying six errors, including the overemphasis on and abuse of impartation via laying on of hands, and the idea that the Church is built on modern-day apostles and prophets. Menzies, *Anointed to Serve*, 324–325.

15. Spencer fully embraced the renewal elements of the "visitation," although he later admitted that he failed to see the extremism some LRM promoters were carrying with them to Pentecostal churches. Elim leaders resumed active involvement in the PFNA a few years later. See Marion Meloon, *Ivan Spencer: Willow in the Wind* (Lima, N.Y.: Elim Bible Institute, 1997), 166–167.

16. Willard H. Pope, "Strange Voices," *Message of the Open Bible* (July-August 1949), 6. See also S. B. Fowler, "A Word From Evangelist Fowler," and Frank W. Smith, "The Revival We Need!" both in *Message of the Open Bible* (September 1949), 2, 5.

17. E. J. Fulton, "Here and There with the General Chairman," *Message of the Open Bible* (December 1949), 15.

18. On the emphases on freedom from fanaticism, see *Policies and Principles*: Amendments through June 2005, published for ministers by Open Bible Churches, 2–3. The article on moderation that had been included in the Articles of Faith was removed after the 2003 national convention.

19. Six months after Fulton's fairly formal public words of correction, OBSC printed a sermon by one of its own leaders strongly advocating "Progressive Revelation for Last Day Revival." See L. E. Welshons, *Message of the Open Bible* (June 1950), 10–13.

20. Sources for this listing include the *Message of the Open Bible*, Mitchell's *Heritage and Horizons*, OBSC credential files, EBC alumni files, and EBC archives.

21. Zelma Argue (daughter of Pentecostal pioneers in Canada; an editor for OBSC *Messenger* in 1920s); Hart Armstrong (EBC dean and EBSC missionary/publisher; left for Assemblies of God in 1940s); Hubert Mitchell (OBSC missionary in 1940s; later worked with ICFG and Youth for Christ); Lottie Anthony (Lighthouse Temple musician/EBC faculty member; became noted Assemblies of God music minister).

22. Bob DeWeese (key pastor and denominational leader); Ron Smith (son of OBSC leader Frank Smith, staff pastor at First OBC in Des Moines); Billy Willard (former OBSC pastor and evangelist, president of Dayton Bible College); Everett J. Fulton (former OBSC general superintendent, EBC/DBC president); Phil Rounds (former OBSC missionary to Japan); Byron Whisler (former pastor at Calvary Temple), and others.

23. Chuck Smith (held OBSC local church credential in CA prior to starting Calvary Chapel movement); Casey Treat (approved for OBSC credentials, never accepted them; became an independent pastor); Wayne Cordeiro (EBC grad/former OBSC minister; became an ICFG pastor/church planter); Eastman Curtis (former OBSC minister; developed an independent TV ministry to youth).

24. Everett P. Fulton (former OBSC national youth director and OBC president; became professor of philosophy and religious studies at University of Wisconsin-

Whitewater); Roger Olson (OBC graduate, more recently professor of theology at Truett Theological Seminary, Baylor University); Wayne Warner (EBC graduate and OBSC pastor; became director of Flower Pentecostal Heritage Center). For some of Olson's personal reflections on his experiences in (and critique of) his former denomination, see Roger E. Olson, "Pentecostalism's Dark Side," in *Christian Century* (March 7, 2006), 27–30, and also Stanley J. Grenz and Roger E. Olson, *Who Needs Theology? An Invitation to the Study of God*, 136–140.

25. Danny Thomas (former pastor of First OBC in Des Moines); Mark Royer (former pastor of Lighthouse Temple, Eugene, OR); Paul Brown (former pastor of Lighthouse Temple, Eugene, OR); Don Lyon (former OBSC pastor in Rockford, IL).

26. Leif Malmin (former key pastor and evangelist; more recently with Ministers Fellowship International); Andy Clark (former missionary; more recently with Ministers Fellowship International); Scott LeLaCheur (EBC graduate, son/grandson of prominent OBSC leaders; more recently with Church on the Rock); Scott Wood (EBC graduate, son of EBC president/OBSC director of world missions; became an ICFG pastor); Nathan Poetzl (EBC graduate from an OBSC church in Iowa, more recently a Seattle-area ICFG pastor); and others.

27. In acknowledging the pain of these lost leaders, at its national convention in 1997 OBSC spent some thirty minutes of a prayer service mentioning the names of those whose loss was felt by one of the ministers or delegates. A microphone was used for the name to be spoken, without any description of why the person was no longer in OBSC.

28. "Statement of Reconciliation," sent to Rev. Dwight L. Baltzell, president of the AFM, Portland, OR, approved by the national board of directors of OBSC, signed on June 27, 1997. Also "Statement of Reconciliation," approved by the national board of directors of OBSC, presented to Dr. John R. Holland, president of ICFG, at the OBSC national convention in Eugene, OR, on June 27, 1997. Found in Cole, "Pentecostal Koinonia," 326–327.

29. "Statement of Reconciliation," in Cole, "Pentecostal Koinonia," 326–327.

30. "Statement of Reconciliation," in Cole, "Pentecostal Koinonia," 326–327.

31. These words were written to John and Louise Richey by Harriet Jordan, then vice-president of ICFG, soon after the ministers from the Midwest notified ICFG of their intent to leave, on September 9, 1932. See Mitchell, *Heritage and Horizons*, 148.

32. Baltzell's letter included some of the following remarks: ". . . Naturally, a parting of ways among God's people is painful. . . Whether something more on our part could have been done, we would have no way of knowing. Hopefully every attempt was made during those days, so that there could be reconciliation. . . after these efforts were made by both parties, (if) there remained a lack of unity in the leadership, then indeed the best course of action was chosen, to separate, rather than to cause further disruption. At this time, we will state that we (AFM) unanimously hold no ill will towards any member of (OBSC) whatsoever. And if there is anything that needed forgiving, we grant it fully and completely. . . ." Read at the OBSC national convention, Eugene, OR, June 27, 1997. See Cole, "Pentecostal Koinonia," 252–253.

33. The plaque's inscription included the following: "We commend. . . the leadership and churches of OBSC recognizing that we are the children of a common revival. Grateful for our shared heritage. . . and united by the Holy Spirit in common fellowship, we. . . covenant ourselves with OBSC in prayer, and the sharing of our mutual faith, love, and hope, as it seeks to fulfill its God-given ministry assignment in the power of the Holy Spirit and the communion of the saints."

34. For further consideration on OBSC's struggle to come to terms with the relationship between Church and Academy as it seeks to fulfill its mission, see David Cole, "Telling the Pentecostal Story: A Brief Essay on Challenges Facing a Denomination," presented at a Wabash University-sponsored colloquium on Resourcing Pentecostalism held at the Assemblies of God Seminary in Springfield, MO April 16–17, 2004, in conjunction with festivities honoring Wayne Warner on the occasion of his pending retirement as Executive Director of the Flower Pentecostal Heritage Center.

35. For an honest sharing of the struggle of a denominational leader to properly respond to a call for organizational restructure, see Jeff Farmer's three pages-long "Restructure Open Bible?" in *Jeff's Journal: Insider Notes, News, Trends, and Resources from the President's Office* (December 2004/January 2005). An update on the restructure process was printed in the October/November 2006 issue of the same publication.

36. As of January 2007 the OBC national board of directors had released the following ten recommendations for denominational restructure to be presented on the convention floor in June 2007 in Spokane, WA: 1) Recognizing mission and vision originate with the local church, the President, elected at a duly called meeting of the Association, is empowered to influence, inspire, encourage, and partner with regions to help churches accomplish mission and vision. 2) The "how to" question of accomplishing mission should be left to the local churches in partnership with the Regional Superintendent and Regional Board. 3) The National Board shall be composed of up to 17 members, but no less than 13. The 13 are as currently configured, with the five, regionally appointed members still being selected by the Regional Boards. The four additional at-large positions (not required to be seated but as needed) would be selected by the members of the National Board. The National Board shall ensure and make provision for ethnic, gender, and emerging leader representation. 4) Regional Superintendents shall be appointed by the President in consultation with the Regional Board, approved by a 2/3 vote of the National Board and ratified by 2/3 of the votes received from credentialed ministers residing in their respective regions. The ministerial vote shall be conducted by mail. 5) Regional board members shall be selected in accordance with the bylaws of each region and ratified by the National Board. 6) The national office will be downsized to ensure missional effectiveness and focus, one goal of which is to generate additional funding for local church health. 7) In keeping with the Open Bible commitment to missional effectiveness, at every level of the Association accountability to mission will be measured. (Local church - by the region; Region - by the President and National Board; President - by the National Board and duly called meeting of the Association) 8) Streamline the governing documents, i.e., separate policy and procedure from the constitution and bylaws. 9) Effective January 1, 2009, all credentialed Open Bible ministers send one-half of their tithe on salary and housing allowance to Open Bible Churches and one-half remains in the local church. 10) The Executive Director of International Ministries shall be appointed by the President in consultation with the Board of International Ministries and ratified by a 2/3 vote of the National Board.

37. Since 1997 Paul Leavenworth has served OBSC as the Executive Director of Leadership Development and Church Ministries.

38. *Policies and Principles*, Articles of Faith, 4–7.

39. Questionnaires were sent to seventeen regional and national leaders in November 2004. Four responses were received.

40. Paul Leavenworth, "Partnership Between OBC and YWAM," *Message of the Open Bible* 87, no. 6 (November-December 2004), 8.

41. Paul Leavenworth, correspondence with the author, December 1, 2004.

42. Jeff Farmer has served as president of OBSC since 1995. He previously served as president of Eugene Bible College for nearly eight years.

43. Jeff Farmer, phone interview with the author, November 17, 2004.

44. After serving as an OBSC missionary to Mexico and El Salvador and as OBSC's Latin America field director, Paul Canfield has served as OBSC's Director of International Ministries for over 25 years.

45. Paul Canfield, correspondence with the author, December 21, 2004.

46. Since 1998 Ross Adelmann has been the Assistant to the Pacific Region Superintendent for OBSC, with responsibilities for Church Health, Church Planting, and Leadership Development for a region of nearly 125 churches.

47. Ross Adelmann, correspondence with the author, December 15, 2004.

48. Available at the Open Bible Churches national office in Des Moines, IA.

Chapter 11

"Follow Peace With All:"
Future Trajectories of the Church of God in Christ

David D. Daniels, III

The twenty-first century provides the Church of God in Christ an opportunity to assert its role as a global denomination. On the global stage, the Church of God in Christ (COGIC) presents a brand of Pentecostalism that mediates some of the fault lines that fracture world Christianity. Various axes criss-cross global Pentecostalism, shaping the contours and content of the different ecclesial communities that constitute Pentecostalism. These axes include liberal/conservative, black/white, white/non-white, racial minority/majority, western/non-western, North/South, rich/poor, and national/global. COGIC is plotted on these axes in manner that defies the categories. For COGIC is a theologically conservative tradition that dialogues with theological liberals and liberationists as well as espouses a liberal political agenda; a black-run religious organization with a multi-racial global membership; a racial minority within the West that identifies with the two-third world majority; a non-white, yet western, denomination; a Northern-based denomination with a majority who reside or are descendents of the Southern hemisphere; a middle-class dominated hierarchy and majority denomination with a significant underclass sector; and a global Pentecostal denomination in a religious movement where the majority of denominations are national in scope.

Within global Pentecostalism, COGIC offers a different trajectory from Pentecostal denominations that conform to the categories of the axes. For instance, COGIC's U.S. white-led Pentecostal counterparts readily conform to these categories with their alliances to white evangelicalism and conservative politics whereas COGIC refuses to be confined to these categories, opting to defy or blend the categories to construct its ecclesial identity, organization, and vision. The role that COGIC will play as a global denomination in its defiance or bending of these categories is related to the ecclesial orbits in which COGIC lodges itself during the twenty-first century.[1]

Beyond North and South

The Church of God in Christ functions in the twenty-first century as a global Pentecostal denomination of approximately 4 million members, residing in over fifty-five nations, with its headquarters in North America. The countries with the largest concentration of COGIC congregations outside of the United States are Haiti, India, Liberia, South Africa, Nigeria, and Mexico. COGIC is a global denomination with its headquarters in United States and jurisdictions or dioceses on every continent. COGIC is a Northern-based denomination while the majority of the countries in which it operates are situated in the Southern hemisphere; more, the majority of its members either reside in or are descendents of the Southern hemisphere. The majority of the countries with a COGIC presence are either in Africa or a part of the global African diaspora. Interestingly, though, nearly a quarter of the countries in which COGIC has a presence are outside of Africa and the African diaspora.[2]

The nationality of COGIC membership on different continents varies according to the country. In Africa, the Caribbean, and Latin America, its members are all nationals. In Asia, its members in such countries as India, Sri Lanka, and the Philippines are also nationals, while most of the members in Japan and South Korea are African American expatriates or military families. The nationality of COGIC membership in certain countries is shaped by immigration. In Europe, Afro-Caribbeans and their British-born descendents are the majority in Great Britain, while Germany and Italy consist of U.S. military families. COGIC membership is also defined by various diasporas. The Jamaican diaspora defines COGIC congregations in Great Britain and Ontario (Canada); the Haitian diaspora shapes COGIC congregations in France, Quebec (Canada), and Florida (United States); the Asian Indian diaspora constitutes COGIC congregations in British Columbia (Canada) and Sri Lanka.[3]

COGIC plays various roles within global Pentecostalism by defying the North-South divide. On the global Pentecostal scene, COGIC was among the earliest Northern-based non-white missionary groups to establish missions and congregations in various regions of the southern hemisphere. By being a non-white global denomination that ministers and relates to people of color as people of color, COGIC anticipated the South-South mission focus. As a U.S. black-led organization, COGIC illustrates the mission-in-reverse movement wherein the people of color as former mission targets spearhead their own missions around the world. Since African Americans are westernized and northern, COGIC introduces another angle into the North-South paradigm. Instead of power issues evolving around the North-South schema constituted by whites and non-whites respectively, within COGIC globally the relationships are structured around African Americans as the North and non-African Americans as the rest of the world. The symbolic politics of these relationships has profound implications for COGIC and global Pentecostalism by shifting the racial axis away from white and non-white towards an ethnic axis of African American and others. As

COGIC moves further into the twenty-first century, this pattern will most likely continue. The impact of this pattern could be powerful as COGIC transgresses the North-South divide, symbolizing a new way of being ecclesial and Pentecostal.

Global yet National

COGIC's demography stands at the core of its globality with the variety of its countries and the diversity of its global membership. As a global organization, though, COGIC structures its ecclesial life around a center-periphery model. COGIC's U.S. sector, which is predominately African American, occupies the center, and COGIC's sectors in other countries constitute the periphery. Throughout the first decades of the twenty-first century, COGIC will need to redefine itself as global denomination in terms of its identity, leadership, and structure. COGIC's identity as a global denomination was formed during the first half of the twentieth century. During the 1910s COGIC began to expand globally. By 1955 COGIC included congregations in such countries as Haiti, Liberia, Canada, South Africa, and Great Britain.[4]

While COGIC grew both nationally and internationally during this time, it was the national growth that forged its identity. The transition from a southern to a national denomination within the United States was applauded as its greatest feat more than its transition from a national to a global denomination or an African American to a global multi-racial denomination. Within its parlance, COGIC refers to its officers as national officials and its denomination as the national church when speaking of COGIC as a global entity; these discrepancies have profound consequences. While holding positions in the international church, leaders are often myopic in scope, routinely advancing a U.S. national denominational agenda as the agenda of the general church. With the abolition of the episcopal entity, the Council of Foreign Bishops, during the 1960s, COGIC is void of a forum where the issues and concerns of non-U.S. jurisdictions or dioceses can be explored without being overwhelmed by the agenda of the U.S. constituency. Structurally, the Mission Department has served as the administrative home for the non-U.S. COGIC leaders, congregations, and jurisdictions. The denominational leadership of COGIC is also firmly within the hands of the U.S. church; the U.S. leaders occupy the vast majority of the current elected and appointed positions on the general church level. While there is an attempt to develop indigenous leadership in non-U.S. jurisdictions, the leadership of many jurisdictions that lie outside of the United States is in the hands of a significant number of U.S. leaders who serve as missionary bishops and supervisors (or the female counterpart to the bishop). In terms of racial dynamics, African Americans run COGIC's general church leadership. So, the non-U.S. COGIC leaders and congregations interface with this leadership in ways that are still unique for most people in the world.[5]

COGIC's global expanse is variously spurred by the mission programs of the General Church, the Women's Department, and mission-minded congregations and jurisdictions. While the triple-pronged approach lacks clear coordination, this approach fits the post-denominational focus on global ministry where congregations connect directly to particular sites of missional partnerships. During the first half of the twenty-first century COGIC will need to assess the various dimensions of its global ministry to provide support especially to countries that are outside of the partnership structure with congregations to support them morally, administratively, and financially. COGIC's character as a global denomination is variously hampered, therefore, by its preoccupation with the U.S. sector, its structural inability to incorporate the non-U.S. congregations into the general church, save the jurisdictions and Mission Department, and the unevenness of its support to COGIC global ministry.

What will be needed to change the structure, redefine the identity, or widen the scope to incorporate more fully the global COGIC reality is unclear. While COGIC's global reality is not a major agenda item at the beginning of the twenty-first century, it is also unclear whether it will become one in the near future. Even with the prominence of the U.S. national constituency in COGIC, COGIC still does challenge the national/global categorization. Whether "national" leaders within COGIC with real global perspectives and commitments can broaden the COGIC debate and scope waits to be seen. The reality of a global-focused zone with the U.S. COGIC sector bodes well for a restructuring of COGIC's national-global relationship. The implications on COGIC's global structure by such a restructuring of the national-global relationship are profound, fostering a global consciousness within COGIC's U.S. constituency who in general tend to be parochial. Yet COGIC will continue to expand globally during the twenty-first century because of the internal dynamics of the general church that initially produced the global thrust.

Beyond Racial Minority and Majority

With the African American constituency constituting the base of COGIC nationally (and globally), COGIC is identified as a faith of a racial minority group. COGIC has entered the twenty-first century in the fore-front of U.S. religious life as a vital organization whose U.S. membership had more than quadrupled since 1960. Having become the largest U.S. Pentecostal denomination during the late twentieth century as well as the second largest U.S. black religious body, it constitutes a dominant presence on the U.S. religious scene. With its sphere of influence extending beyond black America, COGIC has become a recognized institution in U.S. Protestantism, U.S. Pentecostalism, and urban religion. COGIC has a highly visible presence in the United States. While COGIC is clearly a racial minority's organization that confronts racial oppression, in certain arenas COGIC operates as a peer of the majority.[6]

COGIC's place within the Black Church re-enforces its identity as a racial minority movement. Yet as the Black Church functions as a major religious player on the U.S. political and religious scene, COGIC garners more social capital. In a way, COGIC's embrace of the Black Church has changed the Black Church as much as the Black Church has change COGIC. During the 1960s, the Black Church even shifted from defining itself in contradistinction to denominations similar to COGIC to redefining itself inclusive of COGIC and other black Pentecostal denominations. As a key referent, COGIC has participated in the neo-Pentecostalization of African American Christianity. COGIC has made pivotal contributions to the worship and devotional life of the Black Church, including the upbeat liturgical accent, gospel music and praise songs, percussive and rhythmic sound, religious dancing, and the liturgical responses of "hallelujah," "glory," "praise God," "thank you," and "yes, Lord." COGIC has become one of the primary cultural (and liturgical) referents for the identity of the Black Church; a pattern that is expected to continue throughout the early twenty-first century.[7]

COGIC's ecclesial location is a product of its denominational history and is the beneficiary of historical shifts within the United States. Socially, the shift from segregation to desegregation, prompted by the Civil Rights Movement, created new opportunities for the advancement of African Americans, including individual COGIC members, and black institutions such as COGIC. While the emergence of re-segregation has limited these opportunities, re-segregation has also heightened the role of COGIC as one of the most organized national (and global) religious institutions within the U.S. inner city and other urban quarters such as Los Angeles, Oakland, Philadelphia, Chicago, Detroit, Memphis, Milwaukee, Oakland, Dallas, Norfolk (VA), Portsmouth (VA), and Raleigh (NC). COGIC, however, has not achieved this level of influence in cities outside of the United States.

Economically, the doubling of the black middle class, with the opening of the economy to all races and the impact of equal employment opportunity and affirmative action laws during the desegregation of the U.S. society, has included much of the COGIC membership. With more disposal income, COGIC members have been able to utilize their financial resources for the benefit of the Church, especially the building of multi-million dollar edifices, funding of major congregational projects, and the support of global ministry. While the African American community is among the poorest communities in the United States, African Americans are still willing to share with others. During January of 2005, the COGIC presiding bishop, Gilbert Earl Patterson, led a campaign that raised nearly $500,000 to fund relief for the tsunami victims, with special attention to the East African victims. Through the Mission Department, Women's Department, and mission-minded congregation, COGIC supports missions, congregations, orphanages, and clinics. These initiatives join in the transfer of wealth from rich countries to poor countries.[8]

The isolation and entrenchment of the black underclass—though during an era when U.S. agricultural sector was heavily mechanized and U.S. industries either downsized, closed, or relocated as the economy became more service-based—has become a population to which some COGIC congregations have committed themselves as their ministry and underclass neighborhoods have become the location for many of these congregations.

Politically, the emergence of a critical mass of elected black officials during the post-civil rights era with the passing of the Voting Rights Act of 1964 has led to the election of COGIC political officials in addition to the cultivation of the COGIC electoral votes in local, state, and federal elections. For example, during his own presidency, William Clinton delivered addresses at two COGIC conferences. Geopolitically, the collapse of global communion and the subsequent end of the Cold War left the United States, the headquarters' country of COGIC and the home of the majority of COGIC members, as the lone superpower. With its political capital, COGIC can be a voice in U.S. foreign policy, especially regarding Africa and the Afro-Caribbean.

A model of the new COGIC global leader is the first assistant presiding bishop, Charles Edward Blake. Bishop Blake heads *Save Africa's Children*, a Christian relief agency with a commitment to serving the children left destitute by the AIDS pandemic in Africa. Blake is both the pastor of the 25,000-plus member West Angeles Church of God in Christ located in Los Angeles and the bishop of First Ecclesiastical Jurisdiction of Southern California, a diocese of 250-plus congregations. Since 2001, Blake has raised millions of dollars to provide support for 350 grassroots and faith-based projects, including 160 orphanages in Africa. Blake has also assisted over 90,000 AIDS-affected children through funds donated by congregations and individuals across various denominations along with the aid of federal dollars. Blake epitomized a new COGIC global leader who provides leadership on issues of global concern and addresses these global issues in substantive ways.[9]

In the twenty-first century, COGIC will have the opportunity to participate in shaping various arenas. Its racial minority status does limit COGIC in critical ways but its status as a major religious organization provides it access to the chambers of power that eluded the denomination during most of its first century. How well COGIC will navigate the political, economic, and cultural terrain remains an open question.

Beyond Conservative and Liberal

COGIC's theological discourse variously brings into conversation conservative theological concerns, liberal theological perspectives, and progressive political causes. Different COGIC quarters pursue different theological conversations. Some quarters rehearse classic COGIC theological concerns; some quarters debate the teachings of the Word of Faith movement; other quarters participate in the academic study of black theology. The theological gambit of COGIC includes black, womanist, liberationist, contextual, Africentric, and ecumenical theological perspectives along with the more widespread COGIC denominational theology. Classic COGIC theological concerns range from conversion, the holy life, the devotional life, and the anointing to the topics of the Trinity, ecclesiology, and Scripture. COGIC will continue to build upon the theological projects that have engaged COGIC.[10]

Various theological conversations have been pursued in different COGIC quarters. Since the 1970s, COGIC theological scholars have been in conversation with the black theology movement associated with James Cone, Jacquelyn Grant, Gayraud Wilmore, and others who dominated the theological scene within the Black Church. COGIC will definitely continue to engage contemporary black theological currents because COGIC's seminary is a member of the Interdenominational Theological Center, a major center of progressive, African American theological thought in Atlanta, Georgia. The first generation of COGIC theological scholars led by O.T. Jones, Jr., Ithiel Clemmons, James Tinney, Leonard Lovett, Adrienne Israel, Bennie Goodwin, Sherry DuPree, and George McKinney has led to the second generation of COGIC theological scholars that include Robert Franklin, Alonzo Johnson, Michelle Jacques Early, William James, Harold Bennett, Keri Leigh Day, Frederick Ware, and Eric Greaux. These scholars continue to craft a COGIC theological tradition that is in dialogue with black theology, womanist theology, liberation theology, and contextual theology but these scholars also strive to explore the elements within COGIC theological discourse.

As COGIC theological scholars create new moments within COGIC theology during the twenty-first century, their greatest contribution will probably be their crafting a Pentecostal theology whose conversation partners lie outside of fundamentalism and evangelicalism. Whereas white U.S. Pentecostalism holds white fundamentalist, evangelical, and Wesleyan theological discourse as its key interlocutors, COGIC designates black theology as its primary interlocutor. By providing an alternative theological stream with different sources than white U.S. Pentecostalism, for instance, COGIC contributes to the expansion of the theological categories and resources within global Pentecostalism and illustrates the variety of ways of doing theology. With liberation, economic justice, and racial equality being key themes, the COGIC theological conversation will join the voices of other Pentecostal communities with similar concerns.

COGIC's dialogue with black theology and participation in the evolution of black theology will continue further into the twenty-first century because the contemporary COGIC identity remains in the U.S. Black Church. Scholars have deemed COGIC as one of the seven historic black denominations. COGIC as a national U.S. denomination cooperates ecumenically with black denominations and congregations across the theological spectrum from conservative to liberal. COGIC has also embraced the larger ecumenical vision of Black Church, participating in local, state, and national ecumenical bodies. With the appointment of ecumenical officers who have the authorization to interact with ecumenical bodies such as the National Council of Churches and the World Council of Churches, COGIC's ecumenical participation will most likely increase during the twenty-first century.[11]

COGIC's identification with the Black Church also informs its social ethics and embrace of black Christian political activism. As the national leadership of the black community during early twenty-first century makes a complete transition from veterans of the civil rights movement, with strong linkages to black Baptists and Methodists, COGIC and other black Pentecostal leaders are among the new contenders to constitute the new national leadership for Black America. Being thrust into the national spotlight and political arena will strengthen COGIC's turn towards liberal politics. With its commitment to social justice, COGIC and other Pentecostals will add their twist to the national agenda for black people.

On the cusp of the advent of the Christian Right in the United States during the 1970s, COGIC leadership embraced a progressive political vision. At its 1973 General Assembly, COGIC validated progressive political ministry as a legitimate form of ministry. This ministry combined a liberal and conservative agenda together to form the COGIC political vision. On one hand, COGIC leadership advocated the prohibition of alcoholic production and sales and the repeal of legalized gambling, and on the other hand they supported the abolition of capital punishment. They also promoted economic, social, and racial equality as legitimate Christian goals. COGIC leadership resisted needing to join either the conservative or liberal camp fully; they forged their own biblical-based political vision. Political ministry, for COGIC, affirmed the public role of the church in securing equality for all people through participation in social justice movements and the use of Christian persuasion.[12]

Studies have demonstrated that COGIC's commitment to social justice, including civil rights militancy, continues to gain more and more adherents among COGIC clergy and laity, and has already reached the point where the vast majority of COGIC supports social justice. In addition to the COGIC support of social justice, the same study also noted that 78 percent of the COGIC respondents even supported civil rights protest. Throughout the late twentieth century, COGIC retained its pacifist commitments. During the recent Iraqi war, COGIC re-embraced its pacifist heritage. The core of COGIC pacifism is its objection to the war on the biblical injunction against "shedding human blood or taking human life."[13]

During the twentieth century COGIC eluded the ranks of the national civil rights leadership, although COGIC political activism did operate within local and metropolitan arenas, garnering solid city-wide and state-wide influence. Similar to their Baptist and Methodist counterparts, COGIC political activists have achieved access to chambers of political power in all corridors of government where they often pursue their progressive political agenda, focusing on anti-poverty initiatives, urban redevelopment, Africa's AIDS pandemic and other issues. [14]

The progressive Pentecostal faction will continue to expand during the first decades of the twenty-first century. This faction draws upon the COGIC trajectory that promoted education, ecumenism, and social justice and challenged COGIC parochialism. Within COGIC are various factions that compete to define COGIC's role as a global denomination. The competition and its outcomes will shape the COGIC future and influence the future of global Pentecostalism.

Western yet Non-Western

During the century, COGIC will continue to operate within the new historical realities of world Christianity, realities often plotted along a western/non-western axis, realities shaped by demographics. The new moment is defined by the current demography of Christianity. These demographics reflect the presence of Christian congregations across the globe, the shift from the majority of Christians residing in the West to the two-thirds world of Africa, Latin America, and Asia. Christianity became a truly global religion during the twentieth century and Pentecostal-Charismatic Christianity emerged as the second largest Christian tradition within Christianity during the late twentieth century; from these global developments COGIC has gained social capital.

Since the COGIC majority resides in the West, should COGIC be counted within the two-third world? When the West becomes a synonym of European descent, then COGIC with its non-white majority is clearly not western. However, when western is characterized as a particular organizational style, then COGIC is, in a sense, westernized with its organizational ethos and bureaucratic structures. Does COGIC like other denominations within the Black Church anticipate and participate in this shift by being the most organized form of non-western or non-European form of Christianity practiced in the West during the twentieth century?

COGIC transgresses the boundaries between western and non-western. In transgressing these boundaries, COGIC creates space for the designing of an organizational style and culture that it deems appropriate. COGIC simultaneously participates in the definition of western by constructing western and non-western in its own terms as well as erasing the boundaries between the two categories.

Conclusion

During these first decades of the twenty-first century, COGIC occupies a unique place within global Pentecostalism and Christianity as a global denomination that at times defies and other times bend the axes that shape Pentecostalism as a movement. By being a theologically conservative tradition that dialogues with theological liberals and liberationists as well as espouses a liberal political agenda, COGIC breaks the fundamentalist and evangelical stranglehold on Pentecostalism and illustrates Pentecostalism's ability to resist these foreign movements and chart its own course. By being a black-run religious organization with a multi-racial global membership, COGIC challenges the racial assumptions of globality and illustrates the global appeal of African American religious culture in addition to the musical culture of jazz and hip-hop. By being a global Pentecostal denomination in which the majority of the membership, leadership, and program reflect one country and race, COGIC illustrates how even a global denomination needs to overcome various forms of imperialism in order to be truly global in character. By having a middle-class dominated hierarchy and majority denomination with a significant underclass sector, COGIC embodies the class tensions within global Pentecostalism and Christianity as well as strategies for by-passing the rich/poor divide through the transfer of wealth as sign of good stewardship. By being variously a racial minority within the West that connects with the two-third world majority, a non-white, yet western, denomination, and a Northern-based denomination with a majority who reside or are descendants of the Southern hemisphere, COGIC reflects the new moment with global Christianity in which western/non-western and North/South distinctions are erased. COGIC, then, provides for global Pentecostalism and Christianity a trajectory that creates an alternative Pentecostal future in the twenty-first century, a future in contrast to the Pentecostal world of the late twentieth century.

Notes

1. Peter L. Berger and Samuel P. Huntington, eds., *Many Globalizations: Cultural Diversity in the Contemporary World* (Oxford: Oxford University Press, 2002).

2. *Foreign Mission Locations and Administrators* (Church of God in Christ, 1998).

3. Correspondence from Elder Wayne Channer, Toronto, Ontario, March 15, 2005.

4. David Daniels, "Church of God in Christ," *Religions of the World: A Comprehensive Encyclopedia of Beliefs and Practices*, edited by J. Gordon Melton and Martin Baumann (Santa Barbara, CA: ABC-CLIO, Inc., 2002), vol. 1, 318–320.

5. Interview with Bishop Lionel B. Riley, prelate of Ontario (Canada), February 1, 2001.

6. C. Eric Lincoln and Lawrence H. Maimiya, *The Black Church in the African American Experience* (Durham, NC: Duke University Press, 1990).

7. C. Eric Lincoln, *The Black Church Since Frazier* and E. Franklin Frazier, *The Negro Church in America* (New York: Schocken Press, 1974), 106–107.

8. Bart Landry, *The New Black Middle Class* (Berkeley: University of California Press, 1987).

9. See saveafricaschildren.org.

10. Bennie Goodwin, "Social Implications of Pentecostal Power," *Spirit* 1, no. 1 (1977), 31–35; Leonard Lovett, "Conditional Liberation: An Emergent Pentecostal Per-

spective," *Spirit* 1, no. 2 (1977), 24–30; Ithiel C. Clemmons, *Bishop C. H. Mason and the Roots of the Church of God in Christ* (Bakersfield, CA: Pneuma Life Publishing, 1996).

11. Mary Sawyer, "The Fraternal Council of Negro Churches, 1934–1964," *Church History,* 59 (March 1990), 51–64; Lincoln and Mamiya, *The Black Church in the African American Experience,* 191–194; currently Dr. Leonard Lovett serves as the ecumenical officer for COGIC.

12. *Official Manual with the Doctrines and Discipline of the Church of God in Christ* (Memphis: Board of Publication of the Church of God in Christ, 1973), 131–136, 137, 141–142.

13. William B. Holt, comp., *A Brief Historical and Doctrinal Statement and Rules for Government of the Church of God in Christ* (n.p., circa 1917), 10.

14. Lincoln and Maimiya, *The Black Church in the African American Experience,* 224; *COGIC Churches, ITC/FaithFactor Project 2000 Study of Black Churches* (Atlanta: ITC/FaithFactor Project 2000, 2001), 7; Theodore Kornweibel, Jr., "Bishop C.H. Mason and the Church of God in Christ During World War I: The Perils of Conscientious Objection," *Southern Studies: An Interdisciplinary Journal of the South* 26, 4 (Winter 1987), 277.

Chapter 12

Conclusion: Back to the Future: U.S. Pentecostalism in the 21st Century

Eric Patterson

Today many snicker at the caricature of old-time Pentecostals: their injunctions against make-up, their women in hair "buns," their men outfitted with hankies for waving, and the like. Indeed, some consider the appellation "Pentecostal" coterminous with "snake handler," "televangelist," and even "neurotic." Although it is true that twentieth century Pentecostalism, like any religious movement, had its excesses, they were the exceptions. A more realistic portrait of Pentecostalism would appreciate it as the fastest growing religious movement of both the twentieth and twenty-first centuries—a global phenomenon with roots in the United States that is exploding in Asia, Africa, and Latin America.[1]

Classical Pentecostalism was holistic. Unlike many other religious movements which privilege either the head or the heart, classical Pentecostals fused doctrine with experiential discipleship. Classical Pentecostalism focused on engaging the mind through comprehensive Bible study and reflection on key portions of doctrine, while engaging the whole person in participatory worship, Christian service, and personal spiritual experience.

This chapter goes back to the past to identify critical beliefs and practices shared by classical Pentecostals, and then considers the potential of such experiences and values in the future of classical Pentecostal churches in the United States. In order for the classical Pentecostal denominations to transmit key beliefs to their Pentecostal progeny, issues of Biblical authority, cardinal doctrines, and philosophy of evangelism must be addressed. Likewise, classical Pentecostal leaders must reengage discussions about practice and lifestyle: experience versus emotion, the practice of charismata, practical doctrine of holy living, and social engagement within congregations. These two issues, belief and practice, are at the heart of a future American Pentecostalism.

Classical Pentecostal Beliefs: Then and Now

Early Classical Pentecostal Doctrine

Classical Pentecostal denominations are those that trace their lineage or Pentecostal doctrine directly to the 1906 Azusa Street revival: the Church of God in Christ, the Church of God(s), the Assemblies of God, the International Church of the Foursquare Gospel, the Pentecostal Holiness churches, and others.[2] One defining characteristic of classical Pentecostalism was the emphasis on correct doctrine. The religious antecedents of Pentecostalism—Methodism, the Holiness and Divine Healing movements, the revivalist campaigns of the late 1800s—challenged old orthodoxies and called for a reevaluation of key points of Protestant doctrine. With the birth of the Pentecostal movement in 1906, doctrinal scrutiny and controversy ignited regarding the baptism formula, the doctrine of the Trinity, and whether the baptism of the Holy Spirit was a "second" or "third" "work of grace." Of course, these debates simply added to the preceding quarter century's numerous unresolved disputations like pre- versus post-millennialism and whether a believer who prayed for healing could legitimately resort to professional medical treatment.

In any event, classical Pentecostals appropriated four cardinal doctrines from the Holiness and revivalist movements at the turn of the century. Donald Dayton argues that these four doctrines became the key unifying concepts upon which nearly all of the classical Pentecostal denominations were founded.[3] Perhaps the most famous elucidation of those distinctives was by the founder of the International Church of the Foursquare Gospel, Aimee Semple McPherson: "Jesus saves us according to John 3:16. He baptizes us with the Holy Spirit according to Acts 2:4. He heals our bodies according to James 5:14-15. And Jesus is coming again to receive us unto Himself according to 1 Thessalonians 4:16-17."[4]

Students of Pentecostalism are quite familiar with this "foursquare" gospel.[5] The first tenet is a classical idea of salvation: the death and resurrection of Jesus provides atonement for sins, thus an individual who chooses to voluntarily acknowledge Christ as Savior will receive eternal salvation. Second, classical Pentecostals were unified in their belief that the baptism of the Holy Spirit was a spiritual experience subsequent to salvation. The evidence of this Spirit baptism was "speaking in tongues," and glossolalia remained a key distinctive of Pentecostalism throughout the twentieth century.[6]

Third, classical Pentecostals embraced the doctrine that Christ's death provided not only spiritual regeneration but also physical healing in this life. Divine healing, along with Spirit baptism, was seen as important "signs and wonders" testifying to the truth of the primary Christian message: the Lordship of Christ and the individual's need for salvation. Therefore, healing was available from

"Christ as Healer" and Pentecostals expected healings to occur which would validate their religious testimony.

Finally, classical Pentecostals tended to agree that the outpouring of the Holy Spirit, as manifested by tongues, healings, salvation experiences, sanctification, and "deliverance" from various maladies, were harbingers of the soon return of Christ. Most classical Pentecostal denominations developed a premillennial eschatology and believed that the "signs of the times" indicated that they were living in the last days. This created an urgency motivating the Herculean efforts of domestic evangelists and foreign missionaries. Indeed, the doctrine of Christ's return was most important not as a theological consideration but as a motivator to "spread the Good News" before it was too late. Because classical Pentecostals also emphasized that Christ would not return until the Gospel had been preached to the entire world, they took responsibility for taking the Christian message to "unreached nations."

Salvation, Holy Spirit, Divine Healing, the "blessed hope" of Christ's return: four cardinal doctrines that are fundamental to classical Pentecostalism. They are the hallmarks not only of pentecostalized believers in the immediate aftermath of the Azusa Street revival, but are the foundations of the major classical Pentecostal denominations in the United States. Furthermore, for the first several decades of American Pentecostalism it was virtually impossible to attend religious services at a classical Pentecostal church without witnessing a clear presentation of one or more of these key doctrines.

In the past, the cardinal four doctrines were pored over in adult Sunday school classes, sermonized, distilled in "tracts," preached from soap boxes, discussed at denominational conventions, and were the grist for hundreds of pamphlets from fledgling Pentecostal publishers. A question for contemporary Pentecostalism in the United States is how valuable are these doctrines in the life of individual Pentecostal denominations today?[7]

Classical Pentecostal Doctrine Today

Salvation

The doctrine of salvation is the cornerstone of Christian faith, and the Arminian, voluntaristic understanding of individual assent to Christ's lordship remains the bedrock of Pentecostal soteriology. From a creedal standpoint, there has been no change in Pentecostal congregations. That being said, issues have developed in this area. For instance, regardless of what the doctrine is, the practical dilemma facing all classical Pentecostal denominations is their lack of growth. In the United States, these denominations' ability to convert new Christians in the past two decades has been sluggish at best. This may be because many established Pentecostal denominations have "matured" past the exuberant excesses of revivalism and take a less aggressive stance toward evangelism. It may also be that, as Margaret Poloma suggests in this volume, as churches have institutionalized their focus has turned inward to the routinization of their organizations rather than outward in missionary endeavor.[8]

In any case, the doctrine of salvation remains but it is unclear how classical Pentecostal denominations will actualize the doctrine at the community and mass levels through new conversions in the future. Many classical Pentecostals have handed off their revivalist methods of "spreading salvation" to other movements such televangelists, independent crusades (e.g. Greg Laurie's Harvest Crusade), and charismatic churches like the Vineyard Fellowship.

Healing

"The prayer of faith shall save the sick. . . " continues to be embraced by classical Pentecostals.[9] Indeed, one of Pentecostalism's great contributions to U.S. Christianity was the re-awakening of interest in divine healing and its spread throughout the evangelical and mainline Protestant communities.

Nonetheless, as in the case of the doctrine of salvation, we can see important shifts in the way classical Pentecostals handle the doctrine of healing. First, early Pentecostals saw physical healing as one divine intervention among many possible acts of the Holy Spirit (e.g. tongues, prophecy). Today, divine healing is the only physical manifestation of divine agency that is not controversial, whereas phenomena like glossolalia are increasingly marginalized in Pentecostal congregations. Indeed, as Margaret Poloma and Earl Creps note in this volume, such supernatural experiences are less and less likely to happen in Pentecostal churches.

This is not to say that Pentecostals, or the larger evangelical community, have given up on divine healing. Rather, they have moved the practice of divine healing (as well as conversion events and other experiences) out of the Sunday morning service and into well-managed healing situations. The focus of such crusades and retreats is solely on seeking the miraculous. This is not to suggest that venues such as Benny Hinn's miracle crusades have not witnessed some bona fide healings or that the events should be treated with skepticism solely due to their size and popularity. However, it is worth noting that Pentecostals, and American evangelicals more broadly, are often seeking intercession for healing outside their local church rather than in it.

A related point is the nexus of the Word of Faith movement(s) and the classical Pentecostal formulation of divine healing. Classical Pentecostals believed that a sovereign God could choose to heal the sick, and that he often did so out of love for humanity as well as to demonstrate his power to unbelievers. However, a second view has always been lurking in Pentecostal discourse about healing—that the believer has the "right" as a child of God to "claim" their healing. This positive confession approach has always been part of the Pentecostal dialogue, but as Walsh and Patterson point out in this volume, in recent decades it has merged with the prosperity gospel and Word of Faith practitioners into a doctrine of divine entitlement that is distinctly different from the official position of most classical Pentecostal denominations. It is unclear today whether the traditional doctrine of healing or a healing-as-entitlement doctrine will characterize U.S. Pentecostals in the future.

The Second Coming of Christ

For early classical Pentecostals the belief in Christ's imminent return provided a critical schema for evaluating every aspect of faith and ministry. This belief was the chief motivator for the tremendous evangelistic efforts of the twentieth century. Moreover, this belief was dynamic—it was reinforced and reshaped countless times in light of periodic crises in American life. At various times Pentecostals considered the First World War, the Great Depression, the rise of Hitler, the rise of Stalin, the Cold War, and the birth Israel and its successful wars as the harbinger of the apocalypse. Recently, Tim LaHaye's *Left Behind* books and a network television series have rejuvenated interest in the "end times" throughout not only American evangelicalism but pop culture as well.

However, interest is not synonymous with inspiration. In the first several decades of the twentieth century classical Pentecostals were spurred to sacrificially fund foreign missions efforts and sent tens of thousands of their young men and women to serve in domestic and overseas evangelistic posts. The conviction that they lived in the "last days" galvanized their behavior. In contrast, as the centenary of the Azusa Street revival draws close, such urgency is not apparent. True, at times the headquarters of Pentecostal denominations issue missives about "fanning the flame" and "keep the fire burning" "until everyone has heard." Such efforts, like the Assemblies of God's "Decade of Harvest," are more management-generated membership drives than the personal conviction of congregants to dutifully share their faith with their neighbors.

Of course, some sociologists suggest another alternative. Pentecostals at Azusa Street were often the poor and marginalized in society and their hope in Christ's soon return was an expectation of deliverance from destitution.[10] However, as classical Pentecostals have joined evangelicals on the right side of the tracks, natural processes of institutional bureaucratization and comfort in rising standards of living have made the urgency associated with this doctrine less poignant. Moreover, the simple fact is that Christ has not returned, thus, many believers hold onto the "blessed hope" but have contented themselves with living in this world. In any event, as David Bernard observes in his chapter in this volume, negative growth trends foretell a depressing future for most Pentecostal denominations.

Baptism of the Holy Spirit

Certainly the greatest contribution of Pentecostalism to twentieth and twenty-first century Western Christianity is the rediscovery of the supernatural. Early classical Pentecostal pneumatology asserted that the manifestations of the Holy Spirit such as tongues, prophecy, miracles, and divine healing were for the present. Some of these beliefs, primarily healing, have migrated beyond Pentecostalism to most evangelical and some mainline denominations in the United States and are hallmarks of global Pentecostalism. In short, it is absolutely impossible to conceive of a twentieth-century Pentecostalism that did not relish such phenomena.

Of course, the key feature which was believed to demonstrate this "latter day outpouring" of the Holy Spirit was Spirit baptism as evidenced by speaking in tongues. Although Pentecostals have debated among themselves whether Spirit baptism was a second or third work of grace, whether tongues was the (sole) initial, physical evidence of the experience, and the role of tongues in corporate settings, nonetheless they did not question its efficacy for both the individual and the worship community.[11] This has changed. As Margaret Poloma suggests in this volume, it is rare today to hear pastoral teaching on the baptism of the Holy Spirit from classical Pentecostal pulpits and even rarer to witness glossolalia in congregational settings. Moreover, as Earl Creps has noted in his chapter, there seems to be a crisis among many pastors credentialed with Pentecostal denominations about the very essence of the doctrine as well as its applicability in their congregations.

In contrast to many classical Pentecostal denominational leaders, I would suggest that this is not a narrowly defined disagreement about the Pentecostal "distinctive" of tongues. Rather, it is a much broader crisis regarding supernatural agency in the life of individual Christians as well as in corporate environments. Early Pentecostals were marked by their eager expectation and earnest desire for supernatural manifestations in their midst. They believed that such were the hallmarks of effective ministry and that God would act in an environment of faith.

This assumption is clearly lacking in classical Pentecostalism today. Most classical Pentecostal congregations have stories to tell of past spiritual exploits: healings, recovered relationships, the end of substance dependency, messages in tongues and prophecy, and the like. However, they also have stories to tell of "excesses:" when individuals or groups acted in ways that were unduly emotive or lacked wisdom. It seems that in tandem with upward social mobility and institutionalization this second frame of reference has won the day in Pentecostal churches. It is unlikely for Pentecostal pastors to preach about spiritual phenomena as they are increasingly concerned about scaring off "seekers" on Sunday morning. Likewise, congregations seem far less expectant than their Pentecostal forbears with regards to supernatural phenomena and like all Americans are generally far too impatient to "tarry" as Seymour and his parishioners did at the Azusa Street revival.

What made Pentecostalism distinctive in the twentieth century was its welcome of the supernatural in its churches—an interest that has largely waned. In contrast, American pop culture is obsessed with the supernatural, from Harry Potter to television series and movies about the occult. In the end, there will not be a twenty-first century Pentecostalism in the United States, at least not in classical Pentecostal churches, unless that expectation is rekindled.

Biblical Authority

Another essential aspect of Pentecostal belief, indeed perhaps the preeminent one, is that of Biblical authority. The cardinal doctrines all flowed from a veneration of Scripture. Critics of Pentecostal emotionalism usually miss the significant emphasis that classical Pentecostals put on the "Word of God." Pentecostals attended Sunday morning services as well as adult Sunday school, Sunday night evangelistic services, and various meetings during the week. At each event they received teaching. Bible study was stressed at the individual and corporate level. Children were admonished to learn a weekly Bible verse in order to "hide Thy word in my heart that I might not sin against Thee."[12] Parishioners were urged to bring their own Bible to follow along at the services. Indeed, one of the most influential twentieth-century reference Bibles, Finis Jennings Dake's "Annotated Reference Bible," was Pentecostal in orientation, and Thompson's "Chain Reference" Bible was developed by a professor at Aimee Semple McPherson's L.I.F.E. Bible College.

Why this emphasis among classical Pentecostals on the Scripture? The real issue is that of *authority*. On the one hand, classical Pentecostals sought to justify their position that Spirit baptism was for the present by citing Scriptural texts from the Old Testament prophet Joel, the New Testament book of Acts, and elsewhere. On the other hand, Pentecostals referenced Scripture as the authority for condemning many high church practices that they felt were extra-biblical (e.g. infant baptism, confession, prayer to saints, church hierarchy). Christian doctrine, illuminated by careful study of the Scripture, was central to the ethos of the average Pentecostal believer. In short, Pentecostals sought biblical authority for their doctrine and practices to legitimate their distinctive dogma in a largely unsympathetic Western religious milieu.

In contrast, many contemporary churches affiliated with classical Pentecostal denominations have become doctrinally bland in their attempts to catch the biggest market share and not offend potential parishioners. However, Pentecostal churches may be doing their youth and guests a disservice by obscuring the central doctrines of their denomination. Indeed, the historic churches that have stood the test of time (e.g. Quakers, Baptists, Presbyterians) have done so by standing firm on their understanding of biblical and doctrinal authority. Furthermore, churches which provide answers to tough questions may provide needed direction on difficult issues such as the problem of evil and suffering, the need for Christian service, biblical teaching on marriage and family, and the like.

Again, the more fundamental issue here is that of authority. American culture is narcissistic: Americans prefer to put themselves at the center of the universe. Furthermore, the advent of postmodern philosophy challenges the view that there is objective truth and universal moral norms. Many secular Americans are threatened by biblical teaching on moral issues such as abortion and sexual sin. Such moral relativism is increasingly characteristic of American churches as well. By way of contrast, it is difficult to imagine an American Pentecostalism in 2050 that does not explicitly privilege the authority of the Bible.

Philosophy of Evangelism

A third challenge for twenty-first century Pentecostalism is a philosophy of evangelism. Twentieth century Pentecostals were enthusiastic evangelists, often relying on mass media techniques to spread their message.[13] In his chapter for this book, Calvin Johansson calls the philosophy underlying this approach to music and the arts "pragmatism." "Pragmatism is a philosophical disposition which rejects anything that is institutional because of its tradition in favor of modes of expression that accommodate the norms of local culture. The key criterion, then, of pragmatism is functionality: if something works, it is adopted."[14]

Johansson's analysis applies to the question of evangelism in Pentecostal churches today. Pragmatism has been the hallmark of Pentecostal and charismatic approaches to evangelism for the past twenty years: if it works, use it. Debates within congregations over music style, the use of choir robes, "Sunday best" versus dressing down, exterior architecture as well as the use of interior "space," the utilization of guest speakers ("evangelists"), direct mail marketing, sermons "sensitive" to the diverse political attitudes of "seekers," and a-religious events sponsored for the community such as Easter Egg hunts and Harvest Festivals are all evidence of a ubiquitous evangelistic philosophy of pragmatism.

The question for today is two-fold. First, were early classical Pentecostals really so pragmatic? If so, is it really the best theological and philosophical position for twenty-first century Pentecostalism?

Many, but not all, classical Pentecostals had pragmatic tendencies. This was in part due to their instinctive, and often arrogant, rejection of everything "high church" combined with a real concern for effective communication of the gospel message to unchurched audiences. However, effective evangelism may be spiritually powerful as well as socially relevant and culturally sensitive without resorting to least-common-denominator theology.

The fatal flaw of pragmatism is the philosophical dichotomy of ends and means. Pragmatism says that the ends justify (most) means, and that means have no philosophical content in and of themselves. Clearly this is fallacious. Furthermore, pragmatism is chameleonic. A pragmatic church initiates "programs" and alters its "style" to fit in with trends in popular culture. A pragmatic church may grow into a super- or mega-church with thousands of "customers," a religious shopping mall with genres to suit the tastes of targeted audiences.

An alternative to pragmatism is a philosophy based on the doctrine of the Incarnation.[15] An Incarnational approach to evangelism is not cultural accommodation; it is the realization that Christ is Lord of and above all culture. Christ's pattern was to go to sinners, share with them, but not accept the worldview which they functioned in.

Incarnational evangelism means carefully considering context in order to share a transcendent message to individuals. It does not mean that anything goes, because methods do say something about one's philosophy of ends and about one's theology of Christ. Thus, Pentecostals should carefully consider all evangelistic efforts, from scare tactics to charitable contributions to evangelistic Christian rock concerts to see if the message in the means is contrary to the end message.[16]

A corollary within an Incarnational philosophy of evangelism is "indigenization." In this book Jeff Hittenberger identifies three features of indigenization based on the work of missiologist Melvin Hodges: it is self-propagating, self-governing, and self-supporting.[17] A church practicing the indigenization principle will equip new believers immediately to reach out to others in their local community. In other words, parishioners, not advertising executives, will drive church growth. Unlike professional staff-directed organizations, the indigenized church should over time become increasingly self-governing and self-supporting.

In contrast to the prevailing paradigm of pop-cultural, functionalist pragmatism, an Incarnational philosophy of evangelism is contextual, Spirit-led, and transformative. An Incarnational philosophy seeks to present a clear gospel message in a way that is relevant but does not cheapen or shortchange the confrontational and salvationary message of the Bible. Incarnational evangelism does not try to create programs, it seeks to midwife spiritual transformation through a clear and loving Gospel witness. Moreover, like a midwife, the indigenization principle calls for the quick transfer of responsibility for the church's future to local stakeholders so that they can participate in Christian service.

In sum, twentieth century classical Pentecostalism cherished and cultivated Biblical study, doctrinal orthodoxy, Scriptural authority, and an ethic of Incarnational evangelism. Pentecostals were led by pastors, missionaries, evangelists, and lay leaders who took such matters very seriously because of their concern for intimacy with God and correct teaching for their congregations. A twenty-first century Pentecostalism, if there is to be one, must continue to be centered on a core set of values and this worldview will have to be clearly and frequently articulated by leaders, especially at the local level.

Classical Pentecostal Practice: Then and Now

Critics of early Pentecostals, from both fundamentalist and mainline denominations, argued that the experiential component of traditional Pentecostalism was immature, hysterical, psychotic, and perhaps demonic. In order to consider where Pentecostals have been and where they might go in the next half-century, it is useful to consider four topics regarding the practice and behavior of Pentecostals: the question of meaningful experience versus transient emotionalism, charismata, holiness conduct, and social engagement.

Experience or Emotionalism?

It is true that a minority of Pentecostal events were shallow pep rallies or even rigged media circuses. However, this view of Pentecostal experience fails to appreciate the profounder experiential nature of Pentecostalism. When classical Pentecostals were baptized in the Holy Spirit, it was a life-altering event that gave them new perspectives on faith and daily living. This life-changing experience, for many Pentecostals, affected their day to day existence until their death. Such a spiritual experience was simply supernatural.

One wonders how many new attendees of United Pentecostal, Foursquare, and Assemblies of God churches have had such life-changing experiences in the past five years. Two trends in American Christianity have caused Pentecostals to redefine the notion of experience. First, "moments of truth" are out of vogue. In the "old days," the altar call, the sinner's prayer, immediate water baptism, and corporate prayer for tongues were defining and bonding moments in congregational life. In most contemporary churches, these are too unrestrained and therefore are long gone.

Second, Pentecostals have redefined the concept of "experience" to match secular existential or postmodern ideas of experience. For instance, many Gen X churches have built their programs around event-phenomena: concerts, art exhibits, coffee shops, and films. This approach permeates churches where worship is a concert with a mostly passive audience and evangelism is a once-a-year bazaar complete with cotton candy and snow-cones. These attempts at church rely on clever props and technological effects to impress the audience. However, they fail to build community, develop disciples, or create long-term relationships.

The Hollywood moment is increasingly the experience of classical Pentecostal churches: cleverly packaged, well-timed, and sensory rather than cerebral. Sunday morning services are fleeting and emotional, a program of planned, psy-

chological-response moments, events designed for feeling inspired, not undergo-
ing life transformation. Early classical Pentecostals asked one another, "Did you
feel It. . . or Him?" Today, congregants are surveyed, "how did that feel to
You?"

Charismata

Pentecostals derive their identity from their attachment to the day of Pentecost. That day, as recorded in the book of Acts, was a defining moment for the
early Church because believers were empowered for evangelism and experienced supernatural charismata in the form of public displays of glossolalia and
xenolalia. Throughout the twentieth century charismata—chiefly tongues—was
the defining characteristic of Pentecostalism. For Pentecostals to exist in the
twenty-first century, charismata must be present.

Thus the question is not whether or not tongues are the "initial physical evidence" of the baptism of the Holy Spirit. Instead, the essential question is why
have classical Pentecostals stopped practicing and teaching about tongues and
other charismata?[18]

This volume records explanations for why some American Pentecostals
have given up on Pentecostalism. Edmund Rybarczyk observes the movement of
Pentecostals from the periphery of society to the "right side of the tracks." According to Rybarczyk, one of the reasons Pentecostals have abandoned charismata is their embarrassment that tongues is a *faux pas* in middle class America.
David Cole agrees with Rybarczyk but adds an additional dimension: Pentecostal denominations sought religious legitimacy through membership in ecumenical organizations such as the National Association of Evangelicals. Interaction
with their better behaved Reformed evangelical counterparts made Pentecostal
leaders shy away from overt demonstrations of enthusiasm and/or charismata.

Interestingly, Margaret Poloma's chapter offers a structural interpretation of
the loss of charismata in Pentecostal churches. As Pentecostal congregations
aged and grew they institutionalized their services and programs. The standardi-
zation and bureaucratization of services and ministries banished the flexibility
and dynamism of earlier meetings marked by Pentecostal expression and spiritual manifestations. Another structural interpretation may have to do with the
autonomy, and often autocracy, characteristic of Pentecostal pastorates. It is not
uncommon for there to be a high level of control exercised by these pastors over
every part of the church, including the Sunday program. For instance, I recently
visited two modest-sized East Coast Pentecostal churches of different denominations where the senior pastor led every part of the morning service, from the
worship music to the closing prayer, while the other staff members watched
from the front row. In such cases, the "movement of the Spirit" represents something outside the pastor's control and therefore is not welcome.

Earl Creps offers a different analysis. His interviews with the younger generation of Assemblies of God pastors suggests that "younger leaders" sincerely question the spontaneity and accessibility of charismata and have significant reservations about the priority historically accorded to charismata, especially tongues. Indeed, Creps calls a cohort of younger Assemblies of God ministers "post-Pentecostal."

Creps's interview participants correctly point out that their antecedents placed a tremendous emphasis on charismata, particularly the personal transformative experience called the baptism of the Holy Spirit. Critics of the "tongues as initial evidence" position, as well as those embarrassed by emotionalism and unplanned spiritual manifestations, are correct that early Pentecostals did grant privileged place to their "distinctive:" the baptism of the Holy Spirit marked by speaking in other tongues.

However, Creps's "young leaders" and the critics of Pentecostalism misunderstand the rest of the picture regarding charismata. The doctrine of the baptism of the Holy Spirit is not just a "distinctive." It is not simply a quirk, birth mark, idiosyncrasy, or even skeleton in the closet.

Rather, the rediscovery of Spirit baptism is the great contribution of Pentecostalism to global Christianity. Tens of millions have become "pentecostalized" by the second (or third) work of grace. The baptism of the Holy Spirit, for Pentecostals, is an empowering and liberating supernatural work that manifests itself in an intensely personal way, the surrender of verbal control to the Holy Spirit, and should have a sustained impact on the life of the believer. Early classical Pentecostals knew that the baptism of the Holy Spirit was the engine driving evangelistic efforts because it provided individual power for witness. Thus, a position that relegates the baptism of the Holy Spirit to a "nice to have, but not necessary" status in the life of the Pentecostal church is contrary to the missionary impulse that energized classical Pentecostals.

Of course, it may be that the neglect of the practice of charismata is due to muddled thinking about tongues. For instance, it seems that many of the pastors surveyed by Poloma and Creps collapse the individual and corporate uses of tongues into a single category. Classical Pentecostal doctrine distinguished between the baptism of the Holy Sprit and personal use of tongues by every Christian from the gift of tongues (and interpretation) for use by some in the assembly of believers. Thus, we are left with two questions. First, even if pastors are skeptical that tongues is not the only "initial" evidence of Spirit baptism, why have so many discontinued teaching their congregations that the individual baptism of the Holy Spirit with attendant tongues is available to (some) believers? Second, why have Pentecostal pastors banished the corporate charismata (e.g. tongues, prophecy, healing) in their services?

Indeed, one can wonder how silence on charismata is an improvement on over-emphasis on Pentecostal distinctives. Whatever the answer, the historical record is clear: early classical Pentecostals experienced and firmly believed that

Spirit empowerment was responsible for the explosive growth of Pentecostal Protestantism in the United States and worldwide in the twentieth century. Also, scholars observe that the most dynamic areas of growth in contemporary Christendom are precisely in those regions where Pentecostalized Christianity is the primary religious affiliation.[19]

Unless Pentecostals reinvigorate their commitment to a "full gospel" that includes supernatural experience, it seems that there will be no American Pentecostalism in the future.[20] Instead, it is likely that at the local level, congregations within the Assemblies of God, Foursquare Church, Church of God, and other classical Pentecostal denominations will continue to blend in with the broader, blander evangelical "pot of goo" characterized by pop music, well-managed programs, and topical sermons, and from time to time reminisce about that "old-time religion" of their holy roller grandparents.[21]

Holiness

Classical Pentecostalism arose as a branch within the larger reformist and Holiness movements of the nineteenth century. Thus, the focus on righteous living for individuals as well as communities was reflected in not only Christian crusades but also the temperance and abolitionist movements. Of course, holiness movements are nothing new in Christendom: from classical monastic orders to the Reformation to the Jesuits and later the Scottish Covenanters and Massachusetts Puritans, the appeal to righteous and ascetic living as well as separation from "worldliness" is an importation mainstream in the history of Christian discipleship.

The Holiness paradigm reflects on the covenant relationship of the Old Testament nation of Israel with its guidelines for righteous behavior and promise of spiritual intimacy, as a model for Christian living. Indeed, the Old Testament is replete with laws, proverbs, and anecdotes cautioning against immoderate or illicit behaviors (drunkenness, sexual immorality, gambling, cursing). Likewise, the New Testament also provides justification for concern about lifestyle issues such as Christ's admonition to be "salt and light," Paul's concern about male and female modesty, and James' injunctions against gossip.

Many contemporary Pentecostals have reacted against what they saw as the puritanical preference for "do's and don'ts" by their elders. However, it is imperative to understand the real purpose of a theological position mandating a holy lifestyle. First and foremost the objective of the Holiness approach to daily life is an effort to get close to God. A call to holiness is the call to focus one's attention and life work on Christ, without many of the distractions and temptations of this life. The Holiness position recognizes that human beings are prone to gluttony (over-indulging appetites) and idolatry (prioritizing things or others above Christ).

Another motivator of the Holiness movement was Christian witness. Early classical Pentecostals had a keen appreciation that they were Christian, Christ-like, and therefore had to be extremely careful about avoiding hypocrisy before unbelievers. This caution resulted in conservative mores of dress and behavior, including restrictions on alcohol consumption, social dancing, tobacco, and the like. Interesting, classical Pentecostals exercised a genuine concern that their actions not support—directly, indirectly, or tacitly—individuals or corporations that were anti-Christian or worldly. Hence, Pentecostals often refrained from the cinema altogether, lest their financial support of innocent films become the profit that bankrolled racy movies.

So, classical Pentecostals demonstrated a passionate desire to become intimate with a holy God and provide a clear and consistent witness to their neighbors and therefore were extremely concerned about ridding their personal lives of worldly behavior and influences. Of course, at times this position may have been excessive in practice, particularly when injunctions to holy living were expressed as a catechism of expected behavior rather than a philosophy regarding spiritual discipline and Christian witness. Moreover, from a doctrinal standpoint, some classical Pentecostals went too far, straying toward a mild Gnosticism that was anti-Nature and anti-physical in its hyper-spirituality.

The majority of classical Pentecostals in the United States today seem to have embraced, along with their evangelical and fundamentalist siblings and mainline cousins, a casual American materialism focused on comfort. This soft hedonism does not necessarily suggest that "everything goes," but one rarely hears dialogue about how intimacy with Christ might affect personal choices regarding modesty of appearance, language, habits (addictions), and listening/reading/viewing material. For example, I recently overhead a charismatic acquaintance from a theologically conservative church talking about the cigars, beer, and betting at his weekly poker round. Such behavior was frowned upon in early generations of Pentecostalism. Furthermore, key Christian disciplines such as prayer, tithing, water baptism, and regular participatory church attendance are largely absent from the discourse of many classical Pentecostal churches.

For classical Pentecostalism to reassert an identity in the twenty-first century as well as to provide a significant voice of conscience on social and moral issues, it must reconnect itself to a practical doctrine of Holiness. Renewing the Holiness legacy is not an attempt to impose skirt lengths on women and crew-cuts on men. Rather, it is a rekindling of the commitment to abstain from gluttony, idolatry, and questionable behavior that distances the adherent from God and one's fellowman.

Charity, Race, Gender

Classical Pentecostals combined the imperatives of holiness with a belief in the imminent return of Christ. This resulted in a short-sighted understanding of the role of Christians in culture. Pentecostals felt that they should provide the gospel message to the world, but avoid other areas of politics and society. Thus, [many of?] the classical Pentecostal denominations were officially pacifists until the 1960s, [most?] eschewed higher education, and few parishioners became involved in community groups or even voted regularly. This is radical disengagement in order to be separate form the world.

Of course, many classical Pentecostals were from the wrong side of the tracks, making them less likely to be socially engaged as well. Nevertheless, as Pentecostalism faces the twenty-first century, church leaders need to lead the congregations in social engagement. Christ called the church to be salt and light in the local community; it is unlikely that such permeation will result from Pentecostals barricading themselves in their churches four nights a week. Twenty-first century Pentecostals need to strategize about how to positively permeate their society.

Charity

Early Pentecostals took Christ's admonitions very seriously. Of course, Christ's two most important injunctions remain the Great Commandment and the Great Commission. In the former Christ focused the life of the believer around love for God and neighbor. In the second, Christ proclaimed the mission of the post-resurrection Church: "preach the gospel to everyone." Twentieth century American Pentecostals took the Great Commandment and Great Commission to heart, creating the largest domestic evangelism and foreign missionary programs in world history.

However, in so doing Pentecostals consolidated the missives into a single one. In other words, Pentecostals attempted to fill the Great Commandment through the Great Commission—"we'll show God our love by telling others about him and we will show others God's love through evangelization." In so doing some Pentecostals neglected the charitable aspects of the New Testament. Whereas the early Church was reputed for its relief programs for widows and orphans, and although charitable themes are explicit throughout both testaments, classical Pentecostals did not see institutionalized relief services as part of their mandate. In the twenty-first century, Pentecostal churches need to witness Christ's mercy by organized charitable efforts.[22]

Institutionalized charitable programs were not characteristic of most early American Pentecostal denominations. Why were most Pentecostals skeptical of such efforts? Early Pentecostals considered themselves to be living in "the last days" and expected the imminent return of the Messiah. Thus, they interpreted their expression of the Great Commandments (love God and your neighbor) through the Great Commission: go preach, convert, and baptize. They felt that their best efforts and modest resources must be husbanded for domestic evangelism and foreign missions, not diverted to welfare programs. Moreover, it is likely that if local parishioners had a financial need, it would be prayed for in the local body and then assistance would be offered on a private and voluntary basis.

Also, early Pentecostals were suspicious of the Social Gospel of their day. Mainline denominations seemed to have given up on the presentation of the spiritual gospel with Christ's atoning death at its core. Instead, Social Gospel devotees like Walter Rauschenbusch seemed to be arguing, along with socialists and labor organizers, that "social salvation" was possible based on having enough food in one's belly and a roof over one's head.[23] Classical Pentecostals often pointed to the social programs of some churches as symptoms that mainline denominations had forgotten the essence of the Gospel message— salvation in a heavenly kingdom, not social engineering and worldly comfort.[24]

Twenty-first century Pentecostals are doing better in this arena. Contemporary Pentecostals need not dichotomize between "living water" (evangelism) and providing a tangible drink to the thirsty. Christian service need not detract from Christian evangelism. It is obvious that for the past generation Pentecostal missionaries have understood this. Throughout the developing world, many of the most promising Pentecostal efforts are based on meeting the needs of the whole individual, spiritually and materially. Perhaps the best example of this is Latin American Child Care, a network of thousands of schools through Central and South America which provide clothing, healthy meals, clean water, and literacy as well unabashed instruction in Christian living and doctrine. Such programs honor God by demonstrating his love materially and spiritually. U.S. churches should follow this model of prioritizing assistance, spiritually and materially, to those in need.[25]

Race

The 1906 Azusa Street revival that birthed twentieth century Pentecostalism was led by a black man named William Seymour. One of the things that should intrigue us about Seymour's understanding of the baptism of the Holy Spirit was his ecclesiology and hope for racial reconciliation. In the context of Jim Crow, Seymour believed that the gift of tongues symbolized the worldwide unity of the Church and that Spirit baptism laid the groundwork for inter-racial healing and ethnic equality. Seymour was not alone in observing that the blood of Christ had "washed away the color line" at the Azusa Street mission; secular observers of the revival also comprehended the radical nature of race relations at Azusa Street.[26]

The Azusa Street revival was America's best chance at racial reconciliation. Certainly, the social dilemmas caused by slavery and segregation needed supernatural agency to bring about repentance, forgiveness, and reconciliation. And in the first years of the Pentecostal revival, many hoped that would happen. It was not to be. The tragic story of Seymour's mentor Charles Parham's disgust with racial mixing and the quick segregation of Pentecostal denominations within the first decade of the movement (e.g. the black Church of God in Christ and the white Assemblies of God) is well-documented elsewhere.[27]

What of today? I think that it is fair to say on the one hand that most Pentecostals probably love their coreligionists of other colors. Nonetheless, as someone has famously quipped, "11:00 a.m. Sunday morning is the most segregated hour in America." Due to the demographic trends concentrating races in distinct urban neighborhoods as well as historical traditions within specific denominations, it seems likely that many classical Pentecostal churches will remain largely monochromatic, particularly in the South and Midwest.[28] The real question for any Pentecostal church is about how it perceives and interacts with diverse communities and Pentecostal churches in its area. Do white Pentecostal pastors call on their congregations to partner with black Pentecostal congregations to provide relief to the urban poor in their county? Do white and black church leaders preach against any form of racism and misogyny, such as that apparent in rap music?

Women in Ministry

Cheryl J. Sanders writes "On the whole, the Holiness-Pentecostal movement in the United States has made a distinctive contribution to the historical evolution of religion in America by involving blacks, women, and the poor at all levels of ministry."[29] She is one of many scholars who recognize that in the early years of the movement, women served as lay leaders and even as pastors and missionaries. Indeed, perhaps the most famous of the Healing evangelists of the turn of the century was a woman, Maria Woodworth-Etter, and likewise the most famous American Pentecostal was a woman, Aimee Semple McPherson.

However, as Sanders goes on to write, "Over the course of the twentieth century there has been a dramatic and substantial decline in women's ecclesial leadership in the Holiness and Pentecostal churches."[30] For a variety of reasons, Pentecostal churches followed the historic patterns of other Christian churches by increasingly marginalizing women in ministry: the movement relapsed slowly to the patriarchalism prevalent in American society and especially in conservative evangelical churches. Women were incrementally relegated to helping and support roles such as pastor's wife, Sunday school teacher, choir director, and the like.

A twenty-first century Pentecostalism will repent from discriminating against its female members and realize such peripheralization only weakens the movement by restricting the contributions of potential leaders. On the other hand, it will not make the error of some contemporary feminists by suggesting that men and women are identical. Pentecostals started well with regard to relations among the sexes and should have a positive example to provide to American society on this issue. Consequently, an authentic Pentecostalism will return to the egalitarian principles of early classical Pentecostalism—that the Holy Spirit, not denominations or tradition, will choose who will be empowered for ministry. It is likely that choice will often be women.

Conclusion

This chapter suggests that contemporary Pentecostals should mine their past for a vision of their future. While rejecting discrimination based on class, race, or gender, Pentecostals should reinvigorate discussions of cardinal Pentecostal doctrine and biblical authority. Furthermore, this essay suggests that contemporary Pentecostals need to reconceptualize their philosophy of both the ends and means of evangelism based on principles of Incarnation and indigenization.

Likewise, contemporary American Pentecostals must reconnect with the vibrant experiential nature of their faith and recover the awe and expectancy of charismata in their individual and corporate spiritual experience. It is simply impossible to be Pentecostal without the charismata, and yet classical Pentecostal denominations seem to have handed off their gift to younger movements such as the Vineyard and non-denominational charismatic churches.

Will there be a twenty-first century Pentecostalism in the United States? On the one hand, the contributors to this book seem pessimistic that there is the will or vitality left in classical Pentecostal denominations to project a spiritually vital Pentecostalism into the decades ahead. However, the volume also suggests that pentecostalized religion may do best when it returns to its roots, challenges the status quo, and empowers those who seek deep spiritual experiences. It is entirely possible that such Pentecostals do exist in the United States and that a fresh round of revitalized religion, a twenty-first century pentecostalized Great Awakening, lies ahead.

Notes

1. For instance, see Phillip Jenkins, *The Next Christendom: The Coming of Global Christianity* (Oxford: Oxford University Press, 2002); David Martin *Pentecostalism: The World Their Parish* (Oxford: Blackwell, 2002).

2. In this chapter, "early" classical Pentecostalism refers to the people, beliefs, and practices of the first decades of the Pentecostal movement in the United States (roughly through WWII). As Edmund Rybarczyk notes in the introductory chapter of this book, a second wave of people who embraced charismata immediately following WWII were called charismatics. In addition, scholars such as Drogus (2000), Steigenga (2001), and Freston (1995) distinguish between the "classical" or historic Pentecostal churches and the newer, more independent ones of the post-war era. This latter group is sometimes called "neo-Pentecostals." In general, there are few significant doctrinal differences between Pentecostals and neo-Pentecostals, although the latter often form independent con-

gregations. As Walsh and Patterson note in this volume, in North America neo-Pentecostals are associated with a doctrine of prosperity.

3. Donald W. Dayton, *Theological Roots of Pentecostalism* (Metuchen, NJ: Scarecrow Press, 1987), chap. 1.

4. Dayton, *Theological Roots of Pentecostalism*, 21.

5. Some Pentecostals associated with the Holiness movement argued for a five-fold gospel that included instantaneous sanctification as an additional doctrinal point. Such a view of sanctification saw it as a second work of grace following salvation but generally prior to Spirit Baptism.

6. Gary B. McGee, "Early Pentecostal Hermeneutics: Tongues as Evidence in the Book of Acts" in *Initial Evidence: Historical and Biblical Perspectives on the Pentecostal Doctrine of Spirit Baptism*, ed. Gary B. McGee (Peabody, MA: Hendrickson, 1991), 99.

7. I remember a recent visit to a Foursquare church while the pastor, an erudite and well-beloved minister, was vacationing. In his stead, a well-known Foursquare evangelist was to speak. When the enthusiastic and demonstrative preacher took the podium he unleashed an energetic pre-sermon on the core values of the Foursquare denomination. Expecting a response from the congregation, he called out, "the foursquare gospel is Christ as _____ (pause)." No one answered. I quickly looked around the auditorium and suspected that most of the audience had no idea what he was talking about. Then the truly unexpected happened. The evangelist turned to the worship pastor, seated on the front row, pointed a finger at her, and reiterated, "Christ as _____ . . . . . . CHRIST AS _____ . . ." After an embarrassed silence, the worship pastor squeaked, "I don't know." The evangelist, incredulous, flustered, slowly regained his composure and spelled out for the congregation the "foursquare gospel:" Christ as Savior, Baptizer in the Holy Spirit, Healer, and Coming King.

8. Margaret Poloma, "The Symbolic Dilemma and the Future of Pentecostalism: Mysticism, Ritual, and Revival."

9. James 5:14–15.

10. The argument that the poor convert to receive material blessings in times of crisis has recently been applied abroad. See Andrew R. Chesnut, *Born Again in Brazil: The Pentecostal Boom and the Pathogens of Poverty* (New Brunswick, NJ: Rutgers University Press, 1997). That being said, church historians such as Cecil M. Robeck, Jr. (2005) and Grant Wacker (2004) argue that early Pentecostals were not more deprived than those around them, and therefore that the relative deprivation thesis is incorrect.

11. For an overview of these issues, see *Initial Evidence: Historical and Biblical Perspectives on the Pentecostal Doctrine of Spirit Baptism*, ed. Gary B. McGee (Peabody, MA: Hendrickson, 1991).

12. Psalm 119:11.

13. Paul Freston's analysis of global Pentecostalism provides similar observations. Paul Freston, *Evangelicals and Politics in Asia, Africa and Latin America* (Cambridge: Cambridge University Press, 2001).

14. See Johanssen's chapter in this book, 65.

15. See Calvin Johanssen, *Music and Ministry: A Biblical Counterpoint* (Peabody, MA: Hendrickson, 1998), especially chap. 4.

16. The volume which has become a classic account of positive aspects and challenges of contemporary global evangelism is Murray W. Dempster, Byron D. Klaus, and

Douglas Petersen, *Called and Empowered: Global Mission in Pentecostal Perspective* (Peabody, MA: Hendrickson, 1991).

17. Jeff Hittenberger's chapter in this volume cited Melvin Hodges' seminal work, *The Indigenous Church: A Complete Handbook on How to Grow Young Churches* (Springfield, MO: Gospel Publishing House, 1953, 1976).

18. I observed the membership class of a large classical Pentecostal church in southern California regularly visited by denominational officials. Surprisingly, the associate pastor told the inductees that although the church had an organizational affiliation with a denomination (the Assemblies of God), it meant "virtually nothing" with regards to the day to day operation of the church: "we are consciously based on a non-denominational, community church model." If the inductee wanted to learn more about the unique doctrines of the denomination, a brochure could be requested at the end of the membership class: "we're not going to worry about that stuff now." One can barely imagine how the Pentecostal pioneers that founded the church would have responded to that revelation.

19. See Phillip Jenkins, *The Next Christendom: The Coming of Global Christianity* (Oxford: Oxford University Press, 2002); David Martin, *Pentecostalism: The World Their Parish* (Oxford: Blackwell, 2002); Eric Patterson, *Latin America's Neo-Reformation* (New York: Routledge, 2005); David Stoll, *Is Latin America Turning Protestant?* (Berkley: University of California Press, 1990).

20. After three years observing a large, influential Assemblies of God church I had not heard a single sermon on the baptism of the Holy Spirit or any teaching on charismata or spiritual gifts. However, when a group from the church went on a missions trip to India, they sent an email back to the home church asking that the church pray and engage in "spiritual warfare." Indeed, on Sunday morning the associate pastor read the email and asked the congregation to engage in spiritual warfare. My impression was that the majority did not know what he was talking about. Without wasting a breath, he immediately proceeded to announce a church flag football league and took an offering.

21. See Edmund Rybarczyk's chapter in this volume, "American Pentecostalism: Challenges and Temptations."

22. Charitable efforts are one area where Christian political liberals and political conservatives can agree. Liberals tend to prioritize a social gospel for their church, whereas conservatives advocate private donations to and through local churches and non-government agencies. Thus, they can unite in providing for the poor through the local church.

23. Walter Rauschenbusch was the best-known Social Gospel advocate of his day, writing numerous books and articles, including *Christianity and the Social Crisis* (1907), *Christianizing the Social Order* (1912), and *A Theology of the Social Gospel* (1917).

24. Early Pentecostals were extremely wary of "worldly" politics. This has changed since the late 1970s with the blurring of distinctions between Pentecostals and the larger evangelical world. See David C. Leege and Lyman A. Kellstedt, *Rediscovering the Religious Dimension in American Politics* (Armonk, N.Y.: M.E. Sharpe, 1993).

25. A Pentecostal pastor embarrassedly related to me his shock at receiving an irate phone call from a Mormon landlord (Mormon congregations are well-known for taking care of their own). The tenant's family was in serious trouble financially. The landlord wanted to know, "why hasn't your church stepped in? If that individual was a member of our church, we would have provided day care for the kids, put groceries in the refrigerator, and paid the bills 'til they got back on their feet. What kind of Christians are you?"

26. Cecil M. Robeck, Jr. "William Seymour and 'the Bible Evidence'" *in Initial Evidence: Historical and Biblical Perspectives on the Pentecostal Doctrine of Spirit Baptism*, Gary B. McGee, ed. (Peabody, MA: Hendrickson, 1991), 79.

27. See David Daniels, "'Follow Peace With All:' Future Trajectories of the Church of God in Christ," in this volume.

28. Two of the chapters in this volume consider the nexus of ethnic identity and Pentecostalism (Daniels, Walsh and Patterson). There is a wider transnational literature on this topic, such as John Burdick, "What is the color of the Holy Spirit? Pentecostalism and Black Identity in Brazil." *Latin American Research Review* 34, no. 2 (Spring, 1999).

29. Cheryl J. Sanders, "History of Women in the Pentecostal Movement" (paper delivered at the 1996 PCCNA National Conference, Memphis, Tennessee, October 1, 1996), 1. Available at *Cyberjournal of Pentecostal Studies*, vol. 2 (1997), http://www.fullnet/np/archives/cyberj/sanders.html (accessed 1 April, 2004).

30. Sanders, "History of Women in the Pentecostal Movement," 1.

Select Bibliography

Abraham. William J. *The Logic of Renewal.* Grand Rapids: Eerdmans, 2003.

Albrecht, Daniel E. *Rites in the Spirit: A Ritual Approach to Pentecostal/ Charismatic Spirituality.* Sheffield, UK: Sheffield Academic Press, 1999.

Alexander, Kimberly Ervin. *Pentecostal Healing: Models of Theology and Practice.* Blandford Forum, Dorset, UK: Deo, 2006.

———. "'And the Signs Are Following:' Mark 16.9–20—A Journey into Pentecostal Hermeneutics." *Journal of Pentecostal Theology* 11, no. 2 (2003): 147–170.

Alvarez, Carmelo. "Hispanic Pentecostals: Azusa Street and Beyond." *Cyberjournal for Pentecostal-Charismatic Research.* (February 1999) http://ourworld.cs.com /_ht_a/xenoako /alva rez. html

Anderson, Allan. *An Introduction to Pentecostalism: Global Charismatic Christianity.* Cambridge University Press, 2004.

Anderson, A.A. and W.J. Hollenweger, eds. *Pentecostalism after a Century: Global Perspectives on a Movement in Transition.* Sheffield, UK: Sheffield Academic Press, 1999.

Anderson, Robert M. *Vision of the Disinherited: The Making of American Pentecostalism.* New York: Oxford University Press, 1979.

Archer, Kenneth J. "Pentecostal Hermeneutics: Retrospect and Prospect." *Journal of Pentecostal Theology* 8 (1996): 63–81.

Baskett, Thomas A. "The Coming Postmodern Reformation: Toward a Creative Synthesis of Reformed and Pentecostal Theologies." Paper presented at the 28th Annual Meeting of the Society for Pentecostal Studies, March 11–13, 1999. *Toward Healing Our Divisions: Reflecting on Pentecostal Diversity and Common Witness.* vol. 1, 1999.

Beckford, James. "Religion, Modernity and Post-Modernity." in *Religion: Contemporary Issues.* edited by B.R. Wilson. London: Bellew, 1992.

Berger, Peter, ed. *The Desecularization of the World: A Resurgent Religion and World Politics.* Grand Rapids, 2000

Bernard, David K. *In the Name of Jesus.* Hazelwood, MO: Word Aflame Press, 1992.

———. *The Oneness of God.* Hazelwood, MO: Word Aflame Press, 1983, rev. ed., 2000.

Beyet, Peter. *Religion and Globalization.* London: Sage, 1994.

Blumhofer, Edith L. *Restoring the Faith: The Assemblies of God, Pentecostalism, and American Culture.* Urbana and Chicago: University of Illinois Press, 1993.

———. *The Assemblies of God: A Chapter in the Story of American Pentecostalism.* vol. 2. Springfield, MO: Gospel Publishing House, 1989.

Blumhofer, Edith, L., Russell P. Spittler, and Grant A. Wacker, eds. *Pentecostal Currents in American Protestantism.* Urbana and Chicago: University of Illinois Press, 1999.

Bridges, James, ed. *Pentecostal Gifts and Ministries in a Postmodern Era.* Springfield, MO: Gospel Publishing House, 2004.

Brubaker, Malcolm R. "Postmodernism and Pentecostals: A Case Study of Evangelical Hermeneutics." *Evangelical Journal* 15 (Spring 1997): 33–45.

Buller, Cornelius A. "Healing Hope: Healing and Resurrection Hope in a Postmodern Context." *Journal of Pentecostal Theology* 10, no. 2 (2002): 74–92.

Burgess, Stanley, ed. *The New International Dictionary of Pentecostal and Charismatic Movements, Revised and Expanded Edition.* Grand Rapids: Zondervan, 2002.

James T. Burtchaell, *The Dying of the Light.* Grand Rapids: Eerdmans, 1998.

Cargal, Timothy B. "Beyond the Fundamentalist-Modernist Controversy: Pentecostals and Hermeneutics in a Postmodern Age." *Pneuma* 15, no. 2 (Fall 1993): 163–187.

Carroll, Jackson and Wade Clark Roof. eds. *Beyond Establishment : Protestant Identity in a Post-Protestant Age.* Louisville, Ky. : Westminster/John Knox, 1993.

Castleberry, Richard E. "Generating Holiness: Sanctification for a Postmodern World." Paper Presented at the 27th Annual Meeting of the Society for Pentecostal Studies, March 13, 1998. *Purity and Power: Revisioning the Holiness & Pentecostal/Charismatic Movements for the Twenty-First Century.* Vol. 1.

Chan, Simon. *Pentecostal Theology and the Christian Spiritual Tradition.* Sheffield, UK: Sheffield Academic Press, 2001.

———. *Spiritual Theology: A Systematic Study of the Christian Life.* Downers Grove: InterVarsity Press, 1998.

Chiquete, Daniel. "Latin American Pentecostalisms and Western Postmodernism." *International Review of Mission* 92 Issue 364 (January 2003): 29–39.

Clark, Matthew. "Questioning Every Consensus: A Plea for a Return to the Radical Roots of Pentecostalism." *Asian Journal of Pentecostal Theology* 5, no. 1 (2002): 73–86.

Cleary, Edward L. and Hannah W. Stewart-Gambino, eds. *Power, Politics, and Pentecostals in Latin America.* Boulder, CO: Westview Press, 1997.

Clemmons, Ithiel C. *Bishop C. H. Mason and the Roots of the Church of God in Christ.* Bakersfield, CA: Pneuma Life Publishing, 1996.

Coleman, Simon. *The Globalisation of Charismatic Christianity: Spreading the Gospel of Prosperity.* Cambridge: Cambridge University Press, 2000.

Conn, Charles W. *Like a Mighty Army Moves the Church of God.* Cleveland, TN: Pathway Press, 1955, rev. ed. 1977.

Corten, Andre. "The Growth of the Literature on Afro-American, Latin American, and African Pentecostalism." *Journal of Contemporary Religion* 12, no. 3 (1997): 311–334.

Cox, Harvey. "Pentecostalism an Global Market Culture: A Response to Issues Facing Pentecostalism in a Postmodern World." In *Globalization of Pentecostalism.* Edited by Murray Dempster, Byron Klaus and Douglas Petersen. Oxford: Regnum Books, 1999.

———. *Fire from Heaven: The Rise of Pentecostal Religion and the Reshaping of Religion in the Twenty-First Century.* Reading, MA: Addison-Wesley, 1995.

Creps, Earl. "Worldview Therapy." In *Stories of Emergence: Moving from Absolute to Authentic.* ed. Mike Yaconelli. Grand Rapids: Zondervan, 2003.

———. *Communicating with Postmoderns: A Doctor of Ministry Elective Class on Ministry in the Postmodern Context.* D.Min. diss. Assemblies of God Theological Seminary, 2002.

Cross, Terry L. "A Proposal to Break the Ice: What Can Pentecostal Theology Offer Evangelical Theology?" *Journal of Pentecostal Theology* 10, no. 2 (April 2002).

Dayton, Donald W. *Theological Roots of Pentecostalism.* Grand Rapids: Zondervan, 1988.

Deck, Allen Figueroa. *The Challenge of Evangelical/Pentecostal Christianity to Hispanic Catholicism in the US.* Working Paper Series: Cushwa Center for the Study of American Catholicism, 1992.

Del Colle, Ralph. "Postmodernism and the Pentecostal-Charismatic Experience." *JPT* 17 (2000): 97–116.

Dempster, Murray, ed. "Pentecostal Hermeneutics." *Pneuma* 15 (1993): 129–222.

———. ed. "Pentecostal Hermeneutics." [in a Postmodern Age; replies to T. B. Cargal] *Pneuma* 16 (Spring 1994): 101–41.

Dempster, Murray, Byron Klaus, and Doug Petersen, eds. *The Globalization of Pentecostalism: A Religion Made to Travel.* Oxford: Regnum Books, 1999.

Evans, James H. Jr. "African-American Christianity and the Postmodern Condition." *Journal of the American Academy of Religion* 58, no. 2 (1990): 207–22.

Fee, Gordon. "Hermeneutics and Historical Precedent." Perspectives on the New Pentecostalism. edited by Russell P. Spittler. Grand Rapids: Baker, 1976.

French, Talmadge L. *Our God Is One: The Story of the Oneness Pentecostals.* Indianapolis: Voice & Vision, 1999.

Freston, Paul. *Evangelicals and Politics in Asia, Africa and Latin America.* Cambridge: Cambridge University Press, 2001.

Gaines, Adrienne. "Revive Us, Precious Lord." *Charisma* 28, no. 10 (May 2003): 37–44.

Hayford, Jack. *Baptism with the Holy Spirit.* Grand Rapids: Chosen Books, 2004.

———. *The Beauty of Spiritual Language: My Journey Toward the Heart of God.* Dallas: Word Publishers, 1992.

Hayward, Douglas. "Saturday Night in Pasadena: Wholeness, Healing, and Holiness at Harvest Rock Church." In *Gen X Religion.* Edited by Donald E. Miller and Richard W. Flory. Routledge, 2000, 163–184.

Hilborn, David, ed. *Toronto in Perspective: Papers on the New Charismatic Wave of the Mid-1990s.* Paternoster Press, 2003.

Hollenweger, Walter J. "Pentecostalism's Global Language." *Christian History* (Spring 1998).

———. *Pentecostalism: Origins and Developments Worldwide.* Peabody, MA: Hendrickson, 1997.

———. *The Pentecostals,* 2nd ed. Peabody, MA: Hendrickson, 1988.

Hughes, Ray H. *Church of God Distinctives.* Cleveland, TN: Pathway Press, 1968.

Hunter, Harold D., *Spirit Baptism: A Pentecostal Alternative.* Lanham, MD: University Press of America, 1983.

Hustad, Donald P. *Jubilate II: Church Music in Worship and Renewal.* Carol Stream, Illinois: Hope Publishing Co., 1993.

Jacobsen, Douglas. *Thinking in the Spirit: Theologies of the Early Pentecostal Movement.* Bloomington, IN: Indiana University Press, 2003.

Jenkins, Philip. *The Next Christendom: The Coming of Global Christianity.* Oxford: Oxford University Press, 2002.

Johansson, Calvin M. *Music & Ministry: a Biblical Counterpoint,* 2nd edition. Peabody, MA: Hendrickson Publisher, 1998.

Johns, Cheryl Bridges. "Partners in Scandal: Wesleyan and Pentecostal Scholarship." *Wesleyan Theological Journal* 34 no. 1 (1999): 7–23.

———. *Pentecostal Formation: A Pedagogy Among the Oppressed*, JPTS 2. Sheffield, UK: Sheffield Academic Press, 1993.

Johns, Jackie David. "A Yielding to the Spirit: The Dynamics of a Pentecostal Model of Praxis." In *Globalization of Pentecostalism*. Edited by Murray Dempster, Byron Klaus and Douglas Petersen. Oxford: Regnum Books, 1999, 70–84.

———. "Pentecostalism and the Postmodern Worldview." *JPT,* 7 (October 1995): 73–96.

Karkkainen, Veli-Matti. *Toward A Pneumatological Theology: Pentecostal and Ecumenical Perspectives on Ecclesiology, Soteriology, and Theology of Mission.* University Press of America, 2002.

———. *Pneumatology: The Holy Spirit in Ecumenical, International, and Contextual Perspective.* Grand Rapids: Baker, 2002.

Kung, Lap Yan. "Outpouring of the Spirit: A Reflection on Pentecostals' Identity." *Asian Journal of Pentecostal Theology* 4 no. 1 (2001): 3–19.

Land, Steven J. *Pentecostal Spirituality: A Passion for the Kingdom.* Sheffield, UK: Sheffield Academic Press, 1997.

Leege, David C. and Lyman A. Kellstedt. *Rediscovering the Religious Dimension in American Politics.* Armonk, N.Y.: M.E. Sharpe, 1993.

Lehmann, David. *Struggle for the Spirit.* Cambridge: Polity Press, 1996.

Lewis, Donald M., ed. *Christianity Reborn: The Global Rise of Evangelicalism in the Twentieth Century.* Grand Rapids: Eerdmans, 2004.

Lewis, Paul W. "Postmodernity and Pentecostalism: A Survey and Assessment." *Africa Journal of Pentecostal Studies* 1, no. 1 (December 2002): 34–66.

Lincoln, C. Eric and Lawrence H. Maimiya, *The Black Church in the African American Experience.* Durham, NC: Duke University Press, 1990.

Lyon, D. *Jesus in Disneyland: Religion in Postmodern Times.* Cambridge: Cambridge University Press, 2000.

Ma, Wonsuk. "Postmodernism and Asian Pentecostals." *Asian Journal of Pentecostal Studies.* 6 no. 1 (January 2003): 1–2.

Ma, Wonsuk and Robert P. Menzies, eds. *The Spirit and Spirituality: Essays in Honor of Russell P. Spittler.* London & New York: T & T Clark International/Continuum, 2004.

Marsden, George, *The Outrageous Idea of Christian Scholarship.* Oxford: Oxford University Press, 1997.

Martin, David. *Pentecostalism: The World Their Parish.* Blackwell Publishers, 2001.

McClymond, Michael J. *Embodying the Spirit: New Perspectives on North American Revivalism.* Johns Hopkins University Press, 2004.

McGee, Gary B. *People of the Spirit: The Assemblies of God.* Springfield, Mo.: Gospel Publishing House, 2004.

McGrath, Allister E. *The Future of Christianity.* Blackwell Publishers, 2002.

Menzies, William W. and Robert P. Menzies. *Spirit and Power: Foundations of Pentecostal Experience.* Grand Rapids: Zondervan, 2000.

Miller, Donald E. *Reinventing American Protestantism: Christianity at the New Millennium.* Berkley: University of California Press, 1997.

Miller, Donald E. and Richard W. Flory, eds. *Gen X Religion.* New York: Routledge, 2000.

Mitchell, R. Bryant. *Heritage and Horizons: The History of Open Bible Standard Churches.* Des Moines: Open Bible, 1982.

Mouw, Richard J. "Pentecostal Evangelism." *Word World* 16 (Summer 1996): 354–65.

Mullin, Robert Bruce. *Miracles and the Modern Religious Imagination.* New Haven: Yale University Press, 1996.

O'Dea, Thomas. "Sociological Dilemmas: Five Paradoxes of Institutionalization" in *Sociological Theory, Values and Sociological Change,* Edward A Teryakian, ed. Glencoe, NY: Free Press, 1963: 71–89.

———. "Sociological Dilemmas in the Institutionalization of Religion" in *Journal for the Scientific Study of Religion,* vol 1. (1961): 30–41.

Olsen, Ted. "American Pentecost." *Christian History* (Spring 1998): 32.

Olson, Roger E. "Pentecostalism's Dark Side," in *Christian Century* (March 7, 2006): 27–30.

Patterson, Eric. *Latin America's Neo-Reformation: Religion's Influence on Contemporary Politics.* New York: Routledge, 2005.

Penning James M. and Corwin E. Smidt. *Evangelicalism: The Next Generation.* Grand Rapids: Baker, 2002.

Petersen, Doug. "Missions in the Twenty-First Century: Toward A Methodology of Pentecostal Compassion." *Transformation* 16 no. 2 (1999): 54–59.

———. *Not by Might, Nor by Power: A Pentecostal Theology of Social Concern.* Oxford: Regnum Books, 1996.

Pluss, Jean-Daniel. "Azusa and Other Myths: The Long and Winding Road from Experience to Stated Beliefs and Back Again." *Pneuma* 15 (Fall 1993): 189–201.

Poewe, Karla, ed. *Charismatic Christianity as A Global Culture.* Columbia, SC : University of South Carolina Press, 1994.

Poloma, Margaret M. *Main Street Mystics: The Toronto Blessing and Reviving Pentecostalism.* Lanham, MD: AltaMira Press, 2003.

———. *The Assemblies of God at the Crossroads.* Knoxville, TN: University of Tennessee Press, 1989.

Portal, Renee Deloriea. *Pensacola: The Real Thing Hits Brownsville.* New York: Destiny Image Publications, 1997.

Redman, Robb. *The Great Worship Awakening: Singing a New Song in the Postmodern Church.* San Francisco: Jossey-Bass, 2002.

Robeck, Cecil M., Jr. *The Azusa Street Mission and Revival.* Nashville, TN: Thomas Nelson, 2006.

———. "Evangelism or Proselytism of Hispanics? A Pentecostal Perspective." *Journal of Hispanic Liberation Theology.* 4:4 (1997):42–64.

———. "Pentecostal Origins in Global Perspective." In *All Together in One Place: Theological Papers from the Brighton Conference on World Evangelization.* Edited by Harold D. Hunter and Peter D. Hocken, Sheffield, UK: Sheffield Academic Press, 1993, 166–180.

———. "Pentecostals and the Apostolic Faith: Implications for Ecumenism." *One in Christ* 23, no.1–2 (1987): 110–130.

Robey, Steve. *Revival in Brownsville: Pensacola, Pentecostalism, and the Power of American Revivalism.* Nashville, TN: Thomas Nelson, 1998.

Roebuck, David G. and Karen Carroll Mundy, "Women, Culture, and Post-World War Two Pentecostalism" in *The Spirit and the Mind: Essays in Informed Pentecostalism.* Lanham, MD: University Press of America, 2000.

Rybarczyk, Edmund J. "Reframing Tongues: Glossolalia in Apophatic Theology and Postmodern Knowing." *Pneuma* (Fall 2005).

————. *"Beyond Salvation: Eastern Orthodoxy and Classical Pentecostalism on Becoming Like Christ.* Great Britain: Paternoster Press, 2004.

————. "What Are You, O Man? Theo-Anthropological Similarities in Classical Pentecostalism and Eastern Orthodoxy." In *Ancient and Postmodern Christianity: Paleo-Orthodoxy in the 21st Century.* Edited by Kenneth Tanner and Christopher Hall. Downers Grove: InterVarsity Press, 2003. 83–105.

Sanchez Walsh, Arlene M. *Latino Pentecostal Identity: Evangelical Faith, Self, and Society.* New York: Columbia University Press, 2003.

————. *Holy Ghost Setup: Searching for a Latino Pentecostal Identity.* New York: Columbia University Press, 2003.

Sawyer, Mary. "The Fraternal Council of Negro Churches, 1934–1964." *Church History* 59 (March 1990): 51–64.

Shaull, R. and Cesar W. *Pentecostalism and the Future of Christian Churches.* Grand Rapids: Eerdmans, 2000.

Smidt, Corwin E., Lyman A. Kellstedt, John C. Green and James L. Guth. "The Spirit-Filled Movements in Contemporary America: A Survey Perspective." in *Pentecostal Currents in American Protestantism.* Edited by Edith L. Blumhofer, Russell P. Spittler and Grant A. Wacker. Urbana: University of Illinois Press, 1999. 111–130.

Smith, Ron. "Pentecostalism in Comparative Pespective." *Journal of Pentecostal Studies.* 31, no. 2 (1994).

Solivan, Samuel. *Spirit, Pathos and Liberation: Toward an Hispanic Pentecostal Theology.* Sheffield, UK: Sheffield Academic Press, 1999.

Spittler, Russell P. "Are Pentecostals and Charismatics Fundamentalists?" in *Charismatic Christianity as Global Culture.* edited byKarla Poewa. Columbia: University of South Carolina, 1994, 103–116.

————. "Maintaining Distinctives: The Future of Pentecostalism." In *Pentecostals from the Inside Out.* Edited by Harold B. Smith. Wheaton, IL: Victor Books, 1990, 121–134.

Stanley, John E. "Elements of a Postmodern Holiness Hermeneutic Illustrated by the Book of Revelation." *Wesleyan Theological Journal* 28 nos. 1–2 (1993).

Stark, Rodney. "Why Religious Movements Succeed or Fail: A Revised General Model." *Journal of Contemporary Religion* (1996) 11 no. 2:133–146.

Stoll, David. *Is Latin America Turning Protestant?* Berkley: University of California Press, 1990.

Synan, Vinson. *The Holiness-Pentecostal Tradition: Charismatic Movements in the Twentieth Century.* Grand Rapids: Eerdmans, 1997.

————. ed. *Aspects of Pentecostal-Charismatic Origins.* Plainfield, NJ: Logos International, 1975.

Thomas, John Christopher. "Women, Pentecostals and the Bible: An Experiment in Pentecostal Hermeneutics." *JPT* 5 (1994): 41–56.

Villafañe, Eldin. *The Liberating Spirit.* Grand Rapids: Eerdmans, 1997.

Vondey, Wolfgang. "Christian Amnesia: Who in the World Are Pentecostals?" *Asian Journal of Pentecostal Theology* 4, no. 1 (2001): 21–39.

Wacker, Grant A. *Heaven Below: Early Pentecostals and American Culture.* Cambridge, MA: Harvard University Press, 2001.

Walter, Tony and Stephen Hunt. "Introduction: The Charismatic Movement and Contemporary Social Change." *Religion* 28 (July 1998): 219–21.

Yong, Amos. "Pragmati(ci)sm and Theology in a Post/Modern World." Paper presented to the Postmodernism and Evangelical Theology Study Group of the Evangelical Theological Society. 20–22 November 2003.

———. *Beyond the Impasse: Toward a Pneumatological Theology of Religions.* Grand Rapids: Baker, 2003.

———. "On Divine Presence and Divine Agency: Toward a Foundational Pneumatology." *Asian Journal of Pentecostal Theology* 3 no. 2 (2000): 167–188.

Yun, Koo Dong. *Baptism in the Holy Spirit: An Ecumenical Theology of Spirit Baptism.* Lanham, MD: University Press of America, 2003.

Index

About the Contributors

Kimberly Ervin Alexander is Assistant Professor of Theology at Church of God Theological Seminary. Her career spans active work in a variety of church and educational settings. She has served as Instructor in the Ministerial Internship Program and Ministerial Development Program in Southern New England; Guest Lecturer at the Community College of Rhode Island; Adjunct Faculty at Tennessee Wesleyan College; and as Adjunct Faculty at Lee University and Church of God Theological Seminary. In 1996, Ms. Alexander was honored by Furman University for her excellence in teaching. Her published work has appeared in the Ashland Theological Journal and the Journal of Pentecostal Theology and she is an active member of the Society for Pentecostal Studies. Ms. Alexander is completing a doctoral thesis entitled "Towards a Pentecostal Theology of Healing."

David K. Bernard, J.D. is president of Urshan Graduate School of Theology, superintendent of the South Texas District (United Pentecostal Church International), and founder and pastor of New Life United Pentecostal Church of Austin, Texas, out of which twelve other churches have started. He has authored 30 books with over 700,000 printed, including Word Aflame Press's best-seller, *The Oneness of God.* He received a B.A. from Rice University, a J.D. with honors from the University of Texas, and a M.Th. from the University of South Africa in 2005. He is presently enrolled in the doctoral program at the University of South Africa.

David Cole is president of Eugene Bible College in Eugene, Oregon. For over twenty years he has been a minister with Open Bible Churches, having served in a variety of pastoral and leadership roles. His Ph.D. in theology is from Fuller Theological Seminary, and he has written a number of articles on themes related to Pentecostalism and ecumenism. He has participated in several ecumenical consultations and discussions, and at this writing is involved in the international Roman Catholic-Pentecostal Dialogue, as well as a dialogue between the U.S. Conference of Catholic Bishops and Evangelicals.

Earl Creps is a scholar, theologian, and pastor. He has served as a senior pastor in Maine, Florida, and Missouri and as a staff pastor in Vermont. He served as sectional presbyter in the Northern New England District Council of the Assemblies of God. Dr. Creps began his teaching career in the state university system of Vermont and has also served as adjunct faculty for several Christian institutions. He was formerly a faculty member at Assemblies of God Theological Seminary and is the author of numerous articles on the nexus of the contemporary church, postmodernism, and mass communication. Presently he is pastoring a church in Northern California.

David D. Daniels, III joined the faculty of McCormick Theological Seminary in 1987 and was inaugurated Professor of Church History in 2003. He holds baccalaureate degrees from Bowdoin College, a M.Div. from Yale University, and a Ph.D. from Union Theological Seminary. He is a member of various societies including the American Academy of Religion, the Society for the Study of Black Religion, and the Society for Pentecostal Studies. He has served as commissioner for the Faith and Order Commission of the National Council of Churches USA. He is author of various articles on the history of Christianity and book reviews published in *Theological Education, Pneuma, Christianity Century, Encyclopedia of African American Religions*, and *A Sourcebook for the Community of Religions*. He has lectured widely in the U.S. as well as in Nigeria, Senegal, and Canada and he is an ordained minister in the Church of God in Christ.

Jeff Hittenberger is Professor of Education and Director of the Graduate Program in Education at Evangel University. Dr. Hittenberger holds a Ph.D. in Education from the University of Southern California (USC) and a B.A. in English and Biblical Studies from Evangel University. Prior to joining the faculty at Vanguard University, Dr. Hittenberger served as Coordinator/Administrator for Curriculum and Instruction at the Monterey County Office of Education and as Special Consultant and Adjunct Faculty Member at California State University, Monterey Bay. Besides his work with numerous districts and schools, Dr. Hittenberger has served as a consultant and researcher in Cameroon, Mali, South Africa, and Haiti, and has authored numerous articles and curriculum units.

Calvin M. Johansson is a graduate of Houghton College, Union Theological Seminary, and Southwestern Baptist Theological Seminary. A former organist/choirmaster at the Post Chapel, United States Military Academy, Dr. Johansson has had extensive experience as a church music director, teacher (including thirty-nine years at Evangel University in Springfield, Missouri), lecturer, and author. His two books, *Music & Ministry: A Biblical Counterpoint* and *Discipling Music Ministry: Twenty-first Century Directions* are widely used as church music texts in colleges, universities, and seminaries because of their uniqueness in relating Scripture to worldview, aesthetics, and the practice of music ministry.

Frank D. Macchia is Professor of Theology at Vanguard University. He holds the Master of Arts from Wheaton College (Wheaton, Illinois), the Master of Divinity from Union Theological Seminary (New York), and the Doctor of Theology from the University of Basel (Switzerland). He is involved in various ecumenical dialogues, including the ecumenical forum established by the World Council of Churches to dialogue with Evangelicals. He is also a member of the dialogue between the World Alliance of Reformed Churches and the Pentecostal Movement. In addition, he has participated in the North American Roman Catholic/Pentecostal ecumenical meetings. He is Immediate Past President of the Society for Pentecostal Studies and serves as Editor of the Society's Journal, *Pneuma*. His book, *Spirituality and Social Liberation*, was published in the Wesleyan and Pietist Studies series of Scarecrow Press. He has published in the areas of theology and ecumenism in various dictionaries of theology and anthologies of theological essays, as well as in journals such as *Theology Today*, and the *Journal of Pentecostal Theology*.

Eric Dean Patterson is Assistant Professor at Georgetown University and specializes in the nexus of Pentecostalism and socio-political life in international contexts. He is the author of *Latin America's Neo-Reformation* (Routledge, 2005) and editor of volumes *Christianity and Power Politics Today* (Palgrave-Macmillan, forthcoming) and *The Christian Realists* (University of America Press, 2002). He is also the author of numerous journal articles including "Faith in a Changing Mexico" in *Delaware Review of Latin American Studies* (Winter 2004); "Different Religions, Different Politics: Religion and Politics in Brazil and Chile" in *Latin American Politics and Society* (Fall, 2004); "Religion and Political Attitudes in Chile and Argentina" in *Journal for the Scientific Study of Religion* (Fall, 2004); "The Invasion of Sects: Protestantism and Political Participation in Brazil" in *Ethnos Brasil: Cultura e Sociedade*, (Winter, 2001); and "Religious Change and Politics in Chile and Brazil" in *Nordic Journal of Latin American Studies (Iberoamericana)*.

Margaret M. Poloma has written extensively about the Pentecostal charismatic movement. She analyzes how foundational forces of Western thought, modernism, materialism, and instrumental rationality, are challenging its worldview. She is professor emerita of sociology at The University of Akron. She is a member of the steering committee of the Christian Sociological Society (CSS) and of the advisory board of the Lewis Wilson Institute for Pentecostal Studies. The author of more than fifty articles in scholarly journals and chapters in volumes of edited works, she is the co-editor of one book, the co-author of four others, including *The Assemblies of God at the Crossroads: Charisma and Institutional Dilemmas* (1989) and *Main Street Mystics: The Toronto Blessing and Reviving Pentecostalism* (2003).

Edmund J. Rybarczyk is Associate Professor of Systematic Theology at Vanguard University where he is also the director of the Lewis Wilson Institute for Pentecostal Studies. An ordained minister in the Assemblies of God, he is the author of *Beyond Salvation: Eastern Orthodoxy and Classical Pentecostalism on Becoming Like Christ* (Paternoster 2004), a study that won the *Pneuma* book award in 2006. He has authored numerous other publications such as "*Glossolalia* within Apophatic Theology and Postmodern Knowing" (*Pneuma*, Spring 2005); and, "What are you, O man? Theo-Anthropological Similarities in Classical Pentecostalism and Eastern Orthodoxy," in *Ancient & Postmodern Christianity: Paleo-Orthodoxy in the 21st Century—Essays In Honor of Thomas C. Oden*, Christopher Hall and Kenneth Tanner, eds. (InterVarsity Press, 2002); Dr. Rybarczyk also serves as the managing editor for *Pneuma: The Journal of the Society for Pentecostal Studies*.

Arlene Sanchez Walsh is Associate Professor in the School of Theology at Azusa Pacific University. She holds a doctorate in history from Claremont Graduate University and taught courses in religion as well as Latino and Latin American Studies at DePaul University from 2000–2005. She is the author of the book *Latino Pentecostal Identity* (Columbia University Press, 2003), a manuscript on Pentecostalism in American culture, and numerous articles and conference papers on Latino Pentecostalism, evangelical culture, religion, and popular culture. Dr. Walsh is a certified minister of the Assemblies of God and is completing the project "Para De Sufrir: Latino Pentecostal Immigrants, Transnationalism and the Influence of the Prosperity Gospel" for the Institute for the Study of American Evangelicals at Wheaton College.